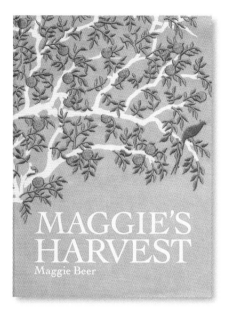

This landmark book from one of Australia's best-loved cooks
was first published in 2007 and will be available
as four seasonal paperbacks.

Available
September 2015

Available
December 2015

Available
March 2016

MAGGIE BEER'S WINTER HARVEST RECIPES brings together 90 of Maggie's signature winter recipes, detailed descriptions of her favourite ingredients and inspiring accounts of memorable meals with family and friends.

The recipes highlight Maggie's philosophy of using the freshest and best seasonal produce available in the Barossa Valley, South Australia, and treating it simply, allowing the natural flavours to speak for themselves. Describing herself as a 'country cook', Maggie cooks from the heart and is passionate about instilling in others this same confidence – to use recipes as a starting point, and be guided by instinct and personal taste.

This collection of recipes from one of Australia's best-loved cooks has been taken from *Maggie's Harvest* and is essential for anyone with an appreciation of the pleasures of sourcing, cooking and sharing food.

✦　✦　✦

MAGGIE BEER is one of Australia's best-known food personalities. As well as appearing as a guest chef on MasterChef and writing books, Maggie devotes her time to her export kitchen in the Barossa Valley, which produces a wide range of pantry items for domestic and international markets. These include her famous verjuice, pâté and quince pastes, her ice cream as well as her sparkling non-alcoholic grape drinks. Maggie was also recognised as Senior Australian of the Year in 2010 for inspiring joy to many Australians through food.

Maggie is the author of eight successful cookbooks, *Maggie's Christmas*, *Maggie Beer* (Lantern Cookery Classics), *Maggie's Verjuice Cookbook*, *Maggie's Kitchen*, *Maggie's Harvest*, *Maggie's Table*, *Cooking with Verjuice*, *Maggie's Orchard* and *Maggie's Farm*, and co-author of the bestselling *Stephanie Alexander and Maggie Beer's Tuscan Cookbook*.

maggiebeer.com.au

MAGGIE BEER'S
WINTER HARVEST
— RECIPES —

Maggie Beer

with photography by Mark Chew

LANTERN

an imprint of
PENGUIN BOOKS

For Colin

CONTENTS

Introduction XI

Cavolo nero 2
Celeriac 7
Chestnuts 12
Crabs 23
Extra virgin olive oil 31
Flour 41
Kangaroo 65
Leeks 70
Lemons and limes 76
Offal 87
Onions 94
Oranges 101
Pigeon and squab 110
Pork 116
Rabbit 127
Riverfish 137
Root vegetables 144
Smoked foods 154
Venison 163
Witlof 169

Basics 177
Glossary 183
List of sources 185
Bibliography 186
Acknowledgements 189
Index 190

INTRODUCTION

MY PASSION FOR FOOD HAS GIVEN ME SO MUCH IN LIFE – a sense of purpose, a delicious anticipation of each new day, and gifts of a much deeper kind than financial. Harvesting the bounty from living off the land, sharing the harvest with my family and friends, and being part of a community are incredibly rewarding – I wouldn't swap my life for anything!

Maggie's Harvest, a landmark book when it was first published in 2007, was the culmination of a lot of hard work and highlights my philosophy of using the freshest and best seasonal produce available at my doorstop in the Barossa Valley. The cover design was heavy with symbolism as well – the pear tree bearing golden fruit, like the one that stands at the bottom of my garden, are what Kylie Kwong called the 'golden orbs' of my life. And the pheasant on the end of the branch dips the hat to my Colin, whose vision to farm pheasants inspired our move to the Barossa, and thus began this food life of mine.

And while the original *Harvest* edition still lives in its beautifully bound, embroidered cover, for ease of use, what better way to approach each new season than with a paperback edition, exclusively featuring the recipes you'll need for the months ahead. More practical in the kitchen – although you need to know how much I love to see splattered copies of any of my books. These seasonal paperbacks celebrate my love for each season and the bounty it brings; accentuating the produce available, beginning with winter.

Winter is about so many things; the aromas of a slow-cooked meal permeating the kitchen when you arrive home from work; the garden full of great root vegetables, and cabbages and kales that thrive in the cold; the citrus, the fruit I certainly couldn't live without, that add so much to the winter table – you need never be short of variety just because of the cooler season.

I love and celebrate each change in the season and the food it brings. I hope you love winter too and that, in turn, you'll collect each of the four seasons.

CAVOLO NERO

 MY FIRST SIGHTING OF CAVOLO NERO, ITALY'S 'BLACK CABBAGE', was at a stall in Florence's San Lorenzo market in 1997. The stall was the most expensive in the entire marketplace and the vendor was so charming to us during the first week of our visit because we bought so much from her.

By the second week we were a little savvier and would circle the market before returning to 'our' stallholder – and she became very bad-tempered when she saw how much we'd bought elsewhere. In fact, she was so cross we almost decided not to buy from her, only to find that she was the only one offering the purpley, greenish-black leaves of the first cavolo nero of the season.

A member of the *Brassica* family (a kale, actually), cavolo nero doesn't form a head but is instead made up of long, loose leaves growing from an upright stem that can be picked a little like silverbeet. Unlike a cabbage, it withstands long cooking, during which time the leaves become almost black, imparting a pleasantly bitter flavour – just right for lovers of savoury things.

I became such a convert to cavolo nero that when I returned home from Italy I brought packets of seeds with me (I declared them, of course), as I had never known the vegetable to be available here. I usually have great intentions of planting seeds and nurturing the seedlings and then in a flurry of chaotic activity forget to water them. Instead, this time I passed the seeds on to Mike Plane of Allsun Farm in New South Wales, who had chased me up after reading of the seeds in an article I wrote. In return, he sent a tray of seedlings with the heads just about to poke through the potting soil. Mike assured me the vegetable was easy to grow, the only problem being a few aphids on the outside leaves (these leaves went to the chooks).

Cavolo nero is now available in specialty greengrocers, though if you go to the trouble of growing it yourself, you can pick the young leaves for salad, before the leaves mature. They are such magnificent plants that they could almost be ornamental features in the garden.

Cavolo nero on bruschetta (see page 4)

Perhaps the best way to enjoy the distinctive flavour of cavolo nero is on bruschetta. This may not be the first dish that springs to mind – but it's a rustic dish for which I would travel miles. Wash and trim a couple of bunches of cavolo nero and chop into 5 cm pieces. Simmer the leaves in chicken stock until softened (this can take up to 30 minutes, depending on the age of the cavolo nero). Toast thick slices of crusty bread and rub these on one

side with a clove of garlic. Dip the toast into the stock briefly to moisten, then put it on a plate and pile on the drained cavolo nero. Add sea salt, freshly ground black pepper and a really good dose of fruity extra virgin olive oil, particularly if you have access to the new season's. Amazing!

Recipes for hearty Ribollita soup (see page 6) usually appear with a note claiming that it is impossible to make it without cavolo nero ('ribollita' simply means re-boiled: the soup can be made one day and reheated the next). I'd made it with Savoy cabbage before our Italian sojourn, which I had thought a good substitute, but, as is so often the case, tradition wins out – it is fascinating to discover that one ingredient can make such a difference. In Italy I used cavolo nero with pork and when making a risotto. Now that I grow my own, I'll find many more applications, but it seems appropriate to include a recipe for a soup here, as this is what I had hoped to cook when scouring the San Lorenzo market for my first taste of cavolo nero.

CAVOLO NERO WITH GOLDEN SHALLOTS AND QUINCE *Serves 4*

1 bunch cavolo nero, washed and chopped
50 g butter
extra virgin olive oil, for cooking
2 small golden shallots, thinly sliced

½ quince, peeled, cored and sliced
lemon juice, to taste
1 teaspoon chopped lemon thyme

Blanch cavolo nero by plunging it briefly in a saucepan of boiling water until just tender, if the leaves are young; if they are older you'll need to cook them a bit more at the end. Drain well and squeeze out any excess moisture. In a large frying pan, heat the butter over medium heat until nut-brown, then add a little olive oil to inhibit burning. Add the shallots and quince slices and cook until tender and golden. Add a good squeeze of lemon juice and the lemon thyme, then add the cavolo nero. If the leaves are older, cook until tender; otherwise, serve straight away.

BRAISED CAVOLO NERO   *Serves 4*

1 bunch cavolo nero, washed and
    roughly chopped
½ cup (125 ml) extra virgin olive oil

1 clove garlic
2 anchovy fillets

Blanch the chopped cavolo nero by plunging it briefly in a saucepan of boiling water until just tender, then drain immediately and set aside.

Heat the olive oil over low–medium heat, then sauté the garlic. Add the anchovy fillets and cavolo nero and season with a little salt and pepper. Sauté slowly for about 5 minutes, until the cavolo nero is tender on the tooth.

I like to serve this as an accompaniment, and it works especially well with a slow-roasted oyster blade.

MINESTRONE WITH CAVOLO NERO   *Serves 8*

Now that I grow cavolo nero in my own garden, I add it to my version of minestrone.

1⅓ cups (275 g) dried lima beans, soaked
    overnight in a deep bowl of water
125 ml extra virgin olive oil,
    plus extra for cooking
20 g butter
3 onions, roughly chopped
3 cloves garlic, roughly chopped
6 large sprigs thyme
2 carrots, roughly chopped
2 sticks celery, roughly chopped
3 rashers bacon, chopped
rind from a piece of Parmigiano Reggiano,
    if available

2 small fresh bay leaves
1 × 410 g can peeled and chopped
    roma tomatoes
2.5 litres Golden Chicken Stock
    (see page 178)
8–10 large cavolo nero leaves,
    stems removed and leaves shredded
2 zucchini, diced
100 g green beans, sliced
sea salt flakes and freshly ground
    black pepper

Drain the lima beans and set aside.

Heat 125 ml olive oil and the butter in a stockpot over medium heat until the butter is nut-brown, then gently sauté the onions and garlic until translucent. Tie the thyme sprigs together with kitchen string and add to the pan with the drained lima beans, carrots, celery, bacon, cheese rind and bay leaves, and toss to coat with the olive oil and butter.

Add the tomatoes and 2 litres of the chicken stock, then stir and bring to the boil over high heat. Turn heat down to low and gently simmer for 1½ hours. You may need to add a little more stock during cooking, so keep an eye on the pan. »

Heat a little olive oil in a saucepan, then add the shredded cavolo nero and toss until wilted. Add to the soup and simmer for another 10 minutes. Shortly before serving, add the zucchini and green beans to the soup and cook until just tender. Season with salt and pepper.

To serve, remove the cheese rind and bundle of thyme, then ladle the soup into warm, wide soup bowls and drizzle over a little extra virgin olive oil.

RIBOLLITA   *Serves 4*

Meaning 're-boiled', ribollita takes leftover minestrone made the day before and extends it with the addition of cavolo nero and extra stock, transforming it into a slightly different dish. I put cavolo nero in my minestrone anyway as I like it so much, but the ribollita still benefits from adding even more.

1 bunch cavolo nero, washed and
   chopped into 5 cm pieces
2 cups (500 ml) Golden Chicken Stock
   (see page 178)
4 large slices wood-fired bread

1 clove garlic
extra virgin olive oil, for drizzling
2 cups (500 ml) leftover Minestrone
   (see previous page)

Simmer the cavolo nero in the chicken stock over low–medium heat for 20–30 minutes or until tender; the time will depend on the age of the cavolo nero.

Grill the bread, then rub on both sides with the cut garlic. Place a slice of grilled bread in each soup bowl and drizzle with olive oil.

Remove the cavolo nero from the stock and set aside. Add the leftover minestrone to the stock and heat over high heat, stirring continuously. When the soup is hot, add the cooked cavolo nero and a good drizzle of olive oil. Serve poured over the grilled bread.

CELERIAC

WHAT A HUGE PREHISTORIC-LOOKING VEGETABLE THIS IS, AND
yet how delicate its flavour. Celeriac is a versatile vegetable available from late
autumn right through winter. It is as ancient a vegetable as celery, so its lack of
popularity is hard to understand, although it has long been part of continental
European cooking. Both celery and celeriac were cultivated from the original wild celery
plant. I love the mild 'celery' flavour of the celeriac – cooked and puréed, it is a natural
accompaniment to game.

While you might buy a bunch of celeriac with four bulbs from a wholesale fruit and
vegetable supplier, it is most often sold individually, which is more appropriate for a small
household (though if you have the chance to buy a bunch of younger, smaller bulbs, then
take it!). As it has a rough surface, it is best to choose the smoothest you can find so that
you don't lose too much of the vegetable in the trimming.

Celeriac discolours on cutting, so put it in a bowl of acidulated water (water with lemon
juice or verjuice added) until you're ready to cook it. If you are going to eat it raw, just rub
the exposed surface with a cut lemon as you would for an artichoke. Sliced finely, celeriac
gives a lovely crunch to salads.

Celeriac cut thickly and roasted to a golden brown in extra virgin olive oil can be added
to a dish of chicken or guinea fowl.

Going through old notebooks of visits to Paris, I found an account of my first ever
Celeriac Rémoulade (see page 9), some years ago now. It was at one of those truly Parisian
bistros – the type that is becoming harder to find these days – with a very limited lunch
menu, checked tablecloths, wine only available in half or full carafes, and lots of tiny tables
crammed together in a narrow room. The food was simply prepared with great flavour and
served with speed and panache. Sometimes I can go a whole winter without remembering
to make celeriac rémoulade, but when I do it immediately evokes the memory of this
French bistro.

In the same notebook I found a description of a warm salad of quail with apple, celeriac, pine nuts, hazelnut oil, a little balsamic and the smallest touch of truffle oil. Just reading through this list of ingredients transports me back to the occasion when I first tried it, and inspires me to make it again.

In this quail dish both the celeriac and apples were raw – peeled, shredded and tossed in lemon juice before being added to the salad. This brings me to the combination of apple and celeriac. It works whether they are raw, cooked together and puréed, or tossed in a pan with some chicken or duck livers. All of these become a real treat when a splash of verjuice is added, though a good squeeze of lemon juice would do.

Celeriac chips are really simple to make, and go beautifully with grilled fish, lamb chops or barbecued chicken. With a firm hand and a sharp knife, or using a mandolin or Japanese shredder, peel and cut the celeriac widthways into 2 cm-thick pieces, then soak in acidulated water for 10 minutes, drain and pat dry. Deep-fry in your favourite extra virgin olive oil until golden brown. Drain on kitchen paper and sprinkle with a little sea salt with grated lemon rind added.

CELERIAC RÉMOULADE
Serves 4

Celeriac rémoulade can be served with cold chicken, smoked potted tongue, a salad of radicchio, apples, walnuts and pancetta, or as Stephanie Alexander says in her culinary bible, *The Cook's Companion*, that I so often refer to, 'this delicious starter is very addictive with a bowl of fat olives and some good bread and maybe a platter of thinly sliced salami'. As it was Stephanie who first introduced me to this dish, I thought it absolutely fitting that I use her method.

1 large celeriac (reject if spongy in the centre after peeling)
1 lemon
½ cup (125 ml) mustard Mayonnaise (see page 38)
1 tablespoon freshly chopped flat-leaf parsley

Peel the celeriac and rub exposed surfaces with cut lemon. Cut into quarters and drop in a bowl of acidulated water. Shred celeriac using the shredding disc of your food processor or a mandolin slicer placed over a bowl containing the mayonnaise. Combine the celeriac and mayonnaise, stir to mix well, then add the parsley.

CELERIAC, APPLE AND WALNUT SALAD
Serves 4

2 small celeriac
juice of ½ lemon
2 small Granny Smith apples, cored and thinly sliced
80 g toasted walnuts
freshly chopped flat-leaf parsley, to serve

DRESSING
¼ cup (60 ml) sour cream
½ teaspoon Dijon mustard
¼ cup (60 ml) extra virgin olive oil
2½ tablespoons freshly grated horseradish
¼ cup (60 ml) walnut oil
1 tablespoon lemon juice (optional)
sea salt flakes and freshly ground black pepper (optional)

Trim the bases and tops from the celeriac, then cut down the sides to peel. Using a strong potato peeler, shave thick slices from the celeriac, dropping them into a bowl of water with the lemon juice added to stop them discolouring. Add the apple to the bowl.

To make the dressing, whisk the sour cream, Dijon mustard and olive oil until emulsified. Add the horseradish, then the walnut oil and stir to combine. Taste the dressing, and add lemon juice, salt or pepper if needed.

Toss the drained celeriac and apples with the dressing, then add the walnuts and some freshly chopped flat-leaf parsley. This salad is excellent served with slices of smoked salmon.

BRAISED CELERIAC *Serves 4*

This dish is best of all when made using four small celeriac, which unfortunately I am yet to see in greengrocers. When made with young ones picked from your own garden, the flavour is extraordinary.

4 small *or* 1 large celeriac	2 tablespoons freshly chopped
lemon juice, to taste	flat-leaf parsley
1 cup (250 ml) Golden Chicken Stock	sea salt flakes and freshly ground
(see page 178)	black pepper
1 tablespoon butter	

Peel and cut the celeriac into slices. Squeeze with a little lemon juice and then simmer in a saucepan with the chicken stock and butter until tender – this will take up to 20 minutes depending on the size of the slices. Remove the cooked celeriac and drain, keeping it warm. Reduce the remaining stock to pour over the celeriac, then finish with the freshly chopped parsley, and salt and pepper to taste.

PURÉE OF CELERIAC TO ACCOMPANY GAME *Serves 4*

This purée can also be made with either just potatoes or apples, depending on what you have to hand and what you are serving it with. Celeriac with apple goes well with pheasant, and celeriac with potatoes is wonderful alongside the best sausages you can buy.

1 medium potato, peeled and cut	50 g butter
into thick slices	150 ml cream
1 large celeriac, peeled and cut	sea salt flakes and freshly ground
into thick slices	black pepper
2 Granny Smith apples, peeled,	
cored and thickly sliced	

Boil the potato and celeriac in a large saucepan of salted water until tender, adding the apples after 5 minutes. Drain well and then purée in a mouli. Whisk in the butter and cream to make a fluffy purée. Season to taste.

VICTORIA'S CELERIAC AND CHESTNUT PIE *Serves 6*

Victoria Blumenstein, formerly of Blumenstein's, came to work for me at the Farmshop in 2002 and stayed for three very eventful years. Victoria and I worked together on so many ideas, and so often it was a case of two heads being better than one. This is one of my favourite recipes from Victoria – a luscious dish for a cold winter's day.

1 × quantity Sour-cream Pastry
(see page 62)
juice of ½ lemon
1 celeriac (about 750 g)
100 g Swiss brown mushrooms,
trimmed and quartered
1 fennel bulb, trimmed and finely chopped
2 large onions, finely chopped
¼ cup (60 ml) extra virgin olive oil
sea salt flakes and freshly ground
black pepper
3 cloves garlic, finely chopped

½ cup (125 ml) verjuice
2 cups (500 ml) vegetable *or* Golden Chicken
Stock (see page 178)
2 sprigs rosemary
2 sprigs thyme
50 g chestnuts, peeled
(frozen, partly precooked chestnuts are
suitable if you can't get fresh ones)
50 g brancolete *or* other goat's cheese,
crumbled
1 egg, beaten with a little milk

Make and chill the pastry as instructed.

Add the lemon juice to a large bowl of water. Peel the celeriac and cut it into 1 cm pieces, then place it in the bowl of water. Place the celeriac in a saucepan of salted water; then bring to the boil and simmer for 4 minutes or until it is almost cooked. Place the mushrooms, fennel and onions in three separate bowls, drizzle each with olive oil and season to taste with salt and pepper. Add the garlic to the onions.

Heat a large frying pan over medium heat, then sauté the mushrooms until cooked, deglaze the pan with a dash of verjuice and transfer to a bowl. Repeat first with the fennel and then with the onion and garlic mixture, deglazing each time with verjuice.

Wipe the pan clean with kitchen paper, then add the stock, herbs and the remaining verjuice and bring to a simmer over medium heat. Add the chestnuts to the pan, reduce the heat to low and poach for 5 minutes or until tender but still whole, then remove chestnuts and set aside. Reduce the stock over high heat until syrupy, then add to the bowl with the sautéed onion mixture. Add all the vegetables and the chestnuts to the bowl, toss to combine, then leave to cool.

Meanwhile, preheat the oven to 200°C. Roll out the pastry and cut out a lid and base for a 24 cm pie mould. Distribute the vegetable mixture evenly over the pastry, then top with the cheese. Place the pastry lid on top, pinch edges to seal and brush with egg and milk mixture. Bake for 20 minutes or until golden brown. Serve with a rocket and shaved Parmigiano Reggiano salad.

CHESTNUTS

I ATE MY FIRST CHESTNUT, TOO MANY YEARS AGO TO WANT TO remember, on a street corner in Vienna during my first European winter. Vendors were roasting them over braziers and serving the hot chestnuts in a cone made from newspaper. It was such a surprise to bite into this smoky morsel and discover a flavour like that of a nutty sweet potato – the chestnuts warmed my hands as I held them and took some of the bitter chill away.

Thinking about this reminds me of when chefs Urs Inauen, Cheong Liew, Tom Milligan and I were in New York in the spring of 1992. The previous year we had won the Seppelt Australian Menu of the Year together, and our 'prize' was to cook a grand dinner for the American press at the Peninsula Hotel. It was unseasonably cold, and snow had brought the chestnut sellers out to ply their wares. The dinner was a mammoth effort, and we were lucky that Urs had arrived ahead of the rest of us in order to source ingredients, as we were beset by disasters (the most memorable of which saw our hare literally flying all over the country – turning up just in time at the last moment!). The night was a great success in the end, but when the dinner finished, the snow had stopped and the chestnut sellers had disappeared from the streets.

And now I have my own chestnut trees. These trees have flourished, even with years of drought and persistent gully winds that would blow a roof off at times. When I think of my long walks in the Umbrian mountains, where wild chestnuts abound without any tending, I guess their hardiness is not at all surprising. They even drop their crop when they are ready. Having said that, timing is everything, and as the chestnuts lose moisture quickly it doesn't pay to leave them on the ground. Pick them up and keep them refrigerated in plastic bags in the crisper section until you're ready to use them – the sooner the better.

Fresh chestnuts (not a nut, in fact, but a fruit) have become readily available in fruit and vegetable shops from late April through to July. The shinier and fuller the chestnut, the

fresher it is. If chestnuts are glossy, a deep mahogany-brown colour and heavy in the hand they will be very fresh. Don't be bothered with withered chestnuts or any that are mouldy. Fresh chestnuts should be cooked very soon after picking as they dry out very quickly, losing weight and flavour.

The area around Myrtleford in Victoria, with the influence of Italian immigrants, abounds with chestnut trees and chestnut festivals. Jane Casey of Cheznuts has a thriving business there, producing frozen, peeled chestnuts, as well as fresh ones, taking all the hard work out of getting your chestnut fix. They are delivered Australia-wide and Jane can be contacted through the website www.cheznuts.com.au. Closer to home for me is Nirvana, a truly beautiful property in the Adelaide Hills where Deb Cantrell and Quentin Jones farm chestnuts and redcurrants.

Because the Australian chestnut industry is so young, many new varieties are being introduced, so if you're looking for a tree for your own garden, check what works well in your area. A variety that performs well in South Australia may not do so in Victoria, and vice versa. The benefit of having such a young industry is that those involved realise the importance of commitment and progress, so much so that all growers pay a levy to fund research. The industry is also aware that the health benefits of chestnuts are a vital market-ing aid: chestnuts contain no cholesterol, are very low in fat (less than 4 per cent), and are 50 per cent carbohydrate and 10 per cent protein (which is very similar to the amount of protein in an egg). You will certainly never get oil from a chestnut! There is tremendous potential for growth in this industry – at the moment the Australian population eats one chestnut per person each year, and although canned chestnuts and a small quantity of dried chestnuts are imported from elsewhere, the only country chestnuts can be imported from fresh is New Zealand.

Most exciting of all, however, is the fact that local chestnut growers are increasingly offering peeled, cooked and frozen chestnuts commercially. My first experience of this, some years ago now, was when I was sent a small hessian sack of fresh chestnuts still in their husks from Richard Moxham and Alison Saunders, who trade as Sassafras Nuts in Griffith, ACT. I was impressed by the fact that Richard had made sure I knew the chestnuts were coming so that I was ready to refrigerate them immediately on receipt, an important issue if their freshness is to be retained. (If you don't have a hessian bag to hand, a brown paper bag is the next best thing for storing chestnuts, in the crisper compartment of your refrigerator.)

The chestnuts came complete with a chestnut knife, the size of a paring knife but with the tiniest blade, which has a sharp protrusion to make cutting into the tough chestnuts much easier. Now, that's what I call clever marketing. In his letter, Richard explained that 'peelability' is the Australian chestnut industry's biggest problem and many growers, like themselves, were regrafting their trees to easier-peeling varieties – in their case to Sassafras Red, a good peeling variety that has a sweet, creamy flavour when roasted.

Chestnuts are notoriously difficult to peel. Collected after they fall from the tree, chest-nuts are encased in a very prickly burr that makes the wearing of gloves essential. If you have your own tree you will need to remove the burr first, then slit the shiny shell beneath it to reveal the chestnut, which has a skin of its own that must be removed. If you buy direct from the farm in season or from a specialist greengrocer, the burr will already have been removed, leaving only the shell and the skin to be dealt with.

My favourite way of eating chestnuts is to slit the shells on the domed side and then roast them over a flame. My friend Steve Flamsteed gave me a chestnut-roasting pan when

he returned from his cheese-making *stage* (training) in France in 1994, though the black pan, with holes about 7 mm across drilled all over its base, hangs the whole year in the pot rack above my marble bench until the chestnut season. So many people are curious about what I could possibly cook in it, and even though it can go over a gas flame it only seems right over an open fire. The holes allow the flames to leap up and lick around the chestnuts. The secret when cooking chestnuts over a fire is to allow them to blacken and then to let them cool just a little (once burnt and crisp, they reach the desired flavour, but if allowed to become cold, the inner brown skin, or 'pellicle', is difficult to remove). One has to be careful not to scorch the chestnuts too much but the crispness this method produces is highly desirable, even if it means burnt fingertips as the skins of the chestnuts are gingerly pulled away.

Unless you have special equipment, the next best method to attain a smoky flavour is to slit the shells and then grill the chestnuts until they are charred, turning them after 15 minutes. They should take about 25 minutes in all to cook this way. Wrap the grilled chestnuts in a tea towel, where they will steam a little, making peeling easier.

If you have lots of chestnuts, they freeze particularly well once blanched and peeled. This is the method to follow if you plan to use the chestnuts in a dish rather than eat them roasted – this way most of the cooking is done in the final dish, so more flavour is taken up, and overcooking the chestnuts, which is quite easy to do and causes them to break up, is avoided. Slit the shiny brown shell with a very sharp knife and peel it away. Bring the chestnuts to the boil in a small saucepan of cold water – they are ready as soon as the water boils; left any longer they go grey, like canned chestnuts (however, should you wish to cook them completely this way, let them simmer for 15 minutes). Remove the pan from the heat then take out one chestnut at a time, and slip off the papery skin. If you are freezing the chestnuts, do so immediately. Thaw them just before they are required, to avoid discolouration.

At present, Australian chestnut growers do not see an immediate market for chestnut flour, although one or two grind their own supply. It is such a limited market, and competing with the small volumes already being imported into Australia would be prohibitive. I love to use chestnut flour to make flat, moist, flavoursome cakes to serve with coffee, as the Italians do (see page 21). The quality of some of the imported flour varies greatly, depending on freshness: one has no idea of the date of harvest and the flour can be full of weevils or rancid. As Australian growers' crops become larger and more viable, we should keep encouraging more of them to grind their own flour, so that those of us who want to use chestnut flour do not need to rely on imports.

Jane Casey of Cheznuts says that in the first four years of growing chestnuts she didn't even eat them. Now she understands that she needs to be passionate about them so she can advise, educate and enthuse her customers. Such a simple matter, and something I've tried to shout from as many rooftops as possible – just imagine what would happen if every producer adopted this philosophy.

Brussels sprouts hadn't been a vegetable Jane had liked at all until she tried steaming them with blanched and peeled chestnuts. They take exactly the same length of time (about 15–20 minutes) and the chestnuts have an inherent sweetness that complements the sprouts, and they also provide great texture. Or try pan-frying blanched chestnuts in nut-brown butter with fresh herbs for 5 minutes, then adding blanched Brussels sprouts that have been cut in half and cooking for another 5 minutes – delicious served with game.

Cooking chestnuts with rice adds another dimension to a stir-fry. Jane uses a rice cooker and merely adds a handful of peeled chestnuts with the usual volume of rice and leaves them to cook (the same result can be achieved if cooking rice by the absorption method). The chestnuts add crunch and their flavour permeates the rice.

Use whole blanched chestnuts in a traditional stuffing for turkey, goose or a really good chicken. Chestnuts, pancetta and rosemary are the perfect combination when cooking guinea fowl. Pot-roast a pheasant or guinea fowl with blanched chestnuts, baby onions, fresh bay leaves, orange rind and juniper berries in a little stock and some sage jelly – the dish will only take about half an hour to cook once you have your ingredients ready. Velvety, nutty chestnut soup (see page 18), a stock-based purée thinned with a little cream, is particularly good with the addition of a little pheasant, pigeon or quail meat tossed in a little oil or butter over heat with tiny onions and fresh herbs.

Take the time to make a chestnut purée as a base for desserts, although I admit it's a tedious job. Boil the chestnuts, reserve the water, and then peel and purée them in a food mill or food processor while still warm. Add some of the liquid to make it easier, if necessary. The purée is great mixed into ice cream or added to choux pastry that is then deep-fried like a doughnut. If you buy canned chestnut purée, check whether it is unsweetened or sweetened – I find the latter overly sweet and prefer to add the sweetness myself. You could use dried chestnuts to make your own purée: cover them with milk, bring to the boil, take off the heat and steep at room temperature overnight. Drain, purée and sweeten to taste.

Of course there is the classic Mont Blanc, a piped mass of sweetened chestnut purée topped with whipped cream; the purée can also be flavoured with a little liqueur and served with créme fraîche alongside.

Going through old notes and scraps of ideas, I came across a mention of a chocolate chestnut cake served with stewed mulberries. My tastebuds remembered it well, but there were no further notes to guide me. How I wish I'd documented all the dishes I've cooked! The problem was that I couldn't remember whether I used a canned unsweetened chestnut purée or chestnut flour; I've certainly made cakes with both. The purée would give a very moist pudding-like consistency, while the flour would produce a moist and nutty Italian-style cake. I would ice both versions with chocolate ganache. I think the purée probably wins out as my more likely choice.

Chestnut and chocolate make a good combination, particularly if you use a very bitter couverture chocolate. A great boon for chocoholics is Peter Wilson's Kennedy & Wilson Chocolates. A winemaker who worked for Bailey Carrodus of Yarra Yering Vineyards for ten years, Peter has made an art form out of this wonderful bitter chocolate, and though the company goes from strength to strength, Peter has now returned to wine-making. Peter was one of our favourite customers at the Pheasant Farm. He went to Roseworthy College to study oenology, and his group was so passionate about their food and wine that they celebrated all their special occasions in our restaurant. My husband Colin allowed them to bring wine in without corkage: they saved up for these dinners, always brought along the best wines they could muster and simply asked me to cook. This group was extraordinary, matched only by Steve Flamsteed's year. It was a delight to cook for them.

The point of all this is that chestnuts are extremely versatile, and this versatility is increased further by the forms in which they can now be bought: fresh, frozen (peeled and par-cooked), canned whole or puréed, dried pieces or ground as flour.

CHESTNUT SOUP   *Serves 6*

1 large onion, finely chopped	sea salt flakes
2 sticks celery, thinly sliced	1.5 litres Golden Chicken Stock
500 g blanched chestnuts	(see page 178)
2 fresh bay leaves	freshly ground black pepper
2 tablespoons extra virgin olive oil	½ cup (125 ml) cream

Sauté the onion, celery, chestnuts and bay leaves in the olive oil in a stockpot over medium–high heat until the onion is golden brown. Season with salt and add the stock, then simmer until the chestnuts are very soft, about 25–30 minutes. Remove the bay leaves and then purée the mixture in a food processor or blender. Season with pepper and check if more salt is needed, then add the cream. Reheat gently and serve immediately.

RAVIOLI WITH CHESTNUTS, MUSHROOMS AND MASCARPONE

Makes 18 ravioli

320 g peeled and blanched frozen
    chestnuts, defrosted
4 sprigs thyme
1½ cups (375 ml) Golden Chicken Stock
    (see page 178)
130 g unsalted butter
320 g Swiss brown mushrooms, sliced
⅓ cup chopped sage
sea salt flakes and freshly ground
    black pepper

640 g mascarpone
1 egg
dash milk
extra virgin olive oil, to serve

RAVIOLI
250 g plain flour
3 egg yolks
2 eggs

For the ravioli, tip the flour onto a bench and make a well in the centre. Whisk the egg yolks and eggs together and pour into the well. Incorporate them into the flour, and knead the pasta dough until it forms a shiny ball and is firm to the touch. Cover the dough with plastic film and rest it in the refrigerator for 30 minutes.

Meanwhile, place the chestnuts, thyme and chicken stock in a saucepan, then poach over very low heat for 10 minutes or until tender. Sauté the mushrooms in the butter over medium heat with the sage, 2 teaspoons salt, and pepper for 5 minutes or until cooked.

Drain the chestnuts, reserving the stock, and combine them with the mushrooms. Chop roughly or pulse once or twice in a food processor, adding 2 tablespoons of the reserved stock to pull the mixture together and make a smooth paste. Fold in the mascarpone, then chill in the refrigerator until firm. Season to taste with more salt and pepper.

Cut the dough into manageable portions. Using a pasta machine with rollers set at the widest setting, feed batches of the dough through the rollers. Reduce the settings on the rollers notch by notch, feeding the pasta dough through until you reach the second-last notch on the machine. It should be very thin, but not transparent (ravioli is often spoilt by pasta that's too thick). Cover each sheet with a damp tea towel to keep moist and continue to roll remaining pieces of dough. The sheets should be even in length – trim if they are not.

Lay the pasta sheets on a bench. Use a small ice-cream scoop or a generous tablespoon to mound spoonfuls of the chestnut filling in rows, 10 cm apart, on half of the pasta sheets. Combine the egg and milk, and brush the pasta sheets with egg wash around the filling and to the edges of the pasta. Lay another sheet of pasta over each of the chestnut-topped sheets, and, starting from the filling edge, press down to remove any air bubbles as you go. Cut into squares 10 × 10 cm, then chill in the refrigerator for at least 2 hours.

Poach the ravioli gently in batches, no more than four at a time, in a deep frying pan of simmering water. They should be cooked in about 5 minutes, but this will depend on the thickness of the pasta. Drizzle with extra virgin olive oil and serve.

SEARED DUCK BREASTS WITH CHESTNUTS, BACON AND VINO COTTO-GLAZED RADICCHIO

Serves 2

2 × 150 g duck breast fillets, skin on

sea salt flakes

1 cup frozen whole chestnuts, defrosted

milk, for cooking

freshly ground black pepper

2 rashers bacon, rind removed

60 g unsalted butter

2 small radicchio, trimmed and cut
  into wedges

1 tablespoon brown sugar

¼ cup (60 ml) vino cotto (see Glossary)

¼ cup freshly chopped flat-leaf parsley

Score the skin of each duck breast diagonally, then sprinkle with salt. If you have time, pour boiling water over the skin and place, uncovered, in the refrigerator overnight – this allows the pores to open and helps the fat under the skin to render beautifully during cooking. If you don't have that much time, even 10 minutes will help.

Simmer the defrosted chestnuts in just enough milk to cover them, for 20 minutes or until tender. Alternatively, if you are short of time, place the chestnuts in a microwave-proof container, add ¼ cup (60 ml) water, cover and cook on high for 2 minutes, then leave them to stand for 10 minutes. Drain and cut in half, then set aside.

Preheat the oven to 200°C. Heat a chargrill pan or heavy-based frying pan over high heat until very hot. Season the duck breasts with salt and pepper and place skin-side down in the pan to sear. Leave until well-browned, then turn over and sear the other side for 1 minute. Transfer to the oven and cook for another 4 minutes, then remove and leave to rest, skin-side down, in a warm place.

Add the bacon to the pan and cook until crisp, then cut into small pieces and set aside.

Meanwhile, heat half the butter in a frying pan over medium heat until nut-brown, then add the chestnuts and toss until light brown and crisp. Season to taste with salt and pepper, then remove and set aside.

For the vino cotto-glazed radicchio, add the remaining butter to the pan, and when nut-brown, add the radicchio. Cook until the radicchio just starts to wilt, then add the brown sugar and season to taste. When the sugar has melted, deglaze the pan with vino cotto and add the reserved bacon and chestnuts.

Carve each duck breast into slices on the diagonal, then fan them out a little. Divide the chestnuts, bacon and vino cotto-glazed radicchio between two plates and top each with a sliced duck breast. Drizzle with the resting juices from the duck, and serve.

CHESTNUT CAKE

Serves 6–8

In Italy, this flat, dense cake is served with coffee. Chestnut flour is available from Italian delis – the freshness of the flour will dramatically affect the flavour of the cake.

⅓ cup (50 g) dried currants
verjuice, for soaking
250 g chestnut flour
1½ cups (375 ml) cold water
¼ cup (60 ml) extra virgin olive oil
pinch salt

⅓ cup (50 g) pine nuts
2 teaspoons finely chopped rosemary
finely chopped rind of 1 orange
Strega (an Italian liqueur, optional) *or*
    mascarpone combined with grated
    orange rind (optional), to serve

Reconstitute the currants, in enough verjuice to cover them, for about 30 minutes. Preheat the oven to 200°C. Sift the chestnut flour into a bowl, then gradually stir in the cold water to make a thick paste (you may not need all of it). Make sure there are no lumps, then add the olive oil and salt.

Dry-roast the pine nuts on a baking tray for about 10 minutes until golden brown (watch them carefully as they burn easily). Reduce the oven temperature to 190°C.

Add the rosemary, orange rind, drained currants and pine nuts to the batter and stir vigorously until amalgamated. Grease a shallow 20 cm cake tin and pour in the batter to a depth of 2.5 cm, then bake for 30 minutes. Serve the cake warm, either moistened with Strega poured over it as soon as it comes out of the oven, or with mascarpone flavoured with grated orange rind alongside.

CHESTNUT AND CHOCOLATE POTS

Serves 8

This is a very rich dessert so I tend to serve it as a treat after supper in small demitasse coffee cups.

1 × 430 g tin unsweetened chestnut purée
120 ml pouring cream
80 g unsalted butter, chopped
30 ml Cognac
2 tablespoons Seville orange marmalade

GANACHE
150 g dark couverture chocolate buttons
    (see Glossary)
85 ml pouring cream

Place chestnut purée and cream in a saucepan and melt, stirring to combine, over low heat. If the purée is extremely thick and difficult to stir, add a little water. Add butter and continue stirring until it melts and combines. Add Cognac, then remove from the heat.

Using a hand-held blender or food processor, purée the chestnut mixture until smooth. Pour the purée evenly into 8 small demitasse coffee cups and refrigerate for about 20 minutes or until firm. »

Meanwhile, for the ganache, melt the chocolate and cream together in a small saucepan over low heat, stirring to combine.

Add 1 teaspoon marmalade to each cup, then cover with chocolate ganache and refrigerate until totally set.

CHOCOLATE AND CHESTNUT LOG

Serves 12

In fourteen years of cooking at the Pheasant Farm Restaurant I hardly wrote down any recipes, but fortunately this chocolate and chestnut log was recorded for posterity. I have no idea where the original recipe came from, as the card it is written on is now almost illegible, after fifteen years' worth of sticky fingers all over it. This dessert is unbelievably rich, so rather than offering cream with it, raspberries would be perfect, when in season, as would candied cumquats.

200 g unsalted butter

2 tablespoons castor sugar

1 large egg

1 tablespoon Cognac

450 g cooked, peeled and sieved fresh
    chestnuts *or* canned unsweetened
    chestnut purée

200 g dark couverture chocolate
    (see Glossary), melted

Using a hand-held electric mixer, cream the butter, sugar, egg and Cognac until light and fluffy. If using fresh chestnuts, purée them until smooth. Add the chestnut purée to the butter mixture and mix thoroughly.

Transfer half the mixture into another bowl and mix in the melted chocolate thoroughly. Spread the chocolate mixture into a rectangle on a sheet of baking paper or foil, then top with the remaining chestnut mixture. Roll into a log and refrigerate until set.

To serve, cut the log with a sharp knife dipped in hot water.

CRABS

A TRIP AWAY SO OFTEN MAKES YOU REALISE JUST HOW wonderful things are at home. There are so many things I've become aware of following my trips overseas, such as the value for money we take for granted in Australia, and the quality of our produce. But we can't kid ourselves either – although superior-quality produce is available, you need to look for it. You have to search out the right seafood merchants, meat suppliers and greengrocers, or gain access to producers via farmers' markets, to be assured of quality. Importantly, you need to know the right questions to ask too, such as what variety it is, where the product was farmed and how, and whether it has been refrigerated.

When it comes to seafood, specialist shops in both the United States and the United Kingdom have over the past few years become exceptional, but I suspect our great advantage in Australia is that those of us who like to fish have access to a wide variety of bounty that would be hard to match anywhere.

For me, in South Australia, nothing stands out more than our blue swimmer crab. Years ago now I was part of a group that travelled to New York to cook a spectacular dinner at the Peninsula Hotel. Unable to bring in our own blue swimmers we had instead to use Dungeness crabs, the famous Californian variety, flown specially to New York. These crabs looked spectacular and were easy to shell, yet the flavour had none of the sweetness and intensity of our blue swimmers caught at Port Parham, on the Gulf of St Vincent near Adelaide, where recreational fishermen can spend an afternoon crabbing on the tidal beaches, then cook the catch in situ to enjoy one of the best meals of their lives. The flavour is wonderful – I prefer it to almost any seafood, as long as the crabs are fresher than fresh.

The crabs swim in as little as 30 cm of water in sandy or weed-covered areas and can be found at night by the light of a lantern, using nets or rakes to scoop them into a large tub of water – we use an old tin baby's bath. They can also be caught from a boat in deep water using drop nets.

Blue swimmer crabs will never taste as good away from the shore. Many years ago, when I first visited the 'beach' at Port Parham where my husband Colin's family has a shack, the flat, wide, desolate expanse of sand that is exposed when the tide is out came as a great shock to me. I had come from Sydney where, as a teenager, I'd travel from the western suburbs to the beach on weekends and was more used to rocky coves, headlands and the sea lapping on the shore. However, over the years I have learnt that, in perfect conditions, Parham can feel like the Greek Islands, and with a meal of crabs on the beach and a bottle of white wine, you can feel at peace with the world. 'Perfect conditions', by the way, means the tide being in at sunset, the water warm enough to wade in, the sun on your back and no one else around – it doesn't happen often but is such a delight when it does that it makes up for all the times you visit in the heat of summer and find there is nowhere to swim.

If you catch your own crabs, bring back some sea water to cook them in – have a bucket handy at the shore to remind you. We have a copper pot set up in the backyard of the shack and our first job is to get the fire started, to bring the sea water to a boil. While you are waiting for the water to boil, stun the crabs in the freezer for 20 minutes. The crabs are then thrown in the boiling water, about 25 at a time, and cooked for 3 minutes only. They are then scooped out and thrown onto an old wire mattress frame kept solely for the crabs to cool down on before eating. They are turned upside-down, with the white underside of the carapace showing, so that all the juices are retained. The crabs are allowed to cool just enough to be able to pick them up – for me, they are at their very best when warm. Any accompaniments you have prepared for them will be superfluous – the crabs are wonderful just as they are.

One of the food delights I experienced in New York was a visit to a fish market where, for the first time in my life, I saw soft-shell crabs for sale. I had read about these crabs for many years: they can be eaten in their entirety and are a great delicacy in America, particularly in Louisiana and in the crab restaurants of Chesapeake Bay. We arranged a detour to Chesapeake Bay just to eat in a crab house, but unfortunately we were a week shy of the fresh crab season and had to make do with frozen crab, which fell far short of our expectations.

Soft-shell crabs are, of course, available all over the world at the time when crabs shed their shells, which is different in every region. Colin likes to tell the story of having crabbed at Port Parham all his life, yet always throwing back these gelatinous specimens simply because he wasn't aware they could be eaten, let alone realising that they were a delicacy.

At Bribie Island in Queensland, exciting research is underway into large-scale commercial production of soft-shell crabs. There they have developed soft-shell varieties which 'moult' to order. As well as opening up huge export opportunities, these will be perfect for the restaurant table, if the sample I've had is anything to go by.

Crabs have to be treated very carefully to get the best out of them, so if you cannot catch and cook them live yourself, then buy them ready-cooked rather than 'green' at the market. Crabs begin to decompose the moment they die. If you are buying a whole cooked crab, make sure it has a fresh sweet smell and no hint of ammonia (a sign that the crab is either

old or has been badly handled), otherwise the crab will be unusable. Cooked crabs have a very short shelf-life and must be kept super-chilled. Freezing crab meat renders it stringy and dry, although it can be used for crab cakes. Cooked crab meat has to be handled with care so that it doesn't become tough.

Whether you pick the crab meat from the shells yourself or buy it ready done, you need only do very little to it for a really special treat if it's super-fresh. For example, cook and drain some dried pasta, then toss through room-temperature crab meat, extra virgin olive oil, loads of freshly chopped flat-leaf parsley or chervil, salt and freshly ground black pepper and serve immediately. Add a little freshly chopped red chilli with the olive oil too, if you like.

POTTED CRAB   *Serves 4*

I'm so incredibly spoilt to have ready access to Port Parham, one of the best crabbing beaches anywhere, that anything less than catching, cooking and eating the crabs within hours just doesn't quite match up. Having said that, after an experience many years ago when Colin and I cooked and picked fresh crabs by ourselves for an entrée for over 100 people, I resolved to investigate commercially picked fresh crab meat (there are times when even I have to be practical). This comes from crabs cooked immediately after catching and the meat is picked as soon as it has cooled, and I can tell you that I prefer this to buying green or cooked crabs from a fishmonger. Just remember that if you buy it vacuum packed, you must remove it from the bag half an hour before use to allow the plastic smell to dissipate.

Whilst potted crab might be thought of as a way of extending the shelf-life of crab, this version, with its thin layer of butter over the top, is meant to be eaten the day after making.

175 g unsalted butter	½ teaspoon sea salt flakes
¼ teaspoon ground mace	freshly ground black pepper
10–12 basil leaves (depending on size)	3 teaspoons verjuice
250 g freshly picked cooked crab meat	4 thick slices bread

In a shallow frying pan, heat 125 g of the butter with the mace and basil leaves until nut-brown. Remove from the heat and allow butter to cool for about 15 minutes, until the solids separate and the flavours are infused.

Shred crab meat using two forks, then mix in the salt and add pepper to taste. Add the verjuice and mix in well. Transfer crab meat to a large bowl, then pour in three-quarters of the clarified butter, being sure to leave the solids behind. Stir through and check seasoning, then pack the meat into 4 small ramekins or 1 large mould, smoothing the surface with the back of a spoon. Pour the remaining clarified butter over the top of each ramekin or the mould, forming a thin film.

Refrigerate until butter is set, then remove from the refrigerator 10 minutes before serving. Brush slices of bread with the remaining butter and bake in a preheated 220°C oven until crisp. Serve the potted crab with toast, some rocket leaves and a wedge of lemon.

PORT PARHAM CRAB SANDWICH *Makes 8 mini-loaves or 1 large loaf*

Making mayonnaise by hand will always give a beautifully silky texture that cannot be matched by a machine. But the difference between homemade, even using a food processor, and shop-bought is so startling that you could start there and work your way up. Use the 'mustard' (innards) of the crab to enhance the mayonnaise.

80 g freshly picked blue swimmer crab meat per person (approximately 1 average-sized crab per person); reserve 1 whole crab claw per serve for garnish

MUSTARD BREAD
150 g burghul
125 ml tepid water
30 g fresh yeast *or* 15 g dried yeast
1 teaspoon sugar
380 ml warm water
2⅓ cups (350 g) wholemeal plain flour
1 cup (150 g) strong flour (see Glossary)
1 teaspoon sea salt
1 tablespoon extra virgin olive oil
⅓ cup (95 g) top-quality wholegrain mustard
1 tablespoon strong honey *or* maple syrup

MAYONNAISE
2 large egg yolks
¼ cup crab mustard (only if you can gather it from fresh crabs)
pinch salt
juice of 1 lemon
1½ cups (375 ml) mixture of extra virgin olive oil and a milder oil to suit your palette (I often use grapeseed oil or a good vegetable oil at half-and-half ratio so that it does not overpower the crab)
freshly ground black pepper

For the mustard bread, first preheat the oven to 200°C. Soak the burghul in the tepid water. If using fresh yeast, place it in a small bowl with the sugar and 80 ml of the water; when it froths, mix it with the flours and salt. If using dried yeast, mix the yeast and sugar with the flours and salt. Add the soaked burghul. In a small saucepan or frying pan, warm the olive oil, wholegrain mustard and honey or maple syrup. Gradually pour this mixture into the balance of the dry ingredients and mix with a wooden spoon. The consistency will resemble that of scone dough. Turn out and knead on a floured chopping board. Leave to rise for 2 hours and then separate the dough into 8 mini-loaves or shape into 1 large loaf. Leave to rise again for 30 minutes.

Bake the mustard bread in the oven for 25–35 minutes for mini-loaves, or 45 minutes for 1 large loaf. »

For the mayonnaise, place the egg yolks, crab mustard, pinch of salt and 1 tablespoon of the lemon juice in a bowl and whisk, or blend well in a food processor. Begin pouring the oil in as slowly as possible for the first 100 ml, then allow it to flow a little faster for the remainder, in a thin but steady stream. When all the oil is added and blended, adjust with as much lemon juice as you need and check for seasoning.

Make the sandwich by slicing each loaf of mustard bread diagonally in two, or cut thick slices if you have made a large loaf. Place the picked crab meat (being very careful that there are no pieces of shell) on one side and the crab mayonnaise on the other. Serve with a wedge of lemon, a crab claw and, for those who must have it, some chilli jam. I usually serve some peppery greens with this, such as mustard cress or rocket.

SALAD OF BLUE SWIMMER CRAB, FENNEL AND PINK GRAPEFRUIT

Serves 4

320 g freshly picked blue
    swimmer crab meat
sea salt flakes
1 large pink grapefruit, segments cut
    free of pith and juice retained
2 tablespoons extra virgin olive oil
½ large fennel bulb
1 bunch rocket
1 punnet baby mustard cress

VINAIGRETTE
2 tablespoons Champagne vinegar
1 golden shallot, very finely diced
½ teaspoon sea salt flakes
½ cup extra virgin olive oil
freshly ground black pepper

Spread the crab meat out on a plate and sprinkle with sea salt, a little of the pink grapefruit juice and some extra virgin olive oil, and set aside for 10 minutes to allow the flavours to mingle.

To make the vinaigrette, mix all the ingredients together in a small bowl.

Cut the fennel into very thin slices using a sharp knife or a mandolin. Toss together the sliced fennel, crab meat, rocket, cress and the vinaigrette (use only enough vinaigrette to just coat the salad leaves – you don't want to drench them). Divide the mixture evenly among 4 plates and arrange equal numbers of grapefruit segments on top of each to serve.

BLUE SWIMMER CRAB RISOTTO WITH VERJUICE

Serves 6

This is a family favourite, and a great way to serve a large number of guests. The risotto is full of flavour and works well as a warm buffet dish. If there is any left over, it can be rolled into balls and shallow-fried the next day.

500 g freshly picked blue
   swimmer crab meat
sea salt flakes and freshly ground
   black pepper
extra virgin olive oil (optional), for drizzling
squeeze of lemon juice (optional),
   for drizzling
1.25 litres jellied Fish Stock
   (see page 177) *or* crab stock

225 g unsalted butter
2 large onions, finely chopped
2½ cups (500 g) Arborio rice (see Glossary)
¾ cup (180 ml) verjuice
¼ cup coriander leaves
2 lemons, cut into wedges

If you have bought vacuum-packed crab meat, transfer it to a dish, season with salt and pepper and drizzle it with olive oil and lemon juice to get rid of any plastic taint.

Bring the stock to a simmer in a saucepan.

Heat 150 g of the butter in a heavy-based saucepan, then gently sweat the onions over low heat. Add the rice, stirring well until it is coated with butter. When the rice is glistening, turn up the heat to high, stir in the verjuice and let it evaporate. Season with salt.

Ladle in some hot stock and stir until it has been absorbed. Continue adding the stock a ladleful at a time, stirring frequently, until the rice is cooked but still firm – this will take about 20 minutes. A few minutes before the rice is cooked, check the seasoning and add salt if you wish, then add the remaining butter and gently fold in the crab meat, taking care not to break it up. Serve this lovely, rich risotto with a grind of black pepper and some coriander leaves, and wedges of lemon alongside.

EXTRA VIRGIN OLIVE OIL

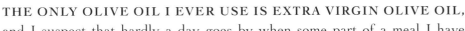

THE ONLY OLIVE OIL I EVER USE IS EXTRA VIRGIN OLIVE OIL, and I suspect that hardly a day goes by when some part of a meal I have doesn't need it. I do at times use incredibly intense walnut, hazelnut or almond oils in small quantities, depending on the dish I'm serving (particularly as they all go so beautifully with verjuice), but it's extra virgin olive oil that is really my life's blood. All extra virgin olive oils are far from being equal, and while you often hear the comment that life is too short to drink bad wine or eat bad food, for me the rest of this adage is that life is too short to use bad oil.

There is a fascinating history to olive farming in Australia. The first groves were planted around 1805 in Parramatta, Sydney. While other states also had some early plantings in the early 1800s, South Australia took the lead in the 1830s, bringing in varieties from similar microclimates in the Mediterranean. To think that in 1851, a South Australian oil won an honourable mention at the London Exhibition, and in 1911 the Stonyfell Olive Oil Company of South Australia won gold medals for the oil they exported to Sicily! Yet the industry failed then, as our Anglo-Celtic settlers saw olive oil as medicinal rather than gastronomical. We have our Mediterranean immigrants to thank for the resurgence of extra virgin olive oil. For those interested in this history, Dr Michael Burr has a chronological account of the olive in Australia in his book, co-written with Karen Reichelt, *Extra Virgin: An Australian Companion to Olives and Olive Oil*.

We in the Australian olive industry have been on a steep learning curve over the past ten years, and although there is still much more to be learnt, I am truly proud of the top-quality extra virgin olive oils produced in Australia.

Dr Rod Mailer is a principal research scientist with the New South Wales Department of Primary Industries and is at the forefront of olive oil industry research. He has worked for many years to define the right harvest times and the best storage conditions to produce optimum-quality olive oil. He has worked closely with the industry to help growers understand oil quality and what they can do to produce the best oil. Currently he is working with Codex Australia and the Australian Olive Association to detect fraud in olive oil labelling, so we can be confident that if it says extra virgin olive oil on the label, then that is what it is. His laboratory does much of the testing for olive producers in Australia, as well as for the New Zealand Olive Association.

In Adelaide, we have Susan Sweeney, the Olive Horticultural Consultant within the Waite Research Precinct, whose work with olives has led to an amazing wealth of practical knowledge. Her research into olive varieties, reported in the Autumn 2006 edition of *The Olive Press*, the Australian Olive Association's journal, is of great importance to anyone considering planting olives for oil.

Given its history and the remnants of the original groves which are still standing, I initially thought that South Australia would have a prime advantage as the leading state for oil production, yet it seems that our lack of water has led many of the bigger players across the border to overtake us.

On our own land, we have 1000 trees, mostly Tuscan varieties, the first of which we planted at the farm in 1995 and, soon after, the balance on our home block. Even though the trees are of much the same varieties, only 5 km apart, the fruit ripens differently – a huge logistical issue for me. The exterior colour of the olives gives only a rough indication of ripeness, and any individual tree will always have olives of varying degrees of ripeness on it.

The biggest challenge I face each year is deciding when to pick my olives. For my estate-bottled oil I always pick early in the season, when the olives are still half green and half ripe, yet not so early that their flavour hasn't developed, even though I know they will yield much less oil. No oil accumulation test in a laboratory will help me with this one. What I strive for in my oil is that perfect balance of fruitiness/bitterness and pungency. It's the oil I choose for that last flourish on a dish and for vinaigrettes and bruschetta, when I'm after a truly full flavour. Just a drizzle of great oil can turn the ordinary into the sublime.

I never fail to be excited by each year's harvest and after making the decision to pick I insist on following the whole process through, going down to Angle Vale for the milling of the olives each day. I wouldn't miss it, as seeing that green-gold liquid run into the tank is almost a sensual experience and the wonderful perfume of the crush permeates my very being. I go to the crusher prepared with a chunk of good wood-fired bread, some sea salt flakes, a pepper grinder and an enamel plate so I can dip the bread into that first cloudy oil with its strong peppery flavour; this is tasting extra virgin olive oil at its absolute best. To me it is nothing short of intoxicating.

OLIVE OILS

As a flavour-driven person who loves to cook, the only olive oil I use is extra virgin, as I've said before. But first let me attempt to explain the difference between the varying grades of olive oil.

EXTRA VIRGIN OLIVE OIL

Extra virgin olive oil is the oil or juice of fresh olives extracted purely by mechanical means. The crushed olives become a paste and the oil is extracted from this paste without the use of chemicals, and with only enough heat to naturally separate the oil, which is lighter than the water and solids of the paste.

Don't be misled by the term cold-pressed oil. This term has virtually no relevance in today's technological age, and the Australian Olive Association recommends that growers not use the term as it is no longer one that reflects modern-day practices. Therefore, if used, it is used incorrectly, and only because it is seen by marketers as being a statement of quality. In my opinion, it is not just a superfluous term that confuses the public but is also misleading in terms of the process alluded to.

To be considered as extra virgin olive oil, on testing the oil must be found to contain less than 0.8 per cent free fatty acids, measured as oleic acid. However, within this definition, there is a huge range of flavour profiles of extra virgin olive oils, from the fruity, aromatic, pungent and yet beautifully balanced, to the other end of the spectrum of mellow and even bland, and everything in between. Knowing that an olive oil is extra virgin should therefore only be the starting point to choosing a good-quality oil.

The level of free fatty acids in olive oil is a result of the degree of ripeness of the olives – oil from early season olives contains the least free fatty acids – and the care taken in handling the fruit between harvest and oil extraction. The quality of an extra virgin olive oil is the result of this, combined with the length of time between picking and crushing, the cleanliness of the olive crusher and the temperature at which the crushing process is carried out. The olive varieties used, as well as the terroir (that wonderful term that signifies the characteristics of the growing environment: the position, soil quality and prevailing weather conditions) also have an impact on flavour and quality. Many producers proudly display just how low a level of free fatty acids their oils contain, often so low as to hardly register – yet these oils, although they will have a longer shelf-life, can lack flavour if picked too early.

With our extra virgin olive oil, we are continually aiming to get the balance right between picking early for longevity, but with sufficient maturity to give flavour. Each year I learn enough to know how much more I need to know. The difference there is in the quality of the oil and its flavour when, having decided that our olives are perfect to pick, I can't get the picking organised until a week later, astounds me.

Although half-ripe fruit yields less oil, which is less economic for the grower, the resulting oil has greater quality, integrity and longevity. Riper fruit yields far more oil, but results in a rapid decline in quality a few months after harvest, whereas oil made from earlier picked fruit, assuming that it meets all the other necessary conditions for quality, is still fresh and sound a year after harvest.

All of this means that, although an oil could be termed 'extra virgin' because of its low level of free fatty acids, if it has flavour defects from processing such as being 'fusty', 'musty' or 'winey' (to name a few), this would deny the oil the extra virgin classification. Even if an oil makes the extra virgin classification because it contains under 0.8 per cent free fatty acids, but is a much riper oil, then it will not have the shelf-life of an earlier picked oil, so it will not necessarily retain its extra virgin status over time, particularly if stored badly. Rancidity, the most common fault in extra virgin olive oil, is usually a fault of bad storage and/or the age of the oil, and is so easy to detect once you've identified it – just think of the smell of sweaty socks, or butter left uncovered in the back of the refrigerator that has absorbed every 'off' odour around it.

Many people, when first beginning to learn about good olive oils, realise that they have only ever tasted what they are now able to identify as rancid oils. I always explain that I first smell any extra virgin olive oil I buy or that I'm offered to taste, just as you might an oyster to make sure it's not off before you slip it into your mouth. I cannot imagine, once you have smelled and tasted a good extra virgin olive oil, that you would ever use a rancid olive oil again.

VIRGIN OLIVE OIL

This is simply olive oil that didn't quite make the grade of extra virgin. Its free fatty acid measurement sits between 0.8 and 3 per cent, and it should be used soon after it is crushed. It will have less flavour and a much shorter shelf-life than extra virgin olive oil. In Europe, a little virgin olive oil is combined with 'pure' or refined olive oil to add some flavour.

OLIVE OIL

Still often referred to as 'pure' olive oil, it is almost at the bottom of the range in terms of quality, so this is really a misnomer. This olive oil is the result of industrial processing, deemed necessary because the oil has not met the above criteria for virgin or extra virgin olive oil. In this process, the olive oil is refined, using a chemical treatment in which peroxides and free fatty acids are removed to make it suitable for consumption. The oil may also be bleached and deodorised to remove any 'off' flavours but, at the same time, this removes many of the natural flavours and antioxidants that are characteristic of extra virgin olive oil. 'Pure' olive oil may be suitable for cooking where a less dominant flavour is required, as it still contains some of the fatty acids that make olive oil nutritionally attractive.

POMACE OIL

Pomace is the residue or olive waste left after the extra virgin olive oil has been mechanically removed from the olive paste. This solid waste product may contain 3–8 per cent oil, which is called pomace oil. The oil is recovered by washing the waste with an organic solvent such as hexane. The recovered oil is then heated to remove the solvent and the oil is subjected to the same refining processes described for olive oil. As with olive oil, bleaching and deodorising removes not just the unwanted odours but also the fruity characteristics of the olive. It strips any flavour, good or bad, out of the oil, and the resultant oil is fatty in the mouth and tastes of the industrial processes it has been subjected to, even though a small amount of virgin olive oil is generally added for flavour. I have no use for this oil, even for a marinade.

LIGHT OLIVE OIL

Light olive oil is a marketing term aimed at the weight-conscious. The only thing light about this oil is that it is light in character – or, to my mind, totally lacking in flavour, colour and aroma. It has exactly the same number of calories or kilojoules as extra virgin and other olive oils but, as it is refined, it lacks the health-giving antioxidants and polyphenols of extra virgin olive oil, as well as the flavour.

CHOOSING AND USING EXTRA VIRGIN OLIVE OIL

Extra virgin olive oil is never more vibrant than when first crushed. Unlike wine, it diminishes with age – although, as mentioned above, the earlier harvest extra virgin olive oils have a longer shelf-life. As a rule of thumb, only buy an extra virgin olive oil if it displays its year of harvest and you are buying within that year. This doesn't automatically mean the oil is no good if it's over a year from its harvest date, but it does mean that unless it has been picked early enough and has enough of that assertive character at the beginning, it will begin to lose its freshness and vitality after a year, and will become 'flat' and more prone to rancidity as it gets even older.

I keep two grades of extra virgin olive oil. The first is my own estate-bottled oil which comes from my own trees or those of other producers I respect – and there are many of those in Australia, I am delighted to say. This is the oil that makes all the difference to a dish when added as a last flourish; my own preference is for a robust, fruity oil for the majority of my food where the olive oil flavour dominates. I also use a less expensive Australian extra virgin olive oil from the supermarket that declares its year of harvest and, even though it is cheaper, it is still fresh and fruity. This is the oil I use when serving more delicate dishes (such as poached fish) or for cooking with, as high temperatures dissipate the flavour of extra virgin olive oil to some extent.

In summary, buy the finest extra virgin olive oil you can afford, and use it generously rather than keeping it for 'best'. I love to have a good extra virgin olive oil on the table at every meal, and either use it in a vinaigrette or simply drizzle it over piping hot vegetables to serve with grilled bruschetta. I also love to use it for dressing sliced raw tuna, moistening goat's cheese and lavishing over sliced tomatoes. With really good extra virgin olive oil you can turn a simple pasta, such as Spaghettini with Parmigiano Reggiano, Garlic, Capers and Flat-leaf Parsley (see page 40), into a spectacular dish. It is amazing how a splash of extra virgin olive oil over a hot bowl of soup or fresh cannellini beans adds a truly powerful dimension that lifts the flavour to another level.

I use my more mellow everyday extra virgin olive oil for sweating onions, coating foods for a marinade or grilling fish, chicken or meat. If I deep-fry (or probably more often, shallow-fry), once again I use this more mellow extra virgin olive oil. Even though it may sound extravagant, it imparts so much more crispness and flavour, as food fried in extra virgin olive oil gains a wonderfully crunchy coating that acts as a seal and prevents excess oil from penetrating further.

STORING EXTRA VIRGIN OLIVE OIL

It is very important to store oil properly to maintain its quality. It should be kept away from light – ideally in dark glass bottles, tins or bag-in-the-box 'bladders' to protect it from light, heat and oxygen. Whatever you do, don't sit the bottle by the heat of the stove or on your windowsill, no matter how jewel-like it may look in the sunshine!

Most importantly, once you open a bottle of extra virgin olive oil, never leave it without a stopper, as exposure to oxygen leads to rancidity. Better still, rather than save it for special occasions, use it frequently – even the smallest amount added to a dish can make such a difference to its flavour.

While I refrigerate my nut oils to control their rancidity, I never refrigerate my extra virgin olive oils as it changes their structure. Although this reverts to a certain extent if the oil is returned to room temperature, I find there is a loss of flavour and 'texture'– a funny word perhaps when talking of oil, but a relevant one nonetheless.

MAYONNAISE   *Makes 375 ml*

Once you've made your first mayonnaise, you'll never want to buy it again. Homemade mayonnaise adds so much to a meal, with very little effort involved – its rich and velvety texture can make a really simple dish sing. Some people are anxious about making their own because they think it's difficult or they fear it will split, but the technique is really very simple (and even a split mayonnaise can be resurrected by starting again in a clean, dry bowl, with fresh egg yolks, before incorporating the split mixture drop by drop).

A basic mayonnaise consists of olive oil, egg yolks, some seasoning and an acidulant such as lemon juice, verjuice or vinegar. I use a mixture of half extra virgin olive oil and half a lighter vegetable or grapeseed oil (this is the one exception I make to my rule about only using extra virgin, as the flavour can be too sharp). The quality of the eggs will have a bearing on the final dish, so free-range eggs at room temperature are best. Mustard is often included but is optional, while salt, I think, is essential. Mayonnaise is at its silkiest when made by hand, but it can also be made successfully in a blender or food processor. Or, you could start using a machine and finish by hand to achieve that 'almost as good as handmade' effect.

Mayonnaise goes with almost every type of meat and fish (particularly when barbecued), not to mention vegetables and salads. Once you master a basic mayonnaise you can use your imagination to change the texture, flavour and colour. Depending on the dish with which the mayonnaise is to be served, you can experiment with verjuice or wine vinegar as the acidulant. Try adding herbs – lemon thyme mayonnaise is great with snapper, and give Sorrel Mayonnaise (see page 180) a go. Garlic mayonnaise (or Aïoli, see page 180) can be made by adding raw garlic, or puréed roasted garlic for a mellower, nuttier flavour. Rouille (see page 181), essentially an aïoli with puréed roasted capsicum, is wonderful added to a fish soup and is simple to make once you are confident with the technique. I serve roasted garlic and quince mayonnaise with kid pot-roasted with lemon, fresh herbs and garlic, so, as you can see, the combinations are endless.

2 large free-range egg yolks	½ cup (125 ml) extra virgin olive oil
(at room temperature)	½ cup (125 ml) vegetable *or* grapeseed oil
pinch sea salt flakes	freshly ground black pepper
1 tablespoon lemon juice	1 tablespoon boiling water (if necessary)
1 teaspoon Dijon mustard (optional)	

Rinse a bowl with hot water and dry thoroughly. Whisk the egg yolks in the bowl with a pinch of salt until thick, then add two-thirds of the lemon juice and the mustard, if using, and whisk until smooth. Continue to whisk whilst adding the oil slowly, drop by drop to begin with. Once the mixture begins to thicken you can add the remaining oil in a slow, steady stream, whisking continuously. When all the oil has been added, taste and add as much of the remaining lemon juice as needed. Season with pepper, and add more salt and lemon juice if needed. Only add the boiling water if the mayonnaise needs thinning and requires no more acidulant.

PEARS, PARMIGIANO REGGIANO AND GREEN EXTRA VIRGIN OLIVE OIL

Serves 6

When each ingredient is perfect, this makes an exceptional end to a meal.

3 pears, halved and cored

1 tablespoon lemon juice

300 g wedge Parmigiano Reggiano, cut into shards

1 bunch rocket, washed and dried

½–¾ cup (125–180 ml) extra virgin olive oil (ideally from an early season crush)

Slice the pear halves, then toss with lemon juice to prevent discolouration. Divide the sliced pear and shards of Parmigiano Reggiano among 6 plates, then add the rocket and drizzle a tablespoon or more of the fruity olive oil over each.

SALMON POACHED IN OLIVE OIL

Serves 4

This is a very special, even sensuous, dish. It works best when the salmon fillets are the same size and weight (ideally from the middle of the fish). The cooked salmon is quite pink inside and warm rather than hot, so make sure your guests don't belong to the 'if it's not piping hot or cooked well-done, it's just not right' school of thought.

about 1 cup (250 ml) mellow extra virgin olive oil (depending on size of saucepan or frying pan)

4 × 120 g trimmed salmon fillets, skin removed

sea salt flakes

juice and grated rind of 1 lemon

80 ml fresh extra virgin olive oil

fresh chervil, to serve

Choose a heavy-based saucepan or deep frying pan large enough to accommodate the fish in one layer; the smaller the pan, the less olive oil you will need to use. Pour the olive oil into the pan, then stand it over the lowest heat possible on your stove-top, bringing it to blood temperature only (briefly dip the blade of a knife in – it should feel warm to the touch, not hot). Salt the fish and rub in the lemon rind.

Slip the fillets into the oil – the fillets should lie just below the surface like submarines – and cook at this gentle temperature for 10–20 minutes (this will depend on how low you can keep the temperature on your stove – use a simmer mat if you have one). The fish should be more set than cooked. If white dots appear on the surface of the fish (these are beads of protein), the oil is too hot, so you'll need to reduce the temperature. Next time, you'll know to cook it less – I promise it's so delicious you'll want to.

Carefully take the fish out of the warm oil and drain. Reserve the oil to use again when cooking fish. Dress the salmon with the lemon juice, fresh extra virgin olive oil and sprigs of chervil and serve.

PIQUANT BREAD SALAD   *Serves 4*

This salad makes an ideal accompaniment for Salmon Poached in Olive Oil (see previous page). Or, served for lunch, it is so satisfying that it makes a complete meal in its own right.

2 slices wood-fired bread, crusts removed,
    cut into large pieces
⅓ cup (80 ml) extra virgin olive oil,
    plus 1 teaspoon for drizzling
½ small red onion, finely chopped
1 cup flat-leaf parsley leaves

1½ pieces preserved lemon, flesh removed
    and rind rinsed and cut into long,
    thin strips
1 tablespoon capers, rinsed and drained
6 green olives, pitted and quartered
freshly ground black pepper

Preheat the oven to 180°C. In a food processor, pulse the bread quickly into very coarse breadcrumbs, then place on a baking tray, drizzle with 1 teaspoon olive oil and toast in the oven for 10 minutes or until golden.

Toss all the ingredients together with enough olive oil to coat, then season with pepper (no salt is required).

SPAGHETTINI WITH PARMIGIANO REGGIANO, GARLIC, CAPERS AND FLAT-LEAF PARSLEY   *Serves 4*

sea salt flakes
500 g spaghettini
1 clove garlic
1 tablespoon capers, rinsed and drained
3½ tablespoons extra virgin olive oil,
    plus extra for drizzling

200 g grated Parmigiano Reggiano
freshly ground black pepper
½ cup freshly chopped flat-leaf parsley
juice of ½ lemon

Bring a large saucepan of water to the boil. Add a generous amount of salt and cook the spaghettini according to the directions on the packet.

Meanwhile, using the flat side of a large knife, crush the garlic with a little salt to make a paste. Fry capers in a small frying pan in 1½ tablespoons olive oil over medium heat, then remove from pan and dry on kitchen paper. Use the same oil to fry the garlic, being careful not to let it burn. Drain the spaghettini in a colander; do not refresh. Be ready with hot plates and all ingredients.

Add 2 tablespoons of oil to the drained spaghettini pan, then add the hot spaghettini, garlic and the cheese. Mix to combine, then add the capers. Season to taste, then add the parsley, lemon juice and a little more extra virgin olive oil to moisten. Pile onto 4 hot plates and serve immediately.

FLOUR

 **FLOUR IS SUCH AN ESSENTIAL PART OF SO MANY OF THE FOODS** we eat every day, yet we tend to take it for granted. However, using the finest-quality flour (determined by the quality of the original grain, the method used to process it, and the amount of processing it undergoes), makes such a vast difference in the final outcome of a dish, both in taste and texture.

BREAD

What is it that makes really good bread? It's a question that deserves a lot of thought, since bread is the staff of life. While devotees beat a path to the handful of great bakeries scattered over this country, to buy bread with character made in wood-fired ovens, unfortunately the greater percentage seem happy to accept the mass-produced, often fairy-floss-like bread that's so readily available.

Wood-fired ovens aren't trendy – they've been in Australia since European settlement. Those that have survived modernisation are usually tended by passionate bakers, who use traditional methods to produce wonderful sourdoughs or crusty peasant loaves and the like. The Apex Bakery, on my doorstep at Tanunda, makes really good white loaves – bread that tastes of the wheat from which it is made.

In earlier times, just about every town had its own flour mill and each area produced a unique flour. This was certainly the case in South Australia – Loxton had a great reputation for the flour from which its bread was made, while the bakers in Mount Gambier would only use the local flour, which was particularly good for biscuits and soft cakes, as it was too expensive to buy in any other sort. But the spread of transport systems and the swallowing up of many of the mills by multinationals has meant the end of this regionalism to a large degree.

Those of us who live in the Barossa have been lucky to have Laucke Flour Mills as part of the Valley's history. I was introduced to Laucke's when I first moved to the Barossa. The business began in 1899, when flour was milled in Greenock – although the actual flour milling is now done at Laucke's in Strathalbyn, the quality remains the same. Mark Laucke, the grandson of the founder, tells of his early working days when the miller had no control over the wheat being delivered, thus requiring the baker to blend flours to ensure the best results. Mark remembers bakers combining three different bags of flour in the one bowl, each bag from a different mill! There must have been a lot of expertise in the baking industry then – today the tables have turned and the miller chooses the wheat to blend into grist before making the flour.

Small, passionate millers are treasured by those of us driven by flavour, including bakers and chefs targeting niche markets. Many bakers have to contend with the price pressures of supermarkets and are often forced to downgrade their products to service the demand for cheap bread. However, there are also a handful of specialist bakers (probably only one or two in each capital city), who stand out from the pack and are making extraordinary bread, in stark contrast to the mass-produced product. Supermarkets will continue to be a fact of life as more and more people depend on them for one-stop food shopping, but even with our much busier lives we would do well to demand and be prepared to pay for better bread, and champion the great bakeries, which will in turn use the small millers so that they too survive. Good bread, like all good food, should be available to everyone.

I've long realised how lucky I am to have access to top-quality, locally made bread, and need no convincing about the merits of bread made in wood-fired ovens. But to understand the rest of the equation – how good bread is actually made – I spent some time observing the process at the Apex Bakery. To give you just a glimpse of the wealth of tradition that abounds here, the patriarch, Keith Fechner (better known as 'Chiney'), started in the bakery as a lad in 1924, the first year of business. In 1948 he bought the bakery, and in 1982 he sold it to his three sons, Brian, David and Johnny. Until just a few years ago, Keith still started the ferment every night with Johnny, while the rest of the team began work at 3 a.m.

Keith has managed to keep a firm hold on the traditions of the bakery, although in truth this is probably more to do with the Barossa ethos that if you can't afford to pay cash then you can't afford a new piece of equipment. In the 1960s he successfully resisted his sons' idea to change over to gas-fired ovens as gas was cheaper than wood. Having had their attempts to modernise foiled, Keith's sons are now every bit as proud of the bakery's traditions – in fact, they still collect Mallee wood from Sedan, a 45-minute drive away, for the firing of the ovens.

I had arranged to visit one evening to observe the fermenting process, and luckily the night I was there was an uncharacteristically cool summer's night, so the crew didn't have to wait too long for the temperature to drop before mixing began. We were able to start as early as 10.30 p.m. – the previous night it had been much hotter and preparations couldn't begin until just before midnight (if the room is too hot, the dough will be too active and will over-prove).

The Fechners like a long, slow prove, so they measure the temperature of the flour and the water to ensure a mixed dough temperature of 76°F (24°C, although nothing is measured in Celsius). I expected rainwater to be used but was very wrong: the harder the water the better the bread, so Barossa tap water is perfect (it's the only good thing about it I can think of!). These days it is Johnny who draws four buckets of water and mixes the yeast and salt, and then the dough. It is not always possible to get the mix right the first time without adjustments – sometimes almost another half a bag of flour is added to the giant mixing bowl. This bowl rotates quite slowly and two huge claws come in from either side, simulating hands grabbing at the flour at the bottom, working the mixture into a moist

dough. It is a little like a volcano erupting – flour puffs up from the sides as it is pulled into the mixture. The machine works even more slowly than if you were mixing and kneading by hand, and the smell of the fresh yeast lingers. I found watching the bowl almost as mesmerising and soothing as kneading dough myself.

No timers are used, instead it is done by feel, and looking for the point when the dough starts to come away from the sides of the bowl. They showed me how to stretch a walnut-sized piece of dough and hold it up to the light – when it was quite transparent yet wouldn't break, it was deemed sufficiently kneaded. A proving ring was then placed on the rim of the bowl to give the dough plenty of room to grow, and a calico cover placed on top to keep out any draughts. The dough was left to rise to the very top, which usually takes four hours. (It was 11.30 p.m. at this stage, so I snuck away to catch some sleep, but Keith and Johnny still had a lot of work to do.)

As soon as the morning shift arrives at 3 a.m., the dough is knocked back and the table is floured. One of the boys pulls the dough out with his hands and then carries it to the table, where someone else cuts it with a dough knife (a blunt knife made especially for this purpose). The pieces of dough are then divided again into weights appropriate to the final loaves, then the ends are tucked under and the dough is rested for 5 minutes. These shapes are then put through a very old machine called a 'ribbon moulder'. A series of rollers, a little like those on an old washing-machine wringer, knocks the air out of the dough, which is then rolled into the rough shape of the final loaf on a small conveyor belt before being shaped by hand.

When I returned at 5.30 a.m. the giant mixing bowls were empty and the trolleys were full of moulds filled with dough – the same moulds that have been used since 1924. The fire in the Scotch oven, which seemed to have stalactites on its huge domed roof, takes a couple of hours to heat. It is an art to have the loaves proved and ready to go straight into the oven when it reaches the right temperature (450°F, according to the Fechners, or 232°C). As the loaves mustn't over-prove, or else they'll collapse and fail, timing is critical. When the fire is first lit, flames leap out from the right-hand side of the oven. This ceases when the wood in the firebox has been reduced to coals – and the oven is ready. The time this takes differs each day, depending on the density of the wood. While a gauge indicates the temperature now, it was broken for twenty years, so instead a handful of flour was thrown into the oven to test the temperature: if it ignited the oven was deemed too hot, and was allowed to cool with its door ajar.

When the decision is made that the oven is ready, the fire door is closed, the bottom of the oven and the flue are blocked off and the chimney is opened up. Again, no timers, no rigid instructions – just feel, rhythm and speed. The dough-filled moulds are put into the oven on long-handled paddles; the oven takes 500 loaves at a time.

I thought for a moment that empty moulds were being put into the oven, then I realised that to get square loaves the moulds were turned upside-down to keep the dough compressed. The oven was filled from the cooler back left-hand corner, where the bigger, high-top loaves that take longer to cook were baked. The day I was there the fire was hot and after 10 minutes the loaves were already golden brown – too soon! – so newspaper hats were placed over the bread to stop it scorching.

Sleepy as I was, the whole process was truly magical: the smell of the bread, the ferocity of the heat, the golden glow of the loaves, the skill of the Fechner boys, and the humour that abounded. I headed home for a bit more sleep with two warm loaves under my arm. But the temptation of the loaves was too great – and soon I was transported back to my childhood when I used to hollow out the warm bread that was delivered by horse and cart. I was embarrassed by how much I had eaten, so on my way home I trimmed the loaf with a bread knife to hide the evidence of my secret feast!

Good bread is truly the sum of all its parts. In the case of the Apex Bakery and others like it, it is all about craft and care: the hard flour full of the flavour of wheat, the dry heat of the wood-fired oven, the fresh yeast, the additive-free recipes that have remain unchanged since 1924, the gentle mixing of the dough, and the slow natural ferment.

Bruschetta is one of my favourite ways to eat bread, but it is only as good as the flour used to make the bread. We eat outside a lot, particularly on the weekend, frequently with our daughters, their partners and grandchildren and, more often than not, we have bruschetta. My husband Colin is the bruschetta-maker in our house and brooks no interference. But he isn't interested in making it unless the family is gathered around, or I'm busy on the other side of the kitchen window getting the rest of the dinner ready. In other words, he must have an audience. He has also become very pedantic, as one needs to be, about the quality of each ingredient used.

We all know bruschetta, but what makes a truly great one? Well, the bread has to be proper bread, with a good crust; if it's a wood-fired, chewy Italian-style loaf, all the better. It also has to be stale. Next is the extra virgin olive oil. Nothing is better than the first oil

of the season – greenish-tinged and peppery, but balanced, of course. A clove of garlic is vital, as is good sea salt and freshly ground black pepper.

The best bruschetta of all is grilled over a wood fire (although a gas barbecue does a pretty good job, too), hence our courtyard picnics. The bread is sliced quite thickly and grilled on each side until charred markings appear. As soon as each piece is done, it is rubbed on one side with a cut clove of garlic before being dipped into the oil (quickly or slowly, depending on your penchant for oil) seasoned with sea salt and freshly ground black pepper. It must be eaten immediately, and the oil running down your chin is part of the pleasure.

If that's all too basic for you, top your bruschetta with your favourite ingredients. Spread the toasted bread with tapenade, add sliced ripe tomatoes and round it off with anchovies, perhaps. Cut a chunk of Parmigiano Reggiano, or spread the bread liberally with goat's curd. Toss some mushrooms in a pan on the other side of the barbecue and top the bruschetta with them. Add a hint of truffle oil (if you can find the real thing), if you want to impress. Roast red capsicums on the fire as well and add the peeled, juicy flesh to the bruschetta. Or perhaps try slow-cooked beans when you need something more filling.

SOME SIMPLE TIPS TO ALLEVIATE THE MOST COMMON BREAD-MAKING PROBLEMS

✦ To make bread by hand, give yourself plenty of space on a cleared workbench and, as for all recipes, have your quantities measured out and standing by. You will need a huge bowl the size of a wash basin, preferably an old ceramic one, although an inexpensive oversized stainless steel bowl from a commercial kitchenware shop will do, but remember a little warmth helps.

✦ There is a huge variation in quality of flour, determined by the original grain, the amount of processing and the method of processing. High-quality bread mixes are readily available from Laucke's Flour Mills (www.laucke.com.au). They have a huge number of variations and you only need to add water and yeast. I also love the wonderful varieties of flour grown and milled by Gavin Dunn's company, Four Leaf Milling of Tarlee (www.fourleafmilling.com.au). It is biodynamic and stone-ground.

✦ Next to the quality of the flour, the temperature of the water is most important, although in truth the more experienced you get, the more casual you can become about this. If the water is too hot, it will kill the yeast, and if too cold, it will not activate the yeast. When a recipe calls for tepid water, this means that your hand should feel comfortable in the water – not cold and not hot (about 34°C on a thermometer). To test this, leave your finger in the water for 10 seconds: if it becomes uncomfortably hot, you will need to add a little cold water. Your utensils and ingredients should be blood warm, even the flour.

✦ Remember, the amount of water needed will alter every time you make bread, depending on the flour and the temperature or humidity. Always begin with less water than a recipe states and add more as required.

✦ I prefer compressed fresh yeast in its block form to dried yeast. It gives a much better flavour to the bread, though dry yeast is easier to handle. Dry yeast is also more concentrated, so you need twice the quantity of compressed yeast.

✦ Not to make bread by hand is to deny yourself an addictive pleasure, but if you use a machine, be sure not to over-mix. When the mixing is finished, the dough should be at about 28°C.

✦ Bring the bread to the first rise on a bench away from any draughts. Cover it with a clean tea towel, with a piece of plastic film sprayed with oil separating the dough from the tea towel so it doesn't stick. In winter you could try putting it in tins in the oven with just the pilot light on, if it is gas, or at about 50°C in an electric oven.

✦ Fat gives a softer loaf and helps the bread last longer. Butter is possibly better than oil as the addition of liquid gives the dough a different structure. The butter should be soft and pliable, not melted.

✦ If you like crusty bread, cut down on the fat content (although this will reduce its keeping qualities) and bake at a lower temperature for longer, say 190°C for 40 minutes instead of the usual 220°C for 30 minutes. You could also try putting a bowl of water in the oven to make steam, but the first method seems to work better.

✦ A small amount of sugar gives a softer texture and adds colour to the crumb. It feeds the yeast, but bread can still be made without it.

✦ For me, salt is very important because it flavours the bread and controls the yeast activity. Too much salt will actually retard the yeast. Saltless bread is possible, but the dough has to be handled quickly or it will go mad.

✦ Freezing bread will dry it out a little, but if you do want to freeze bread, take the hot loaves from the oven and put them straight into bags and into the freezer. The condensation seems to make the bread fresher on thawing out. Splash the thawed loaf with a little water and put it in the oven to re-crisp. Make sure you add some fat to the dough of any bread you intend to freeze.

✦ I have never used natural bread improvers. They are made of vitamin C and modify the gluten so it is more extendable and gives a better crumb and height. The gas given off by the yeast is carbon dioxide – this blows up the gluten and forms bubbles in the dough. Using a bread improver allows a better 'bounce back' after retarding the bread in the refrigerator overnight. This is useful when you want to bake fresh bread in the morning but don't want to wake as early as the bakers.

SOPHIE'S FARMHOUSE LOAF

Makes 2 loaves

When I first worked with her, Sophie Zalokar was Sophie Harris, a young, wide-eyed Barossa girl with an enquiring mind and an ability to turn her hand to almost anything creative and practical. Sophie was a 'bread witch', as we say in the Valley – yeast and flour became magical in her hands. This innate skill, combined with her artistic abilities in painting and weaving, her proficiency in shooting and skinning rodents, and her talent for playing the piano (she would play in the restaurant after service had finished at night), makes her pretty much an all-rounder.

Sophie, like Natalie Paull, Alex Herbert and Steve Flamsteed, were the closest to us of all our Pheasant Farm Restaurant family, and are still part of our lives. After her four-year apprenticeship with me, Sophie travelled, then married, had a family and went to university; she now writes about food too. In 2002 I had the honour of launching her first book, *Picnic* – it is a beautiful book, but I would have expected nothing less.

Poolish is a French bread-making term to describe the 'pre-dough'. Other terms such as levain, biga, chef, sponge, mother and starter all mean the same thing.

POOLISH
½ cup (125 ml) warm water
½ teaspoon dried yeast
115 g strong flour (see Glossary)

FINAL DOUGH
1 kg strong flour (see Glossary),
    plus extra for kneading
2 teaspoons sea salt flakes
½ teaspoon dried yeast
600 ml warm water
1 teaspoon olive oil, plus extra for oiling

For the poolish, place the warm water and yeast in a small bowl and leave to sit for 1 minute, before stirring to dissolve. Stir the flour into this yeasted water until smooth and elastic. Cover with plastic film and leave in a draught-free place for 1 hour, or until mixture has doubled in size.

For the final dough, place the flour and salt in the bowl of an electric mixer. Stir the yeast and the poolish mixture into the warm water. Using a dough hook, slowly add this mixture to the bowl and knead until a soft, elastic dough forms. Generously flour the workbench, tip out the dough and knead it by hand for 5 minutes, using only enough flour to stop the dough from sticking to the bench. Brush the inside of a large bowl with the olive oil and roll the dough in the bowl to coat with oil. Cover the bowl with plastic film and leave in a warm place for about 1–2 hours, or until the dough has doubled in size. (If you want to slow down the rising process, say if the weather is warm, smear the dough with a little olive oil and then press plastic film closely over it before covering the bowl with a tea towel.)

Knead the dough again, then divide it in two (each piece should weigh about 900 g). Dust 2 proofing baskets or ceramic bowls with flour or oil two 1 kg bread tins, then place the dough pieces in them and shape to fit. Place each basket or tin in a plastic bag, seal and leave in a warm place to rise for 1–2 hours, or until the dough has doubled in size. »

Preheat the oven to 230°C. If using proofing baskets or ceramic bowls, gently invert the dough onto a greased and floured baking tray. Quickly slash the tops with a very sharp knife and gently place on the top rack in the oven, as close to the top of the oven as possible but still allowing room for the dough to rise. If using tins, slash the tops, then sprinkle with a little flour and place in the oven as instructed above.

Bake for 20 minutes, then turn the baking tray or tins around, reduce the temperature to 200°C and bake for another 25–30 minutes. Remove the loaves from the tray or tins and return them to the oven directly on the oven rack. Bake for another 5 minutes to crisp the bottom of the loaves. Remove from the oven and place on a wire rack to cool.

GRAPE AND WALNUT BREAD   *Makes 2 loaves*

125 g shelled walnuts	½ teaspoon salt
15 g fresh *or* 7 g dried yeast	2 tablespoons extra virgin olive oil,
1 teaspoon sugar (optional)	plus extra for oiling
1½ cups (375 ml) warm water	2 cups fresh red grapes *or* 1 cup
500 g unbleached strong flour (see Glossary)	dried muscatels

Preheat the oven to 200°C. Dry-roast the walnuts on a baking tray for 6–8 minutes, then rub off their skins with a clean tea towel. Using a sieve or colander, separate the skins from the nuts.

If you are using fresh yeast, mix it to a sludge with the sugar and 1 tablespoon of the warm water in a small container (a cup will do) and set it aside until it begins to froth (this will take about 10 minutes, depending on the weather).

Put the flour into a large bowl and make a well in the centre, then add the salt and olive oil. If you are using dried yeast, add it now (omit the sugar), otherwise tip the frothing yeast mixture into the bowl. Pour in half the warm water and start bringing the dough together with your hands. Add the walnuts and then whatever water you need to form a dough (you may find you need more than you've allowed). Scrape the mixture from the bowl and turn it out onto a floured workbench, then knead it gently for 10 minutes or until the dough is smooth and shiny.

Put the dough in a lightly oiled bowl, then cover the bowl with a loose piece of plastic film. (If you want to slow down the rising process, smear the dough with a little olive oil and press plastic film closely over it before covering the bowl with a tea towel.) Put the bowl in a draught-free spot and allow the dough to double in size; this will vary depending on the conditions of the day – allow about 1 hour, but be prepared to wait longer or retrieve it a little earlier. Remember, the slower the rise the better. Do not over-prove.

Knock back the dough, then tip it onto a floured bench and pat it into a large round. Push the grapes or muscatels into the dough, then fold the dough over them so as few grapes as possible poke through. Divide the dough in half and shape as required. Put the

Grape and walnut bread (left), and flatbread (right, see page 52)

loaves onto a lightly greased baking tray, then cover them with tea towels and allow to double in size again.

Meanwhile, preheat the oven to 220°C. Dust the tops of the loaves liberally with extra flour and bake for 10 minutes, then reduce the oven temperature to 180°C and bake for another 20 minutes.

FLATBREAD   *Makes 6 rounds*

This flatbread can take on all sorts of flavours or it can be served plain. It can be thick or thin, depending on your whim. Try adding slivers of garlic or rosemary leaves to the 'dimples' in the dough before the final rising. It can also be covered with slow-cooked onions and torn basil leaves before baking, and then drizzled with extra virgin olive oil and seasoned with salt and pepper while hot. Or toss a large handful of freshly chopped flat-leaf parsley with a vinaigrette of extra virgin olive oil and lemon juice and pour it over the just-baked flatbread.

15 g fresh *or* 7 g dried yeast	1½ teaspoons salt
½ teaspoon sugar (optional)	¼ cup (60 ml) extra virgin olive oil,
1½ cups (375 ml) warm water	plus extra for greasing
500 g unbleached strong flour (see Glossary)	polenta (optional), for sprinkling
2 tablespoons whole milk powder	

If you are using fresh yeast, mix it to a sludge with the sugar and 1 tablespoon of the warm water in a small container (a cup will do), and set it aside until it begins to froth (this will take about 10 minutes, depending on the weather).

Mix the flour, milk powder and salt in a large bowl, then make a well in the centre and add the 60 ml olive oil and the frothing yeast mixture (if you are using the dried yeast, add it now but omit the sugar). The milk powder gives richness without liquid, but you could use milk instead and then add less water. Pour in the remaining warm water and stir until well combined, then turn the dough out onto a floured workbench and knead for about 10 minutes until the soft dough is smooth and shiny. Put the dough in a lightly oiled bowl, then cover it with a tea towel and allow it to double in size in a draught-free spot (this will take about 1½ hours, depending on the weather).

Turn out the dough, knock it back and knead again for a few minutes, then divide it into 6 pieces. Roll each piece into a ball and leave these to rest under a tea towel for 15 minutes. Grease a baking tray with olive oil or sprinkle a baker's wheel with polenta. Spread each ball of dough into a round about 1 cm thick. Brush the rounds with oil, then 'dimple' the tops with your fingertips. Cover the dough with tea towels and allow to double in size again (45 minutes–1 hour).

Preheat the oven to 230°C with a pizza tile (or unglazed terracotta tile) in it, if you have one. If not, use a baking tray. Bake the flatbread for 10–15 minutes on the tile, or for a little longer on a baking tray.

CHICKPEA FLATBREAD

Makes 1 flatbread

This recipe is great for those who are being careful with their consumption of wheat. I just love the flavour of this bread.

Chickpea flour is made from ground chickpeas and is available from wholefood stores, Italian or Indian grocers. I buy it in small quantities as it tends to turn rancid quickly.

250 g chickpea flour	¼ cup (60 ml) extra virgin olive oil
4 sprigs rosemary	1 teaspoon salt

In a large bowl, mix the chickpea flour with about 500 ml water, whisking to avoid lumping (the dough should have the consistency of thick cream – add more or less water as needed). Add half the rosemary sprigs to steep. Leave overnight.

Next day, preheat the oven to 230°C. Remove any scum from the surface of the mixture, fish out the rosemary sprigs then add the olive oil and 1 teaspoon salt and stir to form a batter. Strip the rosemary leaves from the two remaining sprigs and add to the batter. Pour the batter onto a pizza tile or unglazed terracotta tile (or use a baking tray). Bake for about 10 minutes – it should resemble a very thin pizza-like flatbread.

BREAD AND BUTTER PUDDING

Serves 10

120 g dried apricots, diced	900 ml milk
½ cup (125 ml) verjuice *or* half white wine and half water	600 ml cream
	8 eggs
4 × 1 cm-thick slices good white bread	125 g castor sugar
60 g butter	1 vanilla bean, halved lengthways
220 g prunes, pitted and diced	

Reconstitute the apricots in the verjuice or wine and water overnight, or cheat and use the microwave on defrost for a few minutes. Meanwhile, remove the crusts from the bread, butter it and then grill on both sides until golden. Butter a 22 cm ovenproof dish (I use one that is 7.5 cm deep) and arrange the bread slices over the base. Drain the apricots and sprinkle them over the bread with the prunes.

Preheat the oven to 200°C. Bring the milk and cream to a simmer in a saucepan, then remove from heat. Beat the eggs and castor sugar in a large bowl, then scrape the seeds from the vanilla bean into the egg mixture. Stir the hot milk and cream into the egg mixture, then pour this carefully over the bread. Stand the dish in a larger baking dish and pour in hot water to come two-thirds of the way up the sides. Bake for about 30 minutes until set, then allow to cool a little before serving.

PIZZA

One of the great wood-fired-oven experiences is to be had at Russell Jeavons' fine establishment Russell's Pizza at Willunga, south of Adelaide. A few years ago, I was part of a contingent of more than sixty from the Slow Food Convivium that gathered at Russell's for an olive oil tasting, led by Zany Flannagan, a local with a good nose and palate. After the tasting was complete, a procession of food began, each 'course' served on a wooden board in the centre of the table. No knives, forks or plates were offered or needed, although serviettes were welcomed.

The food, all cooked in Russell's huge brick oven that sits in full sight, came out in waves. The first offering was wood-fired bread, baked that morning. It came with a dish of local extra virgin olive oil, Russell's dukkah, a green salad made with Island Pure kefalotiri and the last of that year's local olives, and a tray of smoked beef and prosciutto. This was all consumed literally within seconds.

But when the first wooden board of what Russell called 'bits' appeared, we all looked for more of the bread to mop up the sauces. Here was duck confit crisped in the oven on pizza trays with pheasant hearts and slow-cooked pork in a highly flavoured jus. A good dab of rosehip jelly (made by Russell, of course) sat in the middle of the board. A plate of Kangaroo Island haloumi came out next, the cheese sliced and caramelised in the oven with olive oil.

And then the pizzas! There were nine tables in the room, and Russell's staff fed us pizza after pizza. When I went into the kitchen to return a few plates (it's that sort of place), there were buckets of dough and several industrious young people rolling and preparing the bases. These bases – thin and tasty – were made of flour from Four Leaf Milling, the organic and biodynamic grain specialist from Tarlee. Each pizza took only five minutes to cook in the well-worked oven. The first pizza to appear used the duck confit again, this time separated into pieces and partnered with sliced par-boiled potato and rosemary and drizzled with extra virgin olive oil. Then came a tomato-based one with anchovies and next a chicken and chilli pizza. The last one was a triumph of seafood: tomato and fennel on the base, then a thick layer of squid caught off Port Willunga, all crowned with oysters in the shell. It was so generous it was almost impossible to cut.

Before dessert was served, Russell talked to us about his tiny place. He sees his brick oven as connecting the history of Willunga with that of the Welsh who first settled the area. And he sees the brick oven as the pivot, the centre of his cooking. Russell has had a more traditional career in the past, but rejected the norm of running a conventional restaurant. Instead, when he opened here in 1993, he decided not to open much at all. Up until recently he has only traded six hours a week, only opening on Friday nights, but since October 2005 he now also opens on Saturday nights much to the delight of his customers.

Russell makes pizzas to suit just about every taste, but the best way is to take pot luck and see what you get. I doubt whether you'll ever see a written menu at Russell's, and I also doubt you'll find a better pizza anywhere.

PIZZA WITH GOAT'S CHEESE, SEMI-DRIED TOMATOES AND BASIL
Makes 6 individual pizzas

For years we played around with our wood-fired oven, but never enough to really get a handle on it. That is until Victoria Blumenstein came to work for me and, as a great cook and passionate advocate of wood-fired ovens, she took over the running of it and showed us just how it was done. Of the many occasions we used the oven, one night stays firmly in my mind as being just so incredibly special. I had agreed to hold a function at home as a favour to Adrian Geering, who had been my mentor on business matters and was someone I admired greatly. The dinner was for thirty of his colleagues, and knowing that, for them, business was more important than food, Victoria and I decided to turn the tables and get them very much involved, as we wanted to bring them firmly into our world for the night.

Our idea was to make lots of different pizzas and to chargrill some seafood on the coals from the wood-fired oven. On the day, the fire was lit in the early morning, and a 10 kg bucket of pizza dough was made in the large mixer at the Farmshop, then punched down with gay abandon every time it looked like over-proving. We pulled a solid wooden table from the shed to put in front of the fire, with all our ingredients laid out on it so we could work quickly and feed everyone at the same time.

We rolled out the dough on a granite bench to one side of the fire into beautifully thin ovals about the size of standard dinner plates, then set them aside with a damp tea towel over them to prevent them drying out. Victoria had made two sauces for the pizza bases, one of basil, preserved lemon and extra virgin olive oil, the other of fresh tomato, garlic and oregano. All the ingredients for the toppings were lined up on enamel camping plates on the table – raw tuna, olives, squid cooked quickly on the coals, four different cheeses, fresh figs, prosciutto and sopresso (a type of spicy Italian salami). There were also fresh scallops speared on rosemary skewers to grill, along with the necessary accompaniments of extra virgin olive oil, sea salt, pepper and vino cotto. We were ready for action.

The guests had simply been told we would be eating outside, but had no idea what they were in for. We made each pizza on the spot, adding ingredients as the mood took us. There is something about a fire that draws people in, and as each pizza came out of the oven – a new taste sensation – they devoured it with hungry delight. One after the other the pizzas came out: raw tuna and olives with just a hint of pepper on a basil base, grilled squid on a tomato base, fig and prosciutto with goat's cheese, the list went on and on. Then, as a finale to the night, we made a dessert pizza of figs soaked in my vino cotto, and a cheese-plate pizza of a mixture of cheeses topped with my cabernet paste, which became a luscious molten mass, giving that sweet–sour zing to finish the night. The buzz of the evening was amazing – everyone got involved in the food, both cooking and eating, and we were all carried away by the mesmerising aura of the fire.

Here's the recipe for my basic pizza base, with a delicious topping – but remember to experiment with different toppings each time you make it. You could use an unglazed terracotta tile or a pizza tile to cook the pizza on, or alternatively a flat oven tray will do the trick.

180 g goat's curd
180 g semi-dried tomatoes
extra virgin olive oil, for drizzling
freshly ground black pepper
basil leaves, to serve

PIZZA BASE
15 g fresh yeast *or* 1½ teaspoons dried yeast
½ teaspoon sugar (optional)
1½ cups (375 ml) warm water
500 g unbleached strong flour (see Glossary)
2 tablespoons whole milk powder
1½ teaspoons salt
¼ cup (60 ml) extra virgin olive oil,
    plus extra for greasing
¼ cup (40 g) polenta (optional), for dusting

Preheat the oven to 230°C or its highest possible temperature, and if using a pizza tile, place this in the oven to warm.

If using fresh yeast, combine it with the sugar and 1 tablespoon of the warm water in a small bowl, dissolve the yeast by mashing it with a fork, then set it aside for 5–10 minutes until frothy.

Mix the flour, milk powder and salt in a large bowl, then make a well in the centre and add the olive oil and the yeast mixture (if you are using dried yeast, add it now but omit the sugar). Pour in the remaining warm water and stir until well combined, then turn the dough out onto a floured bench and knead for about 10 minutes or until it is shiny and smooth. Return the dough to the lightly oiled bowl, then cover the bowl with plastic film and leave in a draught-free spot for about 60–90 minutes, or until the dough doubles in size.

Turn the dough out, knock it back and knead again for a few minutes, then divide into 6 pieces. Roll each piece into a ball and allow these to rest under a wet tea towel for 15 minutes. With a rolling pin, roll each ball of dough into a round about the thickness of your little finger.

Stretch the dough by resting it over your hands, clenched in fists with knuckles pressed together, then gently pull your hands apart, allowing the weight of the dough to stretch itself. This important step allows the air to stay in the dough so you get that lightness in your crust. Alternatively, you could try rolling the dough a little thinner to achieve a similar result. Lightly dust the pizza tile or baking tray with polenta or flour, then lay the dough on it.

Place the pizza in the base of your oven; it is important not to oil the dough at this stage. Pull it out when the dough has set (this should be after about 4 minutes, but will depend entirely upon the oven – you are looking for the dough to change from shiny to a soft, just under-baked look). Scatter dollops of goat's cheese and the semi-dried tomatoes over the base, drizzle with olive oil and season with pepper. Return the pizza to the oven for a few more minutes, then drizzle with more olive oil, scatter with basil leaves and serve.

PASTA

Nothing could be more fun than making pasta – all it takes is a little planning. Buy unbleached, 'strong' plain white flour and choose free-range eggs (for colour and flavour). You'll find strong flour in better supermarkets and good food stores.

If you don't have your own hand-cranked pasta machine, someone in your family or circle of friends might. In any case, they cost under $100 for a basic model, which usually comes with spaghetti and fettuccine cutters. Other implements needed include forks and a pastry scraper – a half-moon-shaped piece of plastic that is readily available and very cheap, and once you've developed a taste for homemade pasta, you'll need it again and again.

Making pasta by hand is like making cement: pouring egg into a 'dam' in the middle of the flour and mixing it bit by bit with the egg, making sure the dam walls don't collapse.

FRESH PASTA   *Serves 4*

About 500 g fresh pasta will serve four adults as a main course. Great pasta doesn't need a sauce. Just drizzle olive oil over the hot pasta, then add some freshly shaved Parmigiano Reggiano, or make a simple, uncooked sauce with fresh tomatoes and basil.

The dough should be tight but malleable. If it becomes too loose, it will still be suitable for making ravioli.

500 g strong flour (see Glossary)	**4 × 61 g eggs**
1 teaspoon salt	**1–2 egg yolks (depending on the flour)**

Mix the flour with the salt, then spread it out into a circle 30 cm in diameter over a clean work surface. Hollow out the centre, leaving just a bank of flour around the edges. Break the eggs into the well, then add the yolks. Using one hand, whisk the eggs and yolks until they're amalgamated, and then, using a fork held in the other hand, scoop the flour a little at a time from the 'banks' into the egg mixture, still whisking with one hand. Keep doing this until the mixture becomes a paste.

Scrape up the dough, 'cutting' it until the mixture is well combined. This involves gathering the mass and smearing it across the bench with the pastry scraper until it all comes together. The dough should then be kneaded for 6–10 minutes, pushing the dough away from you with the heel of your hand, then turning it a quarter to the right, folding the dough over, pushing it away and so on.

Once the dough is shiny and silky, roll it into a ball and wrap it in plastic film. Rest it in the refrigerator for 30 minutes.

Set the pasta machine on a bench, screwing it down firmly. Cut the dough into 10 even pieces and cover with a tea towel. Working in batches, take one piece of dough and press it as flat as you can with the palm of your hand, then feed it through the rollers set on their widest aperture. Fold the rolled dough in thirds, and then pass the narrow end through the machine again. Repeat several times, preferably until you hear a sound that I can only describe as a 'plop' – this is the tension of the dough releasing as it goes through the rollers.

Adjust the machine to the next setting and pass the dough through. Repeat this with every setting until you get to the second to last. As the dough moves through each setting it will become finer and finer and the sheets will become longer and longer; you may need to cut the sheets to make them more manageable.

Unless I'm making ravioli, where I want the pasta to be almost diaphanous, I'll stop at the second to last setting, then adjust the machine, adding the cutters, and run the pasta through the cutters. If I'm making long pasta, I like to have someone help here. Hang the pasta ribbons over the back of a chair or a broom handle to dry.

When ready to cook, bring a large saucepan of water to the boil and add a generous amount of salt. Tip in the pasta and cook until done, testing a strand after 3 minutes. Have a large colander at the ready in the sink, strain the pasta and tip it back into the pan (you may also want to save a little of the cooking water, in case you need it to bind the sauce). Don't rinse the pasta or you'll lose the starch that helps the sauce or oil adhere. If you're not ready to use it immediately, spread out the pasta on a large tray to cool drizzled with extra virgin olive oil – I hate to admit it, but it reheats beautifully in the microwave.

DUCK EGG PASTA WITH SMOKED KANGAROO, SUN-DRIED TOMATOES AND PINE NUTS

Serves 6 as an entrée

I suspect that all cooks have one dish they are most proud of, and that's how I feel about this very simple dish, which starred on my restaurant menu for many years. It was the kind of dish where the total was greater than the sum of the parts. The key to it was the rich silkiness of the handmade duck egg pasta – made fresh every day – and the perfection of the ruby-red cold-smoked kangaroo fillet. I sometimes used roasted flaked almonds rather than pine nuts, to great effect. Of course, the pasta can be made with chook eggs too.

I can also proudly say that I have never had a better smoked kangaroo than the one I brined and cold-smoked at Schulz's Butchers in Angaston, and I regret that it is no longer possible to do this, due to changes in food laws. Rather than attempt this dish with a hot-smoked alternative, use raw kangaroo, venison or beef – freeze it first for 20 minutes to enable you to cut it paper-thin.

½ cup (125 ml) extra virgin olive oil

100 g sun-dried tomatoes (not those in
    cotton seed oil), cut into strips

1 cup (155 g) pine nuts *or* flaked almonds

400 g kangaroo, venison *or* beef fillet, sliced
    as thin as prosciutto

sea salt flakes and freshly ground
    black pepper

shaved Parmigiano Reggiano, to serve

DUCK EGG PASTA (makes 500 g)

3⅓ cups (500 g) strong flour (see Glossary)

4–5 duck eggs, depending on their size

To make the pasta, tip the flour onto a bench and make a well in the centre. Whisk the eggs together and pour into the well, and gradually incorporate them into the flour, following the method described on page 57. Add an extra yolk if needed. Knead the pasta dough until it forms a shiny ball and is firm to the touch. Cover the dough with plastic film and rest it in the refrigerator for 30 minutes. Cut the pasta dough into about 8 equal portions.

Preheat the oven to 200°C. Roast the pine nuts on a baking tray for about 10 minutes or until golden brown.

Before beginning to roll the pasta, bring a large saucepan of salted water to the boil. Set the pasta machine on a bench, screwing it down firmly. Working in batches, take one piece of dough and press it as flat as you can with the palm of your hand, then feed it through the rollers set on their widest aperture. Fold the rolled dough in thirds, and then pass the narrow end through the machine again. Repeat several times, preferably until you hear a sound that I can only describe as a 'plop' – this is the tension of the dough releasing as it goes through the rollers.

Adjust the machine to the next setting and pass the dough through. Repeat this with every setting until you get to the second to last. As the dough moves through each setting it will become finer and finer and the sheets will become longer and longer; you may need to cut the sheets to make them more manageable. Adjust the machine, selecting the widest cutter, and run the pasta through to cut into strips. Hang the pasta ribbons over the back of a chair to dry.

Slide the pasta gently into the boiling water, then partially cover with a lid to bring back to a rapid boil. Stir the pasta gently to keep it well separated. Fresh pasta only needs to cook for 3 minutes or so. Drain the cooked pasta, reserving a little of the cooking water in case you need it to moisten the completed dish. Do not run the pasta under water or you will lose the precious starch that helps the sauce or oil adhere. Generously drizzle the pasta with olive oil immediately.

While the pasta is cooking, make the sauce. Heat half the olive oil in a small frying pan, then add the sun-dried tomatoes and pine nuts or almonds and heat over low heat. Toss the remaining olive oil through the slices of kangaroo.

To serve, pile the pasta on a serving dish or plates, top with the kangaroo, then spoon over the sun-dried tomato and pine nut sauce. Scatter over liberal amounts of shaved Parmigiano Reggiano and serve immediately.

PASTRY

Some years ago I witnessed Betsy Pie, then the organiser of the Brisbane Masterclasses, turn a calamity into a triumph when the star chef backed out only days beforehand. Expecting a dashing Frenchman to appear on stage, the students were instead greeted with a glass of French bubbly.

Betsy went on to tell the amazing story of how she had chased leads from one continent to another as she sought out a top-class presenter who could be lured to Australia on literally a few hours' notice. Clever Betsy managed to whisk Nancy Silverton from the Campanile Restaurant and La Brea Bakery in Los Angeles to fill in for the wayward Frenchman. Nancy was confident, unpretentious in her attitude to food, and had every one of us talking about all she had taught us over the weekend.

Nancy talked to us about pastry-making – very 'down home'. Gathering up the audience into her hands as confidently as she did her dough, Nancy shared her tricks, kept us engaged and, frankly, charmed us. As she demonstrated making dough for a tart, it was as if we were seeing the process for the first time. Nancy made the dough with a certain amount of irreverence – she tossed flour onto the bench with the carefree abandon of someone very sure of her craft. She used a food processor, adding the flour with the sugar sifted into it (at the same time telling us that, if making pastry by hand, you should use only the tips of your fingers). She then added very cold butter to the processor, pulsing it in, before adding egg yolks and cream (stirred together first) and stopped mixing just before the dough came together.

Then – and this was the bit we all loved – Nancy gathered the dough into a ball with her hands and bounced it on the bench! This apparently allows the proteins in the flour to relax so they don't shrink during cooking. As she uses a lot of butter, the pastry then went into the freezer to chill well (or to keep for later use) – this also helps prevent shrinkage. Nancy went on to bash the chilled dough heartily with a rolling pin to flatten it so that it wouldn't crack when rolled.

She urged us not to play with the dough by poking it into the corners and to always trim the pastry case by running a rolling pin over the top rather than using a knife. And, of course, she reiterated the need to chill the rolled-out case, to firm the pastry before baking.

My notebook was thick with scribbled tips. One I particularly liked was that, when blind baking, Nancy uses large paper coffee filters rather than foil to line the pastry before adding weights. The filters don't stick to the pastry and allow you to get the weights right into the corners. They also show you clearly whether the pastry is cooked – if it's not, the weights stick.

Another good idea (for me, anyhow) is to only use a plain flan ring when making a pastry case; I lose the detachable bases regularly and find myself with mismatched bases and rings. To do this Nancy uses a large metal baking tray without a lip, baking paper and an unfluted ring. This allows the cooked tart to slip straight onto a plate from the baking sheet; she then slides the band off gently.

As Nancy is as straightforward a writer as she is a teacher, her books are well worth tracking down. And if you are ever in LA, her restaurant Mozza is certainly worth a visit for the fabulous pizzas and antipasti.

SOUR-CREAM PASTRY
Makes enough to line a 20–24 cm tart tin

This recipe makes a very short, flaky pastry with a light, melt-in-the-mouth texture. It is a great all-rounder and can be used in a whole variety of dishes, both sweet and savoury. It's the pastry I make ninety-nine times out of a hundred because it's not only so good but so easy. I like to chill the pastry case in the freezer, as this ensures it is really well-chilled before it goes in the oven.

This pastry rises beautifully and is really light and flaky, which is great if you're making a tart or a pie, but if you want a flat pastry, like a thin pizza dough, a good trick is to 'inhibit' the pastry as it cooks. To do this, carefully open the oven halfway through the cooking (when the pastry is beginning to rise), take out the tray for a moment and press down on the pastry with a similar-sized tray or a clean tea towel, then return the tray to the oven. This will stop the pastry rising too much.

200 g chilled unsalted butter, chopped into small pieces	250 g plain flour ½ cup (125 ml) sour cream

Put the butter and flour into the bowl of a food processor, then pulse until the mixture resembles coarse breadcrumbs. Add the sour cream and pulse again until the dough just forms a ball. Use Nancy's trick of bouncing the pastry (see previous page) if shrinkage worries you. Carefully wrap the dough in plastic film and leave to rest in the refrigerator for 15–20 minutes.

Roll out the dough until it is 5 mm thick, then use it to line a 20 cm tart tin with a removable base. Chill the pastry case for 20 minutes.

To blind bake, preheat the oven to 200°C. Line the pastry case with foil, then cover with pastry weights. Blind bake the pastry case for 15 minutes, then remove the foil and pastry weights and bake for another 5 minutes.

CHOUX PASTRY-STYLE
GLUTEN-FREE PASTRY

Makes enough to line a 24 cm tart tin

As a friend who is a coeliac confided to me, the thing she most missed after being diagnosed was the lack of a luscious pastry. So, along with Victoria Blumenstein, my chef at the Farmshop at the time, I set about finding something to fit the bill.

This pastry browns beautifully, has a nice crispness and holds in moisture; it also has a lovely potato-ey undertone which is very pleasant. It is great for any type of pie and keeps well in the refrigerator for up to five days.

You could add 2 teaspoons of icing sugar to make a sweet pastry for fruit pies and other pastry-based desserts.

Xanthan gum is derived from corn sugar and acts as a binding agent in gluten-free pastry. It is available from most health food stores.

2 teaspoons salt

90 g unsalted butter

150 g gluten-free flour (I use a mix of
potato flour, rice flour and maize flour),
plus ½ cup extra for dusting

2 g xanthan gum

3 × 57 g eggs

In a heavy-based saucepan, combine the salt, butter and 250 ml water. Bring to a simmer over medium–high heat and add the flour and xanthan gum gradually, stirring with a wooden spoon. Reduce the temperature to low and continue to cook until the pastry is well combined and is coming away from the sides of the pan. Remove from heat and allow to cool to room temperature.

Whisk eggs to combine, then slowly add them bit by bit to the pastry mixture, incorporating fully before adding the next bit; you may not need all the egg mixture.

Turn the pastry out onto a bench that has been dusted with ½ cup gluten-free flour to assist rolling, then knead until shiny. Try to incorporate as little flour as possible so the pastry does not become too crumbly.

Chill the pastry for 20 minutes, then, using a rolling pin, roll the pastry between 2 pieces of baking paper which have been greased on both sides. Roll the pastry until it is 5 mm thick, then use it to line a 24 cm tart or pie tin.

To blind bake, preheat the oven to 200°C. Line the pastry case with foil, then cover with pastry weights. Blind bake the pastry case for 15 minutes, then remove the foil and pastry weights and bake for another 5 minutes.

CRISP GLUTEN-FREE PASTRY

Makes enough to line a 24 cm tart tin

This is a nice base for quiches and cheese tarts – it becomes very crisp when baked. Although this pastry does not need to be rested because it contains no gluten, it rolls more easily when chilled.

Xanthan gum is derived from corn sugar and acts as a binding agent in gluten-free pastry. It is available from most health food stores.

125 g cream cheese, cut into chunks

75 g cold unsalted butter, chopped

1 cup gluten-free flour, plus ¼ cup extra
    for dusting

2 g xanthan gum

2 teaspoons salt

In a food processor, pulse the cream cheese and butter to combine. Slowly add 1 cup of the flour, the xanthan gum and the salt and pulse just to combine. Turn the pastry out onto a bench which has been dusted with ¼ cup gluten-free flour and bring together with your hands, kneading for 5 minutes.

Chill the pastry for 20 minutes, then, using a rolling pin, roll the pastry between 2 pieces of baking paper which have been greased on both sides. Roll the pastry until it is 5 mm thick, then use it to line a 24 cm tart, pie or quiche tin.

To blind bake, preheat the oven to 200°C. Line the pastry case with foil, then cover with pastry weights. Blind bake the pastry case for 15 minutes, then remove the foil and pastry weights and bake for another 5 minutes.

KANGAROO

IT TOOK MANY YEARS FOR ALL THE AUSTRALIAN STATES TO come into line with uniform legislation about kangaroo meat. There are very strict quotas in place, which are necessary to protect the kangaroo population, and stringent requirements for the issuing of 'harvesting' licences. Kangaroo is probably still most widely available in South Australia, where it is readily accepted as a healthy, flavourful red meat. It is best of all when cooked on the barbecue, which certainly suits our way of life and our Mediterranean climate.

I first started serving kangaroo at the restaurant in the mid-1990s. It was much in demand as a uniquely Australian meat, and as such it was overseas visitors who were particularly keen to try it, as well as some interstaters who at the time were unable to eat it in their states and so thought it was somewhat daring. For me, flavour was the real motive, along with the knowledge that kangaroo fed on natural grasses in the wild. Also, as a native species, they are more suited to this fragile land of ours than cloven-hoofed sheep and cattle.

When roo first became available we used to buy a whole saddle and spend hours trimming and stripping sinew. Things are much simpler now and the meat is normally sold as fillets, although you can also buy the leg, tail or whole saddle. However, for home cooking, particularly barbecuing, the fillet is the most convenient cut.

I get quite nostalgic when I talk of or write about smoked kangaroo. In the Barossa I have a wealth of food tradition to draw upon, and smoking is one of the strongest. I was incredibly proud of the smoked kangaroo I used to produce at Schulz's Butchers in Angaston. Then, they were happy to let me brine the roo first, then string it up until I thought it was ready. When finished, it was ruby-red with a dense consistency, and I served it sliced paper-thin like prosciutto. As already mentioned, changes in food laws have placed greater restrictions on the smoking process, and it is no longer possible to have access to the local smokehouses.

I suggest that a barbecue or a ridged chargrill plate on a very hot stove is the best way to cook kangaroo fillets. Place them on a tray or plate with just enough olive oil to moisten them (they have absolutely no fat to speak of, so this is important), sprinkle with freshly ground black pepper, and set aside, covered, for about an hour. I don't use a red-wine (or any other) marinade for roo – it disturbs the natural flavour of the meat. Be sure not to buy more meat than required for your recipe – kangaroo meat oxidises on contact with air more readily than any other meat I know, and will spoil and turn grey quickly. It is usually sold vacuum-packed, so keep it tightly sealed until you are ready to cook and then add the olive oil to protect it.

Preheating the barbecue or pan is essential, as is brushing it with olive oil. Season the roo with sea salt flakes just seconds before cooking. After placing the first side down, leave it until properly sealed (at least 2 minutes); if you play with the meat with your tongs before

then, you will tear the fibres. Repeat on the other side for approximately the same time, and then the fillet will need to rest for at least 5–7 minutes before it is ready (depending on the thickness). The grain of the meat is looser than that of beef or lamb, and it is absolutely essential to cook kangaroo rare and never leave out the resting step. If overcooked, it will be like shoe leather.

A simple anchovy and olive butter or horseradish or wasabi butter would add either a salty or hot component to the dish. Probably my two favourite accompaniments to kangaroo, either together or separately, are my Caramelised Onion Salad (see page 99) and a beetroot dish. Try beetroot either cooked, peeled and deglazed with vino cotto or balsamic, or raw, grated in a salad with extra virgin olive oil and orange rind. In fact, even beetroot from a tin – heaven forbid – would be a great counterpoint to the richness of the roo.

If you want to make it more formal, try a rich red-wine and port glaze with some thinly sliced pickled quinces (and just a bit of the pickling liquor added) alongside creamy mashed potatoes or parsnips flavoured with extra virgin olive oil – combine this with perfectly rare and rested kangaroo and you are on to a winner!

For other ideas for kangaroo, look at recipes for venison in game cookbooks. Kangaroo also marries well with Asian flavours and you can happily substitute it for beef in many dishes.

SALAD OF SMOKED KANGAROO

Serves 6

This is such a refreshing dish. It can be made with commercially smoked kangaroo or venison, but would also work well with raw kangaroo that has been frozen for 20 minutes, then thinly sliced.

100 ml extra virgin olive oil

1 tablespoon red-wine vinegar

1 dessertspoon vino cotto (see Glossary) *or* balsamic vinegar

1 small clove garlic, very finely chopped

3 large witlof, bases trimmed and leaves separated

2 cos lettuce hearts, leaves separated

1 bunch rocket, leaves trimmed

300 g smoked kangaroo, thinly sliced

120 g salmon roe

Make a vinaigrette with the olive oil, red-wine vinegar, vino cotto and the garlic.

Wash and spin the lettuces dry. Divide the lettuce leaves among 6 plates and drape the kangaroo over the leaves. Dress each salad with the vinaigrette, then scatter with the salmon roe and serve immediately.

BARBECUED SUGAR-CURED KANGAROO

Serves 4

Select the thickest fillet you can find for this dish, as the denseness of the meat is important. Ask your butcher to trim off the sinew.

125 g cooking salt

125 g sugar

25 g black peppercorns, coarsely crushed

8 juniper berries, bruised

8 sprigs thyme

1 kg kangaroo fillet in one piece, sinews trimmed

extra virgin olive oil, for cooking

Mix the salt, sugar, peppercorns, juniper berries and thyme. Evenly spread the fillet with the mixture, place in a glass or ceramic dish and wrap to seal well with plastic film. Place a similar-sized dish on top, then place weights, such as cans from the pantry, on top of this, and leave in the refrigerator overnight.

Take the meat from the dish and wipe off any excess moisture. Brush with extra virgin olive oil and cook on a very hot barbecue grillplate. The cooking time will depend on the thickness of the meat and may be as little as 4 minutes, but no longer than 10 minutes – the meat needs to be rare. When cooked, it is essential to rest the meat for at least 15 minutes before serving.

Serve with horseradish cream and a salad of bitter lettuces such as witlof, radicchio and frisée.

KANGAROO TAIL PIE

Serves 8

The late Maurice de Rohan became a firm friend after he asked me to prepare a cocktail party for over 500 people in Paris in 2001. It was to be held at the Australian Embassy to commemorate the 200th anniversary of Nicolas Baudin's expedition to the southern Australian coast. Maurice gave me free reign to make this a totally South Australian gastronomic event, so with the help of the Ambassador's staff, I managed to fly in an amazing array of ingredients. I was determined that this was not going to be just standard 'cocktail food'. Based on the premise that if Matthew Flinders hadn't pipped Baudin at the post by just 5 nautical miles we might have been French, the concept was to feature the 'wild' food that Baudin might have found on his arrival.

Maurice immediately loved my idea of whole Murray cod baked in mud, as if they'd been cooked in coals by the side of the river, being opened in front of the guests by gloved chefs who pulled back the casing to reveal the succulent fish. We made damper to serve it as a sandwich (or 'schnitter', as we say in the Barossa) with Joseph Grilli's extra virgin olive oil and some dukkah. The guests crowded around, loving the theatre of it!

The assembled guests ate voraciously and loved it all. As noisily as they talked through the political speeches, they listened intently when I spoke about the food they were eating and the inspiration behind it. It was without a doubt the most exciting food event of my life. The support and cooperation of the then Ambassador, William Frazer, and his staff, particularly his chef Michael Walker, made the event a great success, but it was Maurice's vision that I was so happy to have made a reality.

I had to use artistic licence in sourcing my ingredients, as the logistics involved in transporting food from the other side of the world for such a large party were enormous. We used farmed Murray cod rather than fish straight from the Murray River, and the razorfish, a wonderful mollusc that is not fished commercially, had to be collected by a volunteer group in return for a 'donation' to their cause. The yabbies came from Western Australia because of technical issues with export licences in South Australia, but happily the oysters were from Coffin Bay, and the kangaroo tail was definitely South Australian!

We were to serve cocktail-sized kangaroo tail pies which, when the Parisian caterers and I trialled them, had turned out beautifully – succulent and delicious. As we were working from a kitchen not much larger than a normal household one, we decided to delegate the cooking of the pies on the night to the caterers, but something must have gone wrong and they turned out to be a disaster. So much so that, even though the guest numbers had increased by an extra 200, after a few tears of frustration I decided to throw most of the pies away because they were so dry. I was determined nothing was going to spoil the evening.

Whenever I've made this dish, whether as small individual pies or larger ones, the results have always been moist and more-ish – I urge you to give it a go.

1 large onion, roughly chopped

1 carrot, roughly chopped

1 clove garlic, roughly chopped

extra virgin olive oil, for cooking

1 cup plain flour

sea salt flakes and freshly ground
    black pepper

2 kangaroo tails, approximately 1.5 kg in
    total, cut into thirds

6 lemon myrtle leaves

500 ml jellied veal stock *or* reduced Golden
    Chicken Stock (see page 178)

375 ml red wine

8 golden shallots, finely diced

4 cloves garlic, finely diced

3 sticks celery, finely diced

PASTRY

1 packet Tandaco suet mix
    (believe me, it works and is terrific!)

2 cups flour

1 cup water

1½ teaspoons baking powder

freshly ground black pepper

1 egg, beaten

dash milk

Preheat oven to 140°C.

In a heavy-based casserole, seal the onion, carrot and garlic in olive oil on medium heat until softened, then remove from pan and set aside. Mix the plain flour with some salt and pepper, and dust the kangaroo pieces with the seasoned flour. Working in batches, gently seal them in olive oil on all sides over medium heat in the casserole. Add all the kangaroo back to the pan, placing the thickest tail pieces at the bottom, then add the vegetables and the lemon myrtle leaves. Turn the heat up to high and pour in the stock and red wine. Bring to a simmer, then cover the dish with a lid or two sheets of foil and transfer to the oven. Cook for 1½ hours, then turn the meat over and cook for a further 2 hours, or until all the tail pieces are cooked and the meat falls easily off the bone.

Once cooked, remove the casserole from the oven and set aside until the meat is cool enough to handle. Remove the meat from the tails and cut into dice, adding a little of the cooking juices to keep it moist. Strain the rest of the juices through a sieve and set aside.

In a heavy-based frying pan, sauté the shallots, garlic and celery in olive oil over medium heat until softened, then turn the heat to high, add the drained cooking juices and reduce for 10–15 minutes, until they begin to thicken. Season well, remove from the heat, and add the chopped tail meat. Transfer to the refrigerator to chill for several hours or overnight.

For the pastry, combine all the ingredients and knead on a floured workbench until the dough is smooth and uniform. Carefully wrap the dough in plastic film and leave to rest in the refrigerator for 20 minutes.

Roll out two pastry circles large enough to line the base and lid of a 28 cm pie dish. Line the dish with the base and fill with the chilled kangaroo mixture. Mix the egg with the milk and brush some of this around the pastry edge, then place the lid on and crimp the edges together with your fingers. Brush the lid with the rest of the egg wash, then chill the pie in the refrigerator for 20 minutes.

Preheat oven to 220°C. Cook the pie for 10 minutes, then turn the temperature down to 200°C and cook for another 10 minutes until the pastry is golden and the filling is hot.

LEEKS

LEEKS ARE NOT CALLED 'POOR MAN'S ASPARAGUS' BECAUSE THEY taste like asparagus but because the delicious thin ones can look similar. Personally, I have always aspired to Georges Blanc's dish *asperge du pauvre*, where the leeks are poached for 10 minutes, then refreshed under cold water and served with Beluga caviar. No longer for the poor man!

Why is it that when leeks are sold in a bunch they are not all the same size? I was trialling a dinner for 100 people for the Adelaide Symphony Orchestra and wanted to serve braised leeks. I had to figure out how many bunches I would need and how long they would take to prepare. In my first bunch I had three fat fresh leeks, one fat old leek and one very skinny young leek. Two of the leeks had lots and lots of dirt in them, while the others were clean. The grower probably put his bunches together according to a standard weight, but I objected heartily to the old leek being thrown in.

You may be thinking that this one example does not make for a definitive survey, but this has happened to me many times over, I can assure you. I would have been very happy if the leeks had all been of the thinner variety (called pencil leeks); in fact, I would have paid a premium for them. Even though you're left with something half the size once you've peeled the outside layers off, discarded the root end and trimmed away the darker leaves, these sweeter, more tender specimens provide twice the pleasure of their larger cousins.

Pencil leeks are now much more widely available in major city markets, but at the wrong time of year, they too can be woody in the centre. The leek is still one of the vegetables I give space to in my kitchen garden, as tender young leeks are so different from the fat, over-mature specimens shops often offer. Young leeks add an extra dimension to slow-cooked winter foods and give a fragrance that immediately excites. So many people try to escape cold winters, whereas I love them, if only to experience the joy of walking into a warm kitchen with a one-pot meal simmering away.

Washing leeks meticulously is essential, as the layers can harbour an extraordinary amount of dirt, and there is nothing worse than gritty cooked leeks. If you want to keep the shape of the whole leek, stand it root-end up in a large jug of water to soak out the grit. Another method is to cut through the leek at the point where the dark and light green meet – this way you'll cut away most of the dirt. Remove the tougher outer layers and make a cut about 5 cm into the top, then immerse the leek in a sink of cold water, shaking it to eliminate any remaining dirt. If you aren't cooking the leeks whole, cut them in half lengthways and rinse them thoroughly. It's a much simpler matter if the leeks are to be chopped up as you can reject or rewash any gritty pieces.

The leek is one of the few vegetables that must be a little 'overcooked' to ensure maximum flavour and texture. A simple, wonderful meal cooked this way by a French friend of mine, for Bastille Day years and years ago, showed me how special this vegetable can be. Choose three or four of the youngest leeks possible, of similar size, and wash them very carefully, keeping them whole but trimming away any dark-green leaves. In a frying pan, bring the leeks to a simmer in salted water, adding a dash of verjuice and a little butter or extra virgin olive oil, and simmer them until they change colour and no longer smell like onion – about 15 minutes. Drain the leeks, then refresh them under cold water and drain again, making sure no water remains. Make a small slit in each leek at the light-green end, so that they can be fanned out on the plate when served, then refrigerate them, covered, until really cold. Make a vinaigrette using 4 parts extra virgin olive oil to 1 part sherry vinegar and add a teaspoon of Dijon mustard, a good dash of cream and a little salt and freshly ground black pepper. Serve the dressed leeks with freshly chopped flat-leaf parsley and crusty bread.

Cooked well, leeks are deliciously sweet and they really do melt in the mouth. They are available all winter, and September is probably the last month to enjoy them before they become woody. The frustrating thing is that a fresh bunch gives no clear indication of that woodiness, so it is a case of buyer beware. (This might be the one time when the ever-increasing practice of selling trimmed vegetables on a polystyrene tray might work to your advantage!)

Try simmering the leeks as explained above, but instead of chilling them, arrange them over the base of a gratin dish. Cover the leeks with a layer of grated pecorino or Parmigiano Reggiano, then dot this with butter and add another layer of leeks, cheese and butter. Bake at 210°C for 10–12 minutes until the leeks are warm and the cheese melts.

Sweat off chopped leeks in a tiny bit of verjuice and butter. This makes a great side dish for pan-fried or poached chicken breast, or pan-fried fish (particularly a meaty one like tuna – try this with a rich, reduced red-wine sauce). Roasted whole leeks are also a great side dish for poultry or fish. I often roast pheasant breasts and bake leeks separately in butter, then arrange the leeks over the breast and glaze the whole with reduced pheasant stock.

Leek soup is a favourite on a winter's night. Slice lots of washed leeks into rings and sweat them in a little butter with peeled, chopped potato and onion until softened. Add chicken stock and a little chervil and simmer until the vegetables are cooked through, then purée the mixture and add a touch of cream and seasoning before serving. You could add some freshly shucked oysters to the soup with a spoon of crème fraîche to make it more of a meal.

There are lots of options for leek tarts. Try layering a warm pastry case with chopped and sweated leeks and topping this with pan-fried globe artichokes and crispy pancetta. You can also caramelise leeks in the same manner you do onions by cooking them slowly with butter and a touch of a quality vinegar. Anchovies can be added or the leeks can be studded with goat's cheese before the tart is heated in the oven.

LEEKS POACHED IN VERJUICE
Serves 4 as an accompaniment

6–8 small leeks, washed
½ cup (125 ml) verjuice
1 tablespoon butter
1 teaspoon salt
freshly ground black pepper
2 tablespoons pitted black olives

2 tablespoons soft cheese such as gruth (a soft, fresh quark)
1 tablespoon freshly chopped flat-leaf parsley
extra virgin olive oil

Trim the roots and tops from the leeks so that you are left with a firm, mostly white leek. Lay the leeks on a chopping board and cut horizontally through the first 4–5 cm of the tops of the leeks. Leave to soak in cold water to remove all remaining dirt.

Once perfectly clean, drain the leeks and place over very low heat in a frying pan just large enough to hold them. Pour in the verjuice and ½ a cup of water, add the butter, salt and pepper to taste, then simmer gently for about 1 hour or until the leeks are cooked all the way through. They should still hold their shape, but be soft to the touch. Add the pitted olives for the last few minutes of cooking.

Taste for seasoning and adjust if necessary, then place the leeks on a serving plate, spoon on the soft cheese and sprinkle with the flat-leaf parsley. Add a last flourish of olive oil, then serve.

LEEK AND PANCETTA TART
Serves 6–8

1 × quantity Sour-cream Pastry (see page 62)
12 tender young leeks, trimmed
butter, for cooking
sea salt flakes and freshly ground black pepper

4 eggs
½ cup (125 ml) cream
60 g thinly sliced mild pancetta, diced

Make and chill the pastry as instructed, then roll out the chilled dough and use to line a 20 cm loose-bottomed flan tin. Chill the pastry case for 20 minutes. »

Preheat the oven to 200°C. Line the chilled pastry case with foil and pastry weights, and blind bake for 15 minutes, then remove the foil and weights and return the pastry case to the oven for another 5 minutes. Remove the pastry case from the oven and reset the temperature to 220°C.

Discard the outer layers of each leek, then wash them well and slice them into rings. Cook the leek in a saucepan in a little butter over gentle heat for about 5 minutes or until softened, then season with salt and pepper. Purée the leek in a food processor, then add the eggs and cream and adjust the seasoning.

Scatter the diced pancetta over the pastry case, then add the leek mixture. Bake the filled pastry case for 20 minutes, watching that the pastry doesn't burn on the edges (cover it with foil if necessary). Allow the tart to cool a little before slicing and serving.

LEEK AND OYSTER PIES   *Makes 30*

Without a foil, the butteriness of a good pastry can be too much when combined with the butteriness of leeks. Here, the iron-like flavour of the oysters cuts into all that richness – although the champagne has a role to play, too, of course. This recipe is a favourite of mine to serve with pre-dinner drinks on those rare days when I have spare time.

I have a tray of tiny pie moulds I bought years ago from Chefs' Warehouse in Sydney that I use for these. It has 30 small indents that are about 3 cm wide and is just perfect.

1 × quantity Sour-cream Pastry
   (see page 62)
butter, for cooking
12 young leeks, cleaned and cut into
   5 mm slices
sea salt flakes and freshly ground
   black pepper

½ cup (125 ml) champagne *or*
   sparkling white wine
100 ml thin, runny cream
30 large Pacific oysters, shucked
1 egg, beaten with a little milk

Make and chill the pastry as instructed. Roll out the dough and use to line 30 small 3 cm-diameter pie moulds, then cut out 30 lids slightly larger than the moulds. Chill the pastry for 20 minutes.

Heat a little butter in a frying pan, then sweat the leeks over low heat until soft and season to taste with salt and pepper. Deglaze the pan with champagne, turn the heat up to medium–high and reduce the liquor by half. Add the cream and reduce a little more, then leave to cool.

Chop oysters in halves or thirds. Put a spoonful of leek mixture into each pie mould, then add 1 chopped oyster and cover with a little more leek mixture. Cover with pastry lids and seal carefully. Chill in the refrigerator for 20 minutes.

Meanwhile, preheat the oven to 220°C. Brush the egg wash over the pie lids. Bake pies until golden, about 15 minutes. Cool for 5 minutes in the tins before turning out and serving.

LEEK FRITTATA

6 tender young leeks

2 tablespoons butter

¼ cup (60 ml) extra virgin olive oil

sea salt flakes and freshly ground
   black pepper

1 sprig thyme, leaves stripped

6 eggs

Cut the tops from the leeks at the point where the light-green meets the dark-green, and discard them. Cut the light-green/white parts of the leeks in half lengthways and wash them well, then chop both parts into 1 cm slices.

Heat the butter and 2 tablespoons of the olive oil in a heavy-based enamelled saucepan until golden brown. Cook half the chopped leeks, and when they begin to collapse, quickly add the rest, then season with salt and pepper and add the thyme leaves. Cook the leeks for about 30 minutes or until soft and cooked through, then remove the pan from the heat and allow them to cool for at least 1 hour.

Beat the eggs in a large mixing bowl, then add the cooled leeks and any residue in the pan. Mix thoroughly.

Heat the remaining oil in a heavy-based frying pan, then carefully add the leek mixture and cook over medium heat. When the eggs have set and the frittata comes away from the bottom of the pan, put a plate over the pan and carefully invert the frittata onto it. Return the pan to the heat, then slip the frittata back into it and cook for just a minute more. Return the frittata to the plate using the same method and allow to cool a little – I prefer to serve frittata warm or at room temperature.

LEMONS AND LIMES

THE VERY CONVENIENCE OF HAVING A SUPPLY OF LEMONS ON a tree is absolutely wonderful: just to be able to walk into the garden when you need a squeeze of lemon for some fresh fish, to make a mayonnaise at the last moment, or if, like me, you sometimes have a squirt of lemon in very strong black coffee in the morning. To say nothing of the natural beauty of the tree laden with fruit and flowers – and don't forget the gin and tonic on a summer's afternoon!

Lemons are as indispensable to my cooking as garlic, verjuice, extra virgin olive oil and quality salt and pepper. I use lemon rind in my game pies; lemon juice squeezed into the cavity of all the game I cook; lemon juice to curdle the milk for banana cake; lemons in jam to increase the pectin content; lemon juice in mayonnaise, hollandaise and vinaigrettes; lemon with all kinds of seafood; lemon juice added to a pan of frying mushrooms; lemon juice added to water to stop vegetables oxidising; lemon juice to add balance and zip to a sauce; lemons squeezed on pancakes sprinkled with sugar and then rolled up tight; lemons in homemade lemonade; lemons for squeezing over grilled offal or a just-cooked risotto; lemons for adding to jugs of rainwater on the table; lemons for cleaning my hands after peeling beetroot; lemons for a burnt-butter sauce with capers and parsley to go with brains; and lemons for lemon curd or lemon meringue pie.

In the Riverland in South Australia, lemons begin their season in late July and continue through to November. The lemon tree in your home garden, however, can bear fruit for much of the year, particularly if it's a Lisbon variety; just thin out the main crop so that you are picking mature lemons alongside the forming baby lemons, and there will be flowers on the tree to keep the cycle going.

Lemons don't like clay, nor do they like wet feet. They need well-drained soil and consistent watering through the hot summer months and, though they shouldn't be overfed, if you see the leaves yellowing it means you need to fertilise. Overfeeding will give very large fruit and will make the skins too thick. Lemons can cope with the hottest spot in your

garden, against the northern side of a fence or shed, but only if you keep the ground moist. Their preference, though, is to have shelter. When the leaves turn yellow, it is often due to a lack of lime in the soil, so adding iron chelate can turn that problem around in a week.

While there are other varieties being trialled and grown, particularly in commercial groves where growers are looking for lemons to extend their production year, the other most common variety is the eureka. It is an upright tree like the Lisbon, and grows up to 5 metres tall. Its fruit is deliciously sour and is used for commercial juicing, as the fruit is large and easy to pick, with a thicker skin and barely any thorns. Lisbon lemons only have a thick skin when the tree is young and growing vigorously. As the tree gets older, the skins become thinner.

Then there is the meyer lemon, a lemon that adapts particularly well to pots and comes into fruit before the Lisbon. As I write this, I am looking out of the huge picture window of my piano room and can see five mature meyer lemon trees, which are so abundant with

almost-ripe fruit that they would make a beautiful still-life painting. I'm particularly partial to the meyer lemon, especially for desserts. It is deep yellow in colour, with the smoothest skin and a handsome round shape. Although sweeter than the conventional lemon, it still has a wonderful tang. Meyer lemons sliced super-fine and similarly thin slices of fennel, dressed with peppery, green extra virgin olive oil, salt and freshly ground black pepper, make a perfect salad to serve alongside grilled quail or barbecued lamb or kid.

I've just returned from a trip to California, where meyer lemons are very popular and are used in countless dishes. Whilst there I delighted in a meyer lemon *pot au crème*, as smooth as smooth yet with a delicious bite to it, and a meyer lemon semifreddo served with berries and meyer lemon curd. Consult Alice Waters' *Chez Panisse Menu Cookbook* for lots more ideas on how to use this wonderful variety.

A handy tip for extracting more juice from a lemon or lime is to pour boiling water over the whole fruit and leave for 5 minutes before squeezing it. Or if you have a microwave, heat the fruit on medium for 1 minute and leave to cool a little before squeezing. This is a particularly handy tip for limes (as they are often sold dark green and unripe and hence yield little juice) when you require enough juice for a refreshing summer drink of lemon, lime and bitters or, after a hard day, something more exotic such as a daiquiri or a margarita.

I find so many uses for lemon rind (the coloured part of the skin, not the white pith) that I try to be disciplined enough to peel any lemon before squeezing it. If not using the rind immediately, it can be kept in castor sugar until you are ready to use it, or it can be frozen in a plastic bag. I'm partial to dried rind and use it when making game sauces, stuffing chooks, preparing soup, or making risotto. And I add a few pieces to a bath of walnut oil into which I put grilled wild mushrooms. Drying lemon rind is easy – if you don't have a dehydrator, a low 120°C oven for a few hours will do the trick, as will the hot sun in summer.

Preserved lemons are also a regular part of my cooking. It's amazing how their salty–sour flavour enhances food. I find them incredibly versatile, quite apart from their use in traditional Moroccan fare: scrape out the pulp, quickly rinse and dry the rind, then chop it finely and toss it through a salad of peppery greens; or roast quarters with a whole chook; or bake chook thighs topped with slices of preserved lemon.

I seldom cook pork without using preserved lemon, as they cut through the richness of the fatty meat, but they also work well with chicken, lamb or fish. Make a salsa verde-style sauce to serve with chicken by adding preserved lemon – but go easy on the capers to balance out the salt.

You can add preserved lemon to a warm marinade to serve with fish: cook golden shallots in wine or verjuice and a little fish stock, then reduce and add finely chopped preserved lemon rind and fresh chervil at the end of the cooking. Off the heat, swirl in some extra virgin olive oil, then pour this over grilled or pan-fried fish. Try the same with a breast of chicken, pan-fried – and with the skin on of course – using chicken stock rather than fish stock.

Stuff a whole small fish with sliced preserved lemon and fresh dill or fennel before baking it. Or rub the skin of a whole fish with the oily juices from the preserving jar, along with a little olive oil, and grill on the barbecue. Turn the fish frequently to make sure you don't burn the skin.

If you ever make labna by draining yoghurt overnight so it can be worked into small balls, try rolling the balls in a mixture of finely chopped preserved lemon, finely sliced garlic and lots of chopped flat-leaf parsley to make a sort of gremolata ball. Serve these with slow-cooked or grilled lamb or kid, and couscous or polenta. Exceptional!

Make a warm lentil salad by adding diced preserved lemon, fennel, celery and carrot to freshly cooked lentils and then toss through masses of just-plucked coriander leaves. Dress this with a vinaigrette of extra virgin olive oil and lemon juice and serve with grilled quail.

The lemons I preserve have nothing more than salt and lemon juice added. While most dishes only call for the rind, I return the flesh of the lemon back to the jar for using when I'm slow-cooking lamb shanks or making a casserole. The pulp lasts forever in a jar in the refrigerator; just remember when you use it that you probably won't need to add any extra salt to the dish, but tasting the dish will tell you.

Whether lemons are squeezed, grated, zested or preserved, the uses for them are endless. I love them best of all simply sliced thickly, brushed with oil and grilled on the barbecue, to add a sweet zestiness to grilled meat.

PRESERVED LEMONS

Makes 8 lemons

I love the piquant yet mellow, sweet yet sour flavours of preserved lemons. Most people use only the rind, discarding the pulp before they rinse and finely slice or chop the rind. But it's all a matter of taste. The flesh can actually be kept aside in the jar (in the oily preserving liquid) and then be added to slow-cooked casseroles, particularly if you're using pork or lamb, or rubbed over a leg of lamb before baking. I tend to add it a fair way into the cooking, and don't add any other salt.

Use unwaxed lemons for preserving. If you can't buy them this way, scrub them well with hot water first.

8 lemons	juice of up to 4 extra lemons
150 g coarse kitchen salt	bay leaf *and/or* cinnamon stick (optional)

Make the lemons as juicy as possible by warming them in the microwave for 1 minute on medium, and leaving to cool a little. Cut each lemon in quarters, but not right through, stopping 1 cm from the bottom. Place 1 tablespoon of salt in the base of the preserving jar, then push the remainder of the salt inside the cut lemons, pushing each one back into shape afterwards. Place each lemon in the jar, pressing down as firmly as possible to release the lemon juice. Squeeze as many of the other lemons as you need to immerse the lemons completely in juice.

Leave in a cool, dry place for up to 6–8 weeks, depending on the weather, for them to mature (the warmer it is, the quicker they will mature). They will keep for years – the longer you keep them, the more intense the flavour. After opening, pour a layer of olive oil over the lemons and keep them in the fridge – they will last out of the fridge, but they will oxidise.

PRESERVED LEMON VINAIGRETTE

Makes about 125 ml

1 preserved lemon quarter, flesh removed, rind rinsed and finely diced	1 teaspoon vino cotto (see Glossary) *or* balsamic vinegar
⅓ cup (80 ml) extra virgin olive oil	1 tablespoon torn basil leaves
1 tablespoon good-quality red-wine vinegar	freshly ground black pepper

Toss all the ingredients together, then check for seasoning (the preserved lemon will add salt).

This vinaigrette is good simply served with peppery salad greens or with grilled fish or chicken.

SPINACH WITH LEMON AND CURRANTS
Serves 4

This is a wonderful accompaniment to grilled red meat, chicken and of course fish. The sweet sharpness of the reconstituted currants makes a delicious addition.

1 bunch spinach (about 200 g after cleaning
  and trimming off the first 2.5 cm of stem)

⅓ cup (80 ml) extra virgin olive oil

2 cloves garlic, bruised

½ cup currants, reconstituted in verjuice *or*
  water overnight

sea salt flakes and freshly ground
  black pepper

juice of ½ lemon

Reassemble the bunch of spinach, then cut into 6 pieces, including the stems. Toss quickly in a frying pan with the olive oil and the bruised garlic cloves over high heat until the spinach is just limp. Add the currants and season. Remove from the heat and toss until well incorporated, then add the lemon juice. The spinach should be only just cooked and should retain its colour.

MEYER LEMON RISOTTO WITH MASCARPONE AND SCAMPI
Serves 8

1–1.5 litres ginger-based Fish Stock
  (see page 177) *or* Golden Chicken Stock
  (see page 178)

40 g butter

1 red onion, finely chopped

400 g Arborio rice (see Glossary)

½ cup (125 ml) verjuice

2 meyer lemons *or* other thin-skinned
  variety, cut into thin slices, then each
  slice cut into quarters

125 g mascarpone

1½ cups firmly packed nasturtium leaves,
  sorrel *or* baby rocket

SCAMPI

8 raw scampi, halved lengthways and
  vein removed

½ teaspoon Ceylon tea (optional)

2 tablespoons extra virgin olive oil

2 teaspoons lemon juice

sea salt flakes and freshly ground
  black pepper

Bring the stock to the boil in a saucepan; keep warm over low heat. Melt the butter in a large, heavy-based saucepan over low heat, then add the onion and sauté until translucent. Add the rice, making sure there is enough butter to coat the grains.

Turn the heat up to high and add the verjuice. Reduce the heat to low and add one ladleful of heated stock at a time, stirring often until each is absorbed. Keep a close eye on the temperature, maintaining a simmer. After about 15–20 minutes, when the rice should

Lemon tart

be close to cooked and most of the stock has been absorbed, stir in the lemon pieces and cook for another 5 minutes.

Meanwhile, for the scampi, preheat the oven to 230°C or the highest temperature possible. Either grind a little Ceylon tea to a powder by simply rubbing it between your fingers, and sprinkle it over the scampi (I learned from Tetsuya Wakuda that this brings out the sweetness), or just brush the scampi with olive oil. Place on two baking trays and cook one tray of scampi at a time for about 3 minutes. The scampi are ready as soon as they feel hot to touch; they only need to be cooked about three-quarters through, until translucent. Make a vinaigrette with a little olive oil and lemon juice and toss the scampi through, then season.

Adjust the risotto seasoning and then fold in the mascarpone and nasturtium, sorrel or rocket leaves and serve with the roasted scampi.

LEMON TART   *Serves 8*

For freshness at the end of a meal, this tart, inspired by Sydney chef Tony Bilson's recipe, never fails to delight. I bake it in a deep-sided quiche tin. This tart deserves a little practice to get the texture of the filling just right, as so many factors can influence the set. The first time you make it, start well in advance so that you can refrigerate the tart for an hour or so if the filling does not set. This is pretty delicious served with clotted cream.

1 × quantity Sour-cream Pastry (see page 62)	⅓ cup (80 ml) lemon juice
	grated rind of 1 lemon
150 g castor sugar	600 ml cream
9 egg yolks (from large, fresh free-range eggs)	icing sugar (optional), to serve

Make and chill the pastry as instructed. Roll out the chilled dough and use to line a 20 cm flan tin with a removable base. Chill the pastry case for 20 minutes.

Preheat the oven to 200°C. Line the chilled pastry case with foil and pastry weights and blind bake for 15 minutes. Remove the foil and weights and bake for another 5 minutes.

Reduce the oven temperature to 180°C. Meanwhile, beat the sugar, egg yolks, lemon juice and rind until smooth, then fold in the cream. Fill the warm pastry case with the lemon mixture, taking care not to overfill it. Bake until the filling is set around the edges but still wobbly in the middle (this will take anywhere from 25–45 minutes, depending on your oven). Remove the tart from the oven and set aside to cool to room temperature to allow the filling to set completely – it should be the consistency of a very ripe brie, yet firm enough to cut into portions. Refrigerate for an hour or so if necessary to help set the filling. Serve dusted with icing sugar.

LIMES

Limes have a very special flavour of their own. They fruit at the same time as lemons and are well worth a position in the garden or in a pot, although they do not do as well in Mediterranean climates as lemons. Although limes are most successful in tropical climates, they are still worth growing, even if only in pots. Limes are aromatic and have a strange coconut smell about them. They are interchangeable with lemons for most uses, bringing an extra tang to a dish as they are stronger in flavour.

Growers of Tahitian limes are struggling with the fact that the market demands green limes. However, a green Tahitian lime is simply under-ripe, while the lime picked ripe from the tree is yellow and has so much more aroma, flavour and juice. Whilst it's handy to know that you can get more juice from an under-ripe green lime by putting it in the microwave, it does make you wonder why they are not sold ripe. You need to ask for ripe yellow Tahitian limes – you'll delight yourself and make the growers very happy!

Mrs Beeton's Book of Household Management has a recipe for half lemon and half lime cordial where the juice and rind are reduced on the stove with sugar to taste and then kept cold in the fridge and diluted with a jug of iced water. For those of us who love lime cordial but don't have the time to make it, there is the truly South Australian institution of Bickford's Lime Juice Cordial, widely available throughout Australia. Bickford's have been producing this top-class product since 1874. The base of lime concentrate actually has to come from the West Indies because no one in Australia can supply them with adequate quantities of limes. The cordial is a golden brown colour because when it was originally transported from the West Indies a hundred years ago, the limes oxidised en route, and since then the public has become familiar with this colour. Bickford's managing director suggests that to change the colour now would be like making Coca-Cola clear!

LIME VINAIGRETTE
Makes about 375 ml

My daughter Saskia, Victoria Blumenstein and I made this incredibly simple vinaigrette for a cooking demonstration recently, and it was extraordinarily good served with freshly sliced raw kingfish. It is also great as an all-round salad dressing, or tossed through green beans with finely chopped almonds.

1 lime	1 tablespoon chervil leaves
1 clove garlic	½ cup (125 ml) verjuice
2 tablespoons flat-leaf parsley leaves	¾ cup (180 ml) extra virgin olive oil
5–6 mint leaves	

Remove the lime rind and chop finely, then, if the lime is under-ripe, microwave it on medium for 1 minute before juicing. Combine the lime rind and juice with the remaining ingredients in a food processor, then leave to stand for 1 hour before using, to allow the flavours to develop.

SCALLOPS WITH LIME RIND AND SEA URCHIN BUTTER   *Makes 24 canapés*

When planning parties I want my offerings to delight and surprise. My favourite finger food of all – well, at the moment at least – is this delicious morsel on a shell. Of course you need to be organised and have a wine bucket, or similar, to collect shells as soon as the scallops have been eaten, but that's no more trouble than having a dish for olive pips or toothpicks, and much more interesting.

I use Port Lincoln scallops – they are so sweet and nutty (as long as they haven't been frozen) when barely cooked. Sea urchin roe is now being harvested in South Australia for the first time. It has long been a delicacy in Japan and France (and probably many more places I haven't yet travelled to), but here it is still considered anything from odd to incredibly adventurous.

For me, this recipe is one of the taste sensations of my life. I always leave the brilliant orange scallop roe on, both for colour and flavour: the sea urchin butter with its slightly metallic taste (like that of an oyster) and deep ochre colour gives such a perfect finish to the scallop that I'm always left wondering whether I should actually save any for my guests.

24 Port Lincoln scallops on the half-shell, roe intact	SEA URCHIN BUTTER
finely chopped rind of 1 lime	75 g butter, softened
2 tablespoons extra virgin olive oil	roe from 2 sea urchins *or* about 2 tablespoons harvested sea urchin roe
sea salt flakes and freshly ground black pepper	sea salt flakes and freshly ground black pepper
120 g unsalted butter	1 tablespoon lime juice
100 ml verjuice	
chopped chervil, to serve	

To make the sea urchin butter, combine all the ingredients and set aside.

Clean the scallops by pulling the meat away from the shells and cutting out the intestinal tract. Reserve the shells, then wash and dry them. Place the scallops, lime rind and a drizzle of olive oil in a bowl and season with salt and pepper.

In a frying pan, cook the butter a tablespoon or two at a time until nut-brown, adding a dash of olive oil to inhibit burning. Seal the scallops in several batches over high heat for about 30 seconds on each side, wiping the pan clean between each batch. Do not cook too many scallops at once as you want to sear, not poach, them. When they are all cooked, wipe out any butter from the pan, then return all the scallops to the pan with half the verjuice and deglaze over high heat for just a moment. Remove the scallops and set aside, then add the rest of the verjuice and reduce to a sauce.

Preheat the oven to 220°C or a griller to high. Place a scallop on each half-shell and dot with sea urchin butter. Place in the oven or under the hot grill for about 1 minute or just until the sea urchin butter begins to melt. Sprinkle with chervil and serve with the reduced sauce.

LIME POSSET WITH LIME CONFIT
Serves 6

Either limes or meyer lemons are terrific for this posset. The confit is best made with really ripe limes whose skins have turned yellow.

550 ml cream

150 g castor sugar

finely chopped rind of 2 limes

½ cup (125 ml) lime juice, strained

LIME CONFIT

660 g castor sugar

4 ripe limes, scrubbed and thinly sliced

Combine the cream, sugar and lime rind in a saucepan, then bring to the boil over high heat and boil, stirring, for 3 minutes. Transfer to a bowl and leave to cool.

Once the cream mixture is cool, whisk in the lime juice to aerate the mixture as much as possible. Continue whipping until the mixture begins to thicken. Pour into six 100 ml-capacity cups or moulds, then chill in the refrigerator for 4–5 hours or overnight.

Meanwhile, for the lime confit, preheat the oven to 150°C. Make a sugar syrup by combining the sugar and 750 ml water in a saucepan, then stirring over low heat until the sugar dissolves. Increase the heat and simmer for 5–10 minutes or until the liquid reduces to a syrupy consistency.

Lay the lime slices in a baking dish so they are just overlapping. Pour over the sugar syrup and cover with baking paper, then cover with foil. Bake for 1 hour. Remove the foil and baking paper and return to the oven until the syrup is reduced and the limes are caramelised; this will take another 30 minutes–1 hour. Cool and then refrigerate.

Serve the lime posset topped with a little of the lime confit. Any leftover lime confit will keep well in the refrigerator for up to 1 month.

OFFAL

I LOVE OFFAL SO MUCH THAT I CANNOT GO PAST IT WHEN I see it on a menu, and have even been known to have three offal entrées instead of an entrée, main course and dessert. I share this passion with a group of like-minded offal fanatics, but whilst offal certainly gladdens the 'hearts' of many, it can also be particularly divisive at the dinner table.

As much as I love it, I'm aware that you have to choose your guests carefully when you serve it as it isn't everyone's cup of tea. Offal is far from revered in Australia, but for me it's an absolute favourite.

During the first Slow Food Convivium in the Barossa in 2004, my daughter Saskia and I prepared an offal brunch featuring six different offal dishes, all matched with magnificent wines from Seppelt's Winery. The dishes ranged from brains in a burnt-butter sauce, lemon and capers, to braised pig's ears stuffed with sweetbreads and mushrooms (a dish firmly embedded in my taste memory from the moment I first had it at Berowra Waters Inn what seems like a lifetime ago now, cooked by the incredible Janni Kyritsis).

This was such a success that we did it again for the March 2006 Barossa Slow feast, with the help of Richard Gunner of Coorong Angus Beef, who not only assisted, but supplied the offal. This time the six different offal-based dishes started with rabbit liver crostini with vino cotto and onion jam, progressing to lamb kidneys wrapped in *crépine* (caul fat), and then finishing with slow-braised intercostals (the rich meat between the ribs) in shiraz.

Generally I find the most adventurous eaters are offal lovers. In France, offal reigns supreme as a delicacy; the French word for it is *abat*, from 'abattoir'. The French are wonderfully resourceful in using every part of the animal. Because there is only a small amount of offal per animal and it is so highly prized, offal is quite expensive in France (and in Italy), whereas in Australia it is an amazing bargain for the cook.

Your attitude to offal as food will often depend on your upbringing – it was the very first food I learnt to cook. Many Australians shun it, however I have heard that some abattoir workers who understood the attraction of offal used to take home special 'treats' such as sweetbreads and calves' brains. These days, things are much more regulated, supposedly for our safety, and abattoirs must have special rooms if they want to keep the offal, otherwise they are forced to throw it away. (Although as the whole of the abattoir should be hygienic, I do not understand how offal dissected in a separate room makes it 'safer' for us.) As a result, offal is relatively scarce – for example, pig's ears are hard to find, but are still available if you organise yourself in advance; always try a Chinese butcher. A suckling pig served at a feast doesn't look the same minus the ears, so take the trouble to order your pig intact from a specialist source. Many years ago now, for our tenth anniversary party at the Pheasant Farm Restaurant, I had Schulz's Butchers of Angaston pickle a whole pig for me to serve as the centrepiece of the banquet. It was delivered *sans* ears not long before proceedings began, so some deftly draped grape leaves had to suffice for ears. It didn't spoil the taste, but often the visual effect is also important.

Our sensibilities seem to call for subtle euphemisms for the more confronting organ meats. We call lamb's liver 'lamb's fry' and bull's testicles 'prairie oysters', while the thymus gland and pancreas become 'sweetbreads'; at least an ear is an ear, when you can get it.

There are so many possibilities with offal that are such delicacies to the initiated. There is the heart, which you can stuff; the caul fat or *crépine* (the lining of a pig's stomach), which you can wrap delicate food in before baking or pan-frying; kidneys, which can be grilled or roasted, either encased in their own fat, or trimmed and sliced.

Pig's ears make the most wonderful eating, braised slowly in stock, cooled and then stuffed with sweetbreads or chicken, dipped in egg and breadcrumbs and baked dotted with butter. Pig's trotters are essential to my stock-making but I also love them slowly braised and served with lentils. I think my favourite offal is sweetbreads – I prefer calf's to sheep's, as the tiny lamb sweetbreads lack the nutty characteristics of the veal ones.

Then there is tongue, which was a firm favourite on my restaurant's menu. I often served it brined and smoked (from Schulz's Butchers), simmered gently with stock vegetables and light veal stock until soft to the touch. I simply let it cool a little, enough to be able to handle it, peeled and sliced it while still warm, then served it with pesto or a salsa verde. If you want to prepare it in advance, cut it into slices and cover with plastic film until you are ready to use it, then quickly toss it in a tiny bit of butter in a heavy-based pan over high heat. This caramelises the tongue, which is fabulous served with a salsa verde or pickled plums.

As a child I could never bear to even look at tripe in the traditional white sauce. Then years ago, in a session on rice at a Melbourne Masterclass, Stefano de Pieri cooked a tripe risotto. He had talked to me about it before and I suggested tripe might be too divisive, but he charged ahead and I had to eat my words. He used veal tripe, a delicacy in itself, and softened it further by making the risotto with milk (as often served to children in kindergartens in Italy). He braised the tripe with tomatoes for seven hours and then added this

Brains in caper butter (see page 90)

fragrant stew to the risotto. The two dishes could have been eaten separately, Stefano said, but he combined them as an alternative to the much-maligned tripe in white sauce. There must have been 150 people in the audience, and everyone seemed willing to give the tripe a go – so much for my prediction.

Lamb's brains are among the most accessible and delicious of all offal. The secret is to deal with a good butcher who will supply you with rosy-pink, fresh (or freshly frozen but not yet thawed) brains if you order well in advance. They must be cooked as soon as they thaw out if frozen, or within a day of buying them fresh from the butcher. But before they can be cooked, they must be soaked: soaking the brains in lightly salted water for a few hours gets rid of the blood.

BRAINS IN CAPER BUTTER

Serves 6 as an entrée

A trick to maintain the shape of the brains during poaching is to wrap each one in a small rectangle of foil, twisting each end like a Christmas bon-bon.

6 sets brains
1 dessertspoon lemon juice
1 bay leaf
pinch black peppercorns
70 g butter

sea salt flakes and freshly ground
    black pepper
30 g capers
1 tablespoon freshly chopped
    flat-leaf parsley

The brains should be very fresh – shiny and sweet smelling. Soak them in lightly salted water for several hours before use. Wrap each brain in foil so that they keep their shape while cooking.

Place the parcels in a saucepan of water with a little of the lemon juice added, the bay leaf and a few peppercorns. Start off the poaching in cold water then bring to a simmer over medium–high heat. The cooking time depends on how 'done' you like them (I like them only just set, which takes about 12 minutes). Take the brains out of the water and leave them to set overnight in the refrigerator before unwrapping, then cut in half lengthways. I usually find that by cooling and cutting them in half, then frying them cut-side down, the brains need absolutely no trimming.

Put the butter into a large frying pan and allow it to turn nut-brown over high heat with a touch of extra virgin olive oil to prevent burning. Seal the brains on their cut side. Be careful not to have too many in the pan at once or they will poach and turn soggy. As soon as they brown, turn them over. While the pan is still on the heat, season with salt and pepper. Add capers and parsley and deglaze with remaining lemon juice. Serve immediately.

TRIPE WITH SURPRISE PEAS, VERJUICE AND PANCETTA

Serves 6–8 (it's very rich)

When we decided to do a segment on tripe for the TV series *The Cook and The Chef* last winter, I wanted to cook a very different tripe dish to any I'd done before, to show that there was great potential in combining tripe with different flavours. It was suggested that we should set up a stall at the Barossa Farmer's Market one Saturday morning and offer the general public a taste of tripe, to see if anyone was game to try it.

It was one of those wonderful occasions when I suspect the producers expected people to be horrified or, at the least, put off by the idea of the dish, but they underestimated the people of the Valley and their interest in food. We set up a trestle table, handwrote a sign that said 'Tripe cooked in verjuice with peas and pancetta', and offered to give passers-by a taste. I was bowled over by the number of people who said, 'I've never been keen to taste tripe but I'll have a go.' We got a great reaction to it, and most people loved the dish, with

Tripe with surprise peas, verjuice and pancetta

only a couple of exceptions. The most delightful thing of all, though, was the number of children who tasted it and loved it – you couldn't fake a child's reaction if you tried, and there for all to see were these youngsters hoeing in and coming back for more!

1 kg honeycomb tripe (ask your butcher for
    partially cooked tripe)
1 tablespoon butter
extra virgin olive oil, for cooking
8 small leeks, white part only,
    sliced into rings
1½ cups (375 ml) verjuice

2 tablespoons chopped lemon thyme
3 cups (750 ml) chicken stock
sea salt flakes and freshly ground
    black pepper
1 cup Surprise peas
12 thin slices pancetta

Soak the tripe in cold water for about 30 minutes before cooking. Drain and dry thoroughly, then cut into 2 cm × 3 cm strips. Heat butter in a large saucepan over medium–high heat until nut-brown, add a dash of olive oil to prevent burning, then add the tripe and seal on all sides until well-coloured. Remove the tripe and set it aside. Add the leeks and cook for about 10 minutes or until the leeks are just soft. Return the tripe to the pan. Deglaze the pan with verjuice over high heat, then add the lemon thyme and chicken stock and season to taste with salt and pepper.

Reduce the heat to low, then simmer gently, covered with a tight-fitting lid, for about 75 minutes. Add peas and cook over high heat for another 30 minutes or until the liquid has reduced and is syrupy. Adjust seasoning if desired.

Meanwhile, preheat the oven to 200°C. Lay pancetta on a baking tray and bake for about 10 minutes or until crisp.

Garnish tripe with the slices of crisp pancetta and serve.

TRIPE WITH TOMATOES AND OLIVES
Serves 6

This recipe is inspired by 'Tripe Prepared My Way' by Antonio Carluccio, in *An Invitation to Italian Cooking*. It was the dish that converted me! The slow-cooking in tomatoes and wine is light years away from the hated tripe and white sauce of my childhood.

1 kg honeycomb tripe, cut into 2 cm pieces
2 carrots, roughly chopped
3 celery stalks, roughly chopped
3 onions, roughly chopped
2 cloves garlic, thinly sliced
extra virgin olive oil, for cooking
2 sprigs oregano, chopped
2 sprigs rosemary, chopped

1 cup (250 ml) red wine
2 × 400 g cans chopped Italian tomatoes
100 ml Golden Chicken Stock (see page 178)
sea salt flakes and freshly ground
    black pepper
120 g kalamata olives, pitted
⅓ cup freshly chopped flat-leaf parsley

Most butchers sell tripe blanched and already partially cooked. If your tripe has not been prepared in this way, it needs to be boiled several times, in fresh water each time – giving the tripe about an hour's cooking time in total before proceeding with the recipe.

Toss the carrots, celery, onions and garlic with a little olive oil in a large frying pan over high heat until softened, then remove from the pan and set aside. In the same pan, toss the tripe with the oregano and rosemary in a little more oil. Add the wine and tomatoes and reduce rapidly.

Add the chicken stock and simmer, uncovered, over low heat for about 1 hour. Season with salt and pepper, then add the olives in the last few minutes. Serve with lots of chopped flat-leaf parsley.

GRILLED INTERCOSTALS *Serves 4–6*

As mentioned, intercostals are the muscles which sit between the ribs and hold the lungs in place. The membrane on the inside of the intercostals needs to be trimmed off; the meat can then be chargrilled, stir-fried or braised. Their flavour is fairly rich and almost gamy.

6 intercostals

cornflour, for dusting

2 sprigs rosemary, leaves removed and
    finely chopped

6 bamboo skewers, soaked in cold water
    for 30 minutes

½ cup (125 ml) extra virgin olive oil

2 tablespoons red-wine vinegar

sea salt flakes and freshly ground
    black pepper

Trim away the inside membrane from the intercostals.

Preheat a chargrill plate over high heat until very hot. Combine the cornflour and rosemary, then dust the meat with the cornflour mixture. Thread the meat onto the skewers, then grill on each side for 3 minutes or until well-browned. Place in a dish with the olive oil and red-wine vinegar and leave to rest for 10 minutes. Season to taste with salt and pepper and serve.

ONIONS

OF ALL THE VEGETABLES WE EAT, ONIONS ARE PROBABLY THE most ubiquitous, and so we often forget that they, too, have their own season. Onions are at their best in autumn and winter, although, given the vastness of this country and the variations in climate, this season can be extended significantly.

For most of my cooking needs, I insist on clean, shiny, firm golden-brown onions, but I know that at certain times of the year, such as early spring when only the last of the season's onions are left, these are hard to come by. (Especially if you are a pâté producer, and use some 250 kg of onions each week – and even more now that we make caramelised onion commercially.) It is at this time that onions can start revealing the inner green shoot that signals they are past their best. These onions can still be eaten but can give a bitterness to dishes: the green is simply the leaf forming for the next planting (and a sprouting onion can in fact be planted) but its presence is a reminder of how we demand produce year-round without a thought for the seasons. For a food producer it means changing recipes to accommodate the difference in the onions or, as we do for our caramelised onion, stockpiling supplies for several months so we never have to use inferior onions. Not an easy logistical matter.

Shallots, golden shallots or eschallots (depending on which state you live in) are formed in small clusters a little like garlic and have a flavour that is reminiscent of both onion and garlic. They are naturally sweet and wonderful caramelised: cover the base of a tiny saucepan with peeled shallots, then dot them with butter and add a touch of sugar before covering them with a little water. Bring the pan to the boil with the lid off to reduce the liquid, tossing the shallots to make sure they all become glazed.

I like using raw red Spanish onions in a salsa. I love it even more if they are finely diced and cooked for just a few minutes in butter or extra virgin olive oil; I deglaze the pan with lemon juice, which turns the onion dice a brilliant crimson so that they look like sparkling jewels.

At home I store my onions in a string bag hanging on a nail in our garage. This not only keeps them in the dark, which slows deterioration, but also prevents their odour permeating the kitchen. Actually it is only when an onion is cut that its odour becomes truly penetrating. I refuse to leave a partially used onion anywhere in the house, even wrapped in plastic film in the refrigerator, much to my husband Colin's frustration.

I have peeled a lot of onions in my time and have been given masses of advice on how to make it a less distressing job: under running water, with goggles on, under the canopy of a strong exhaust fan (this last one really works too, as long as the stove isn't on at the same time) and so on. The variety used and time of year also have a bearing on how tear-provoking the onions will be, and some people are just more susceptible than others.

In the days when we made our pâté in a small room on the farm within sight of the restaurant, I found the best way to deal with the masses of onions needed was to do the job outside. The pâté-making girls, Esther and Rita, and I would sit on boxes and peel the onions together, unconsciously pitting ourselves against each other, and the fresh air and sunshine really helped. The trick is to use a very small and sharp serrated knife. If you have to cut the onion in half anyway, do so with the skin on, then it's simply a matter of prising off the skin and the outside layer of the onion at the same time. (Before my conscience pricks me, or my trusted pâté room lieutenants laugh heartily, I should declare that I don't do much peeling of onions these days, but I did my fair share back then.) Now that we have the state-of-the-art export kitchen in Tanunda we are actually not allowed to peel onions on the premises because of a possible mould under the skin, so we have to buy them in already peeled. Things continually change.

The aroma of onions frying immediately makes me feel hungry, no matter when I last ate. But the most luscious of all is slow-cooked onion: the transformation from crisp and sharp to caramelised and sweet is hard to credit. Use warm Caramelised Onion (see page 99) to line a just-baked pastry case (the Sour-cream Pastry on page 62 is good for this), then dot it with goat's cheese or gorgonzola and return it to a 180°C oven for 10 minutes to warm through and melt the cheese. Serve the tart (or individual tarts) with a salad of peppery greens and lunch is ready.

Caramelised onion makes an excellent base for a barbecued meal, too. Cook a kangaroo fillet, brushed with extra virgin olive oil and seasoned with freshly ground black pepper, for a couple of minutes a side on a hot barbecue. Allow the meat to rest for 5–10 minutes before serving it with caramelised onion and a dish of soft polenta or creamy mashed potato.

Sofregit, another slow-cooked onion preparation, has been part of Catalan cuisine since medieval times, and is something I have found invaluable in the cooking of game. There is nothing better than a camp oven for cooking sofregit. Pour extra virgin olive oil into the camp oven to a depth of about a centimetre, then add three finely chopped large onions and put the pot on the slowest possible burner. Stir the onion now and again – it may take an hour or more to colour. Tomatoes, garlic and leeks or lemon can also be added, but it is the slow cooking of the onion that makes the dish. I often add chopped garlic and grated lemon rind after the onions have collapsed and then use this mixture as a base in which to pot-roast older game, usually with the addition of fresh herbs and maybe stock, wine or verjuice.

Renowned Spanish cookery writer Néstor Luján, quoted in Colman Andrews' *Catalan Cuisine*, says that the onions in a sofregit 'should ideally reach the strange and mysterious colour that, in the School of Venice, the brushstrokes of the great master Titian obtained', which is a perfect description of the colour I look for.

Sofregit can become a topping for a flatbread, pissaladière or focaccia. Prepare the dough for the Flatbread (see page 52), then just before baking cover it liberally with sofregit. Add a tablespoon of torn basil leaves, then drizzle extra virgin olive oil over and sprinkle on some sea salt flakes. To make a pissaladière, arrange a pattern of anchovies and olives on top of the flatbread (on a traditional pissaladière the anchovies are criss-crossed to make a diamond pattern and the olives are centred in each diamond).

A caramelised onion or onion marmalade or jam can be made using much the same method as for sofregit. While thickly sliced onion is slowly cooking, add sugar, then stir in red-wine vinegar to counteract the sweetness. Caramelised onion or onion marmalade is a perfect accompaniment to duck confit or any grilled or barbecued meat. Peeled and sliced quince can be added, when in season, and will cook slowly with the onion and almost melt into a purée. This quince version is especially good with pork of any kind.

A rabbit dish I used to serve in the restaurant included tiny onions that had been cara-melised in some verjuice and a little butter. The combination gave a delightful sweet–sour piquancy. The idea could be extended by adding muscatels and roasted pine nuts to the onions and serving the lot with a roasted chicken – or pot-roast the chicken with the same ingredients and some stock.

Try baking large red onions for 45 minutes to 1 hour at 180°C, then cut them in half and remove their centres. Purée the centres and mix with mustard mayonnaise, fresh bread-crumbs, lots of flat-leaf parsley and chopped anchovies. Pile the mixture back into the onion halves and serve them at room temperature as an entrée.

Baby onions roasted in vino cotto

CARAMELISED ONION SALAD
Serves 4 as an accompaniment

Although the onions for this dish need long, slow cooking, they can be prepared in advance and left at room temperature. This salad is wonderful with tongue or grilled steak or sausages. If you are using the caramelised onion in a tart, as suggested on page 96, you may want to exclude the dressing. You might need to warm the tart without the cheese first if the onion is at room temperature rather than hot.

5 large onions

2 sprigs rosemary, leaves stripped

100 ml extra virgin olive oil

1 clove garlic, finely chopped

2 teaspoons balsamic vinegar

2 tablespoons freshly chopped
flat-leaf parsley

sea salt flakes and freshly ground
black pepper

Preheat the oven to 150°C. Trim the ends of each onion, leaving the skins on, then cut the onions into 1 cm-thick slices. Mix the rosemary with 2 tablespoons of the olive oil.

Line a shallow, heavy-based roasting pan with baking paper, then brush this and both sides of the onion slices with the rosemary oil. Bake the onions for 30 minutes, then check whether they are starting to colour. When the onions are a deep caramel colour turn with a spatula and discard any burnt pieces. Remove the pan from the oven when all the onion has caramelised on both sides. This can take between 1 and 2 hours. Allow the onions to cool a little, then remove the skins and place the onions in a serving dish.

Mix the remaining olive oil with the garlic, vinegar, parsley, salt and pepper and pour over the onions while they are still warm. Serve at room temperature.

BABY ONIONS ROASTED IN VINO COTTO
Serves 4 as an accompaniment

500 g baby onions, outer skin removed

¼ cup (60 ml) extra virgin olive oil

½ cup (125 ml) vino cotto (see Glossary)

sea salt flakes and freshly ground
black pepper

sprigs of lemon thyme, to garnish

Preheat the oven to 180°C. Cut the onions in half. Line a roasting pan with a large piece of foil (enough to fold over the onions), then place the onions in the centre of the foil. Whisk together the oil and vino cotto and pour over the onions, then season. Fold the foil over the onions and seal to form a parcel, then roast for 1 hour or until the onions are soft.

Increase the oven temperature to 200°C. Open the foil parcel then return the pan to the oven for a further 10 minutes, to caramelise the onions. Garnish with lemon thyme and serve as an accompaniment to roasted or grilled meats or fish, or dot with goat's cheese and flat-leaf parsley and serve with crusty bread.

SQUID WITH ONION, PARSLEY AND ANCHOVY STUFFING — *Serves 4*

4 × 300 g squid

4 onions, finely chopped

extra virgin olive oil, for cooking

10 g fresh white breadcrumbs

1 cup freshly chopped flat-leaf parsley

4–6 anchovy fillets, finely chopped

sea salt flakes and freshly ground
   black pepper

100 g thinly sliced mild pancetta

4 handfuls mixed baby lettuce leaves,
   washed and dried

VINAIGRETTE

60 ml extra virgin olive oil

1 tablespoon red-wine vinegar

Clean each squid by first removing the head and tentacles. Pull and twist the tentacles away from the body – you will find the guts will come away too. Chop off the tentacles and discard the head, guts and cartilage. Peel the skin from the body and tentacles under running water, then finely chop the tentacles.

Sauté the onions gently in a little olive oil in a frying pan over medium heat until softened and translucent. Drain off the oil and mix the onion with the chopped tentacles, breadcrumbs, parsley and anchovies, then season with salt and pepper. Stuff the squid tubes two-thirds full (the tubes will shrink during cooking) and close the ends with toothpicks. Pour the olive oil into a heavy-based enamelled casserole to a depth of 1 cm, then place the stuffed squid in the oil in one layer. Braise the squid, covered, over low heat for 5–10 minutes until the side in the oil is opaque, then turn the squid over and cook the second side for another 5–10 minutes. Remove the squid and allow to cool to room temperature. Return the squid to the cooled oil to keep moist until required.

Preheat the oven to 220°C and crisp the pancetta on a baking tray (this can also be done in a dry frying pan over high heat). When you are ready to serve, arrange the lettuce leaves on serving plates and cut the squid into 1 cm slices. Add the squid and crisped pancetta to the lettuce, then dress with a vinaigrette made with the extra virgin olive oil and red-wine vinegar. Serve immediately.

ORANGES

THE FRAGRANCE OF ORANGES IS BEAUTIFULLY HEADY – FROM the once traditional orange blossoms at weddings, to the juicy, thirst-quenching orange of the sports field. Remember that squirt of juice cooling your overheated body, your nose buried sensuously in the flesh as you gulped every bit of juice, drained it and grabbed the next quarter? When I am in the kitchen zesting a juicy orange and the citrussy tang sprays in my face like champagne, I'm often reminded of 'quarter time' as a teenager playing hockey.

Although oranges are available throughout the year, they are at their best in winter from our local crops. Navels come on the market about the last week in May and are available until August. They have no pips and a thick skin that makes them easier to peel, and are sweeter than the Valencia, whose green-tinged skin is a characteristic of the variety, not an indicator of ripeness. The Valencia has pips and a thinner skin, and is the best orange for juicing (that is, unless you are lucky enough to have a surfeit of blood oranges), and the juice keeps well for days. The Valencia arrives in August and lasts right through until the following April. It's one of the great sights and smells to drive through the Riverland in South Australia when the groves are heavy with fruit; the trees in flower at the same time produce the most heavenly scent in the air.

Blood oranges, when dark red inside, are the sweetest of all oranges, but with a refreshing tang. Juiced, they are absolutely delicious. They are harder to grow to a size deemed acceptable for sale in supermarkets, and are also very climate-specific. They are therefore expensive and not widely available, and their colour and quality can be erratic.

There is no doubt that citrus fruit is better in some years than others, particularly when it comes to the colour of the blood orange. I have a blood orange tree grown in a pot that took several years to develop colour. I became convinced that its colour improved with age, and was looking forward to this year's crop as last year's was the best ever, but there's hardly a stain of red to be seen. So it seems the Barossa climate is a bit hit-and-miss for this wonderful fruit. Even without the ruby red colour, though, I love its flavour, sweet yet sharp.

It has taken years for blood oranges to become generally available, and I don't think I'll ever lose the excitement I feel when I see them. Nor will I ever tire of maltaise sauce, a hollandaise mixed with blood orange juice. The sharpness of the juice cuts the richness of the butter wonderfully. Make a maltaise mayonnaise by adding the finely grated rind and juice of two blood oranges to your homemade mayonnaise. Freeze the juice and grated rind so that you can try maltaise sauce with the first asparagus of the season, or the mayonnaise with cold poached chicken in spring. Or try a glass of blood orange juice, Campari and ice. It is one time I wish the seasons were reversed as it would so suit a hot summer's day. A jug of this heady mixture brought out as the sun sets really fits the bill.

One of the most successful, and indeed the most beautifully shaped, citrus trees in my orchard is the poor man's orange. The rind of this fruit is an amazing addition to my game pies all winter long. It deserves a place in any garden simply for its looks: its strong, bold trunk supports symmetrical leaves and large, thick-skinned, flat-topped, deep-orange fruit.

Arabs first planted the bitter orange in Seville in Spain during the seventh century. Today huge commercial groves there supply fruit for the English marmalade market. While the first Australian Seville oranges were listed as being grown in the Sydney Botanic Gardens as early as 1828, today very few are grown commercially, even though the trees withstand frost better than the more readily available oranges. The Seville is the most aromatic member of the citrus family.

Seville oranges are available in South Australia from July to the beginning of September. They are hard to find – and they are definitely not an orange to pluck heavy off the tree and eat fresh. But if you love your marmalade they are worth seeking out, or try growing your own if the climate in your area is suitable. They tend to be smaller and very deep-coloured, with more pips than you want to know about, but the intense bitter flavour makes the best marmalade ever (see page 109) – although cumquat marmalade runs a close second. Our Maggie Beer Seville Marmalade now has an amazing following and our orchardist is in planting mode.

Although Sevilles make a wonderfully bitter marmalade, it's a tricky preserve to make in anything but small to middling quantities, and as the citrus industry is as susceptible to changing fashions as any other, you may not find the marmalade readily available. If you are a real marmalade freak and can't track down one of the small handful of almost 'cottage' producers, then you will probably need to make your own. It is well worth doing – just 2 kg of fruit will give you a good supply.

I love all citrus. The length of time the fruit will hang on the tree until I need it makes it so accessible. Being loathe to waste a thing, if I haven't used all the fruit before it starts to get blousy with age, I'll have a cook-in and candy the rind, then squeeze the juice to freeze and use when cooking Muscovy duck or guinea fowl, which I love to serve with sauce bigarde.

To make sauce bigarde, heat some unsalted butter in a saucepan until nut-brown, then add an equal quantity of plain flour and cook, stirring, for several minutes until golden brown.

Add enough verjuice to make a smooth paste, then gradually stir in some chicken stock. Bring the sauce to the boil, simmer and reduce to whatever consistency you prefer. Peel a few Sevilles (or poor man's oranges, or a couple of small navels and a lemon) and cut the rind into fine strips. Put the rind into a saucepan and just cover with water, then boil until tender. Drain the rind, then add it to the sauce. Squeeze the oranges and add the strained juice to the sauce, then taste for seasoning and add another tablespoon of butter just before serving.

The thick, aromatic skin of the poor man's orange and Seville orange are superior for candying. If you have ever tried candied orange peel in Italy you'll know what I'm talking about – it is simply amazing, and you'll never be able to make do with commercial peel again.

To make candied Seville orange peel, cut young, sound fruit in half lengthways. Leaving the pith attached to the peel, remove the flesh. Put the peel into a heavy-based enamelled or stainless steel saucepan and cover it with water, then bring to the boil. Pour off the water and repeat this process twice to remove unwanted bitterness. Drain the peel well and weigh it, then return the peel to the saucepan with an equal weight of sugar. Starting over a low heat, dissolve the sugar and then simmer until the peel is translucent – this may take up to 1 hour. Drain the peel from the syrup and spread it on a cake rack to dry. Turn daily until dried, then store in an airtight container. With a quality dark chocolate, this peel is one of the great flavour combinations.

Orange rind contains a natural sunscreen, so when the rind is exposed to too much sun it will naturally turn green, while the fruit inside is mature and ripe to eat. This often causes problems when marketing the fruit, as consumers assume the green-tinged orange is not ripe. To counter this, as Lee Byrne from Australian Citrus Growers explained to me, both navels and Valencias are gassed with ethylene, a natural plant hormone that affects the growth, development and ripening of all plants. This gas changes the colour of the rind from green to an all-over orange, yet doesn't affect the maturity or taste of the fruit.

As with most foods, if you buy in the peak season, the fruit is at its best flavour and lowest price. There is some flavour variation in quality of crop from year to year, but the yield and size for the grower varies a lot, particularly with Sevilles.

Like the grape industry, the citrus industry has gone through peaks and troughs, but once again times are difficult for the grower. News abounds of tonnes of oranges being fed to cattle as the industry struggles to compete with foreign imports. We should be doing everything we can to protect our local industry by eating more oranges, as it will be our loss if the growers give up and opt for a more reliable crop. When buying orange juice, look for a label that says '100% Australian orange juice'. Labelling regulations now make it mandatory to clearly declare if juice has been reconstituted from imported frozen concentrate.

The vitality of orange makes it a very important ingredient in my cooking. It marries so well with guinea fowl and, of course, duck. I use orange juice in my everyday marinades for pheasant and put the rind into my game pies. I make pasta with orange rind, as well as salads, cakes and desserts. I add orange rind to the perfect scrambled eggs or when serving kalamata or green olives tossed in extra virgin olive oil.

CHICKEN WINGS WITH ORANGE PEEL
Serves 6–8

2 teaspoons Sichuan peppercorns

rind of 2 oranges, removed in strips
  with a potato peeler

2 cloves garlic, finely chopped

2 teaspoons minced fresh ginger

2 golden shallots, finely chopped

2 tablespoons soy sauce

¼ cup (60 ml) peanut oil

¼ cup (60 ml) sesame oil

2 kg (about 20–30) chicken wings

Preheat the oven to 220°C. Roast the peppercorns in a dry frying pan until fragrant, then crush using a mortar and pestle. Make a marinade by mixing together all the ingredients except the chicken wings. Place the chicken wings in a large bowl or ceramic dish, cover with the marinade and leave in the refrigerator to marinate for 4 hours.

Place the chicken wings and marinade in a baking dish, then roast for 12 minutes or until the chicken wings are golden and cooked, being careful they don't burn. Rest for 10 minutes before serving.

ROAST DUCK WITH SEVILLE ORANGE
AND PROSCIUTTO STUFFING
Serves 4

15 g butter

90 g duck *or* chicken livers, cleaned

100 ml extra virgin olive oil, plus extra
  (optional)

1 large onion, finely chopped

finely chopped rind and juice
  of 1 Seville orange

⅓ cup flat-leaf parsley, finely chopped

1 tablespoon finely chopped rosemary

1 tablespoon finely chopped thyme

1½ cups coarse breadcrumbs, toasted

65 g prosciutto, chopped

2 tablespoons pistachios

sea salt flakes and freshly ground
  black pepper

1 × 2.5 kg duck

1 tablespoon finely chopped rosemary

Preheat the oven to 150°C. Melt the butter in a frying pan over medium heat, then add the livers and seal until golden brown on the outside but still very pink in the middle. Remove the pan from the heat, transfer the livers to a large bowl and leave to rest for 5 minutes then, when cool, cut them into large pieces and return them to the bowl. Add 80 ml of the olive oil to the pan, then cook the onion over medium heat for 5 minutes or until golden. Deglaze the pan with most of the orange juice.

Add the orange rind, herbs, breadcrumbs, prosciutto, pistachios and onion to the bowl with the livers, then season with salt and pepper. Fill the cavity of the duck with the stuffing, then place on a trivet in a roasting pan (or you could make a bed of thick slices of potato to soak up the roasting juices). Prick the breast skin, then rub in rosemary, 1 tablespoon salt and the remaining olive oil.

Roast the duck for 1 hour, then reduce the oven temperature to 120°C and roast for another 1½–2 hours; the meat should be soft to the touch. Remove the pan from the oven, then drain the pan juices into a tall jar and place in the freezer for 20 minutes to solidify the fat.

Meanwhile, if the skin isn't caramelised, increase the oven temperature to 210°C. Brush the skin with some combined orange juice and olive oil and return to the oven for 10 minutes or until caramelised.

Remove the duck from the oven and leave to rest for 20 minutes, breast-side down, in the roasting pan. Meanwhile, remove the fat from the pan juices then place the juices in a saucepan and reduce over high heat until syrupy. Remove the stuffing from the cavity. Carve the breast from the bone and remove the legs. Serve a quarter of the duck per person with some stuffing and a little of the reduced pan juices.

OLIVE OIL BRIOCHE WITH CANDIED SEVILLE PEEL *Makes 2*

1 cup (250 ml) warm water

1½ teaspoons castor sugar

15 g fresh yeast *or* 1 teaspoon dried yeast

675 g unbleached strong flour (see Glossary)

3 × 55 g free-range eggs

¼ cup (60 ml) extra virgin olive oil

3 teaspoons salt

1 cup candied Seville peel (see page 105), roughly chopped

1 free-range egg yolk

1 tablespoon milk

In a bowl, combine the warm water, castor sugar, yeast and 2 tablespoons of the flour and whisk to combine. Set aside for 5–10 minutes or until frothy.

Whisk the eggs, then add the olive oil and stir to combine. Combine the remaining flour and the salt in a large bowl and make a well. Combine the yeast and egg mixtures and pour into the well. With your hands, gently fold in the flour until everything is combined and the dough starts to form a ball. Add the candied peel to the dough.

Turn the dough out onto a floured bench and knead for 10 minutes until soft and satiny, adding a little extra flour if it becomes too sticky. Return the dough to the bowl and cover tightly with plastic film, then refrigerate for 12 hours until doubled in volume.

Remove the dough from the refrigerator and let it return to room temperature (this will take about 1 hour). Knead the dough lightly for 1–2 minutes, then divide it into 2 portions and put into greased loaf tins or large brioche moulds. (This dough does not need to be knocked back – dough with a higher fat content struggles to rise again if knocked back.) Leave to rise in a draught-free spot for about 40 minutes or until it is 1½ times its original volume.

Preheat the oven to 220°C. Mix the egg yolk with the milk and brush this over the tops of the loaves. Bake for 10 minutes, then reduce the temperature to 180°C and bake for another 20 minutes. Turn the loaves out onto a wire rack and leave to cool.

ORANGE AND ALMOND TART
Serves 8

1 × quantity Sour-cream Pastry (see page 62)	50 g plain flour, sifted
	finely grated rind and juice of 1 orange
150 g almonds	2 tablespoons lemon juice
150 g castor sugar	8 egg yolks
200 g butter	mascarpone, to serve

Make and chill the pastry as instructed. Roll out the chilled dough and use to line a 25 cm tart tin with a removable base. Chill the pastry case for 20 minutes.

Preheat the oven to 200°C. Line the chilled pastry case with foil, then weight it with pastry weights and blind bake for 15 minutes. Remove the foil and weights and bake for another 5 minutes. Roast the almonds on a baking tray for 6–8 minutes, cool and grind them in a food processor.

Using an electric mixer, cream the castor sugar and butter until pale and then slowly, with the mixer on medium speed, add the ground almonds. Add the flour, orange rind and juice, then add the lemon juice and one egg yolk at a time, beating well after each addition. Pour the mixture into the pastry shell and bake for 30–45 minutes. The mixture should still be a little wobbly when taken out of the oven. Allow to cool a little and serve with mascarpone.

MARMALADE-À-LA-LIZZY
Makes 2 × 380 ml jars

Before I found my Seville orange grower, my favourite marmalade was a recipe given to me by an old friend by the name of Liz, with whom I've since lost contact. Another very special friend, Hilda Laurencis, who worked with me for years, always saw that my larder was well stocked with this marmalade. This is Hilda's version of Marmalade-à-la-Lizzy – a runny but wonderfully flavoured marmalade. It's the nicest way to start the day.

The whisky gives it that bitter edge (and a kick, of course) if you can't find Sevilles.

6 oranges, thinly sliced	900 g sugar
3 lemons, thinly sliced	1 cup (250 ml) whisky

Combine all the ingredients, except the whisky, in a large heavy-based saucepan or preserving pan, adding enough water to cover. Boil over high heat until the marmalade reaches setting point. Test by putting a spoonful of marmalade on a saucer in the refrigerator for a few minutes. If it wrinkles when you push it with your finger, the marmalade is ready. Cool a little, then add the whisky. Stir well and transfer to sterilised glass jars (see Glossary).

SEVILLE ORANGE MARMALADE
Makes 8 × 300 g jars

Marmalade is perhaps the most difficult preserve to make. Buy unwaxed fruit if you can, and do not refrigerate it. Although it is a fairly painstaking process, there is no substitute for hand-cutting the fruit to make a really great marmalade.

The trick is to cook the marmalade at as high a heat as possible; the quicker it reaches its setting point, the fresher the flavour will be. Marmalade is very susceptible to overcooking, leading to a caramelised quality that lacks the freshness of citrus.

Having said that, a marmalade should always be cooked until the rind of the oranges is soft to the touch but still intact. Adding lemon juice increases the natural pectin content, and as much of a problem as pips can be, these contain much-needed pectin too, so they are a necessary evil.

This is a marmalade that responds particularly well to being cooked in a pressure cooker, following the manufacturer's instructions carefully.

2 kg Seville oranges
1.4 kg sugar

juice of 1 lemon

Cut tops and bottoms off the oranges and discard. Slice fruit into thin rounds. Cover with 1 litre of water and leave to soak overnight, weighted down so all the fruit is immersed but only just covered. If you can, separate the pips as you cut, gather them together in a muslin bag and add to the soaking fruit; there will always be a pip or two that gets through!

The next day, transfer the oranges, soaking water and bag of pips to a heavy-based saucepan. Cook over high heat until the rind is just tender.

Heat the sugar in a preserving pan over low heat to dissolve, then add to cooked orange mixture, stirring and skimming off any scum as it comes to the surface. Add the lemon juice. Bring to a rapid boil until marmalade has reached setting point. Test by putting a spoonful of marmalade on a saucer in the refrigerator for a few minutes. If it wrinkles when you push it with your finger, the marmalade is ready.

Let the marmalade cool just a little before bottling in sterilised jars (see Glossary) – the fruit will float to the top if the marmalade is too hot.

PIGEON AND SQUAB

 THERE IS OFTEN CONFUSION ABOUT THE DIFFERENCE BETWEEN squab and pigeon. Squab is baby pigeon, killed before it leaves the nest. It is plump, as it hasn't flown, and very tender. Squab is reared by some farmers in Australia especially for the table; it is fairly expensive but really worthwhile for a special occasion. Pigeon, on the other hand, is caught wild and is of indeterminate age. It is inexpensive but erratic in its availability and quality. With wild pigeons you also need to consider whether they might have been feeding on sprayed crops.

Early in my food career in the Barossa I remember becoming excited by a phone call from Adelaide offering me hundreds, even thousands, of pigeons. I was delighted at such a find until it became clear to me that not only were the birds still alive, but I would also have to go and trap them myself. The call was from an enterprising member of the Adelaide City Council who thought it a perfect solution to both the council's problems and mine. I refused the kind offer.

I use squab and pigeon in totally different dishes and prefer not to compare them. Pigeon makes one of the best pies I have ever eaten and is also great in a ragoût or pasta sauce. Squab can be served elegantly with just a game jus, grapes and verjuice, or it can be barbecued and made into a warm salad. It can also be used in all the same ways as pigeon, although I find that a little too extravagant.

Squab is a truly exceptional bird. It is very easy to prepare – and it is always handy to know how to make a really spectacular dish with next to no effort. The squab available in Australia through Ian Millburn of Glenloth Game in Victoria or Game Farm in New South Wales is superb.

The differences in taste and texture between squab and pigeon are enormous. Tasting them side by side you could be forgiven for thinking they were entirely different species. Both require very specific cooking methods. Once you understand the principles, cooking them is simple.

The meat of the squab is thick and buttery and the breast should be served rare – though not 'blue', as it too often is. I insist on my squab being really pink, as I find that 'blue' has a more limited taste, whereas if overcooked, the meat is tough and 'livery'. Cooked rare, it is tender, moist and delicious. Squab is usually cooked very quickly at a high temperature followed by a long resting time. Pigeon, on the other hand, has to be cooked very slowly until the meat almost falls off the bone, otherwise the flesh can be dry. The flavour is strong and gutsy and the texture is fine when it has been cooked with loving attention. I prefer to use a crockpot or pressure cooker for pigeon, or the 'confit' method, where the bird is cooked in duck fat at barely a simmer for between 1–4 hours, depending on the age of the bird.

Pigeon should be cooked so slowly that each quarter seems just to 'lift off' the carcass. Even so, I am very careful, after having lifted the meat off the bone, to make sure that it is immersed skin-side down in some cooking liquor while it rests so it doesn't dry out. I then make a well-reduced pigeon glaze with the chopped bones of the carcass, chopped raw chicken bones, stock vegetables and veal stock.

Chestnuts are a wonderful accompaniment to pigeon. I used to buy dried chestnuts from Italian grocers and reconstitute them, but these days I'd opt for frozen cooked chestnuts, although fresh chestnuts in season would be the ultimate if you have the patience to cook them and peel them. The piquancy of pickled walnuts is also very good with pigeon. First cook the pigeon gently in some stock, with just a dash of pickled walnut juice, up to the stage of taking it off the bone and making the sauce. Reduce the pigeon stock, adjust it very carefully with some more pickled walnut juice, then cut the walnuts widthways and add to the sauce in the last few minutes with a little cream. (Commercially pickled walnuts will disintegrate very quickly.) Rosemary complements these flavours very well.

Another favourite recipe for good-sized pigeons is to stuff them with some sausage mince, perhaps studded with olives, to help keep them moist during cooking. Add some good-quality canned, peeled tomatoes, lots of herbs and some chicken stock and cook in a pressure cooker or crockpot. When the pigeons are cooked so that the meat is just coming away from the bone, transfer them to a plate to rest (upside-down to retain moisture) and cover to keep warm. Meanwhile, reduce the cooking liquid, then toss in some more olives at the last moment and serve with polenta.

Squab is a great restaurant dish and it is hard to resist on the menu of any serious chef. The most sensationally presented squab I ever had was when French chef Joël Robuchon was still running Jamin, in Paris. These are my notes from the night: 'Pigeon presented in flambé dish and then carved at the table using wooden board with deep ring around for juices. Fresh pepper ground. Hearts and livers spooned out on to a crouton. Finely cut, crisp game chips served with sauce "just a jus". MAGNIFICENT.'

WILD PIGEON

Serves 4

extra virgin olive oil, for cooking

2 tablespoons chopped rosemary

4 × 240 g wild pigeons

80 g butter

sea salt flakes and freshly ground
   black pepper

3 shallots, peeled and chopped

200 g field mushrooms, cut into thick slices

1 teaspoon chopped thyme

1 cup (250 ml) red wine

3 cups (750 ml) Golden Chicken Stock
   (see page 178)

80 g bacon, rind removed, cut into
   2.5 cm strips

2 small bay leaves

flat-leaf parsley, to garnish

Mix a small amount of olive oil with 1 tablespoon chopped rosemary, and rub all over the pigeons. In a large heavy-based frying pan, melt about a third of the butter, then add the pigeons and a pinch of salt, and seal slowly and evenly over low heat. Once the birds have browned all over, remove them from the pan and set aside in a crockpot or pressure cooker.

In the same frying pan, brown the chopped shallots in oil and add to the crockpot. Add the rest of the butter to the pan and sauté the mushrooms and thyme for a few minutes. Season well and add to the crockpot or pressure cooker. Deglaze the pan with the red wine over high heat, reducing it a little. Add the chicken stock and reduce further for 5 minutes, then transfer to the cooking pot. Wipe the pan dry and render the bacon, then add to the pot, along with the bay leaves and 1 tablespoon rosemary. (If using a crockpot, cook on low for 5 hours or overnight. For a pressure cooker, cook on the lowest setting for 20 minutes before first checking. Take out any birds that are done, making sure to keep them moist with a little of the cooking juices, and continue to cook the rest, checking every 10 minutes.) The cooking time will depend on the age of the birds, and wild pigeons are of indeterminate age so cooking times will vary. The pigeon is done when it is tender to touch but still intact enough to pull away the breast and the legs from the carcass in one piece.

Strain the juices from the crockpot and reduce to the desired consistency in a saucepan. You can either serve the pigeon whole, or take the meat off the bone for your guests. Spoon over the reduced juices and serve topped with freshly chopped flat-leaf parsley.

SQUAB WITH FRESH FIGS AND GINGER
AND LEMON BUTTER
Serves 2

Squab is a bit of a luxury, and this is the sort of dish I would cook for a beautifully indulgent meal. For really tender, moist meat, it's important not to overcook the birds, and to rest them after cooking.

As a variation, instead of using fresh figs you could serve this with couscous dotted with verjuice-soaked currants and butter, and blanched spinach.

2 × 350 g squab

extra virgin olive oil, for cooking

½ cup reduced Golden Chicken Stock
    (see page 178), warmed

4 black figs, each cut into 3 slices

butter, for cooking

2 sprigs rosemary, leaves picked

sea salt flakes and freshly ground
    black pepper

GINGER AND LEMON BUTTER

2 tablespoons preserved ginger

¼ cinnamon stick, ground

80 g unsalted butter

grated rind and juice of 1 lemon

freshly ground black pepper

To make the ginger and lemon butter, mix the ginger, ground cinnamon, unsalted butter and grated lemon rind together using a food processor or mortar and pestle. Add lemon juice and freshly ground black pepper to taste. Chill the butter in the refrigerator until ready to use.

Preheat the oven to 230°C. Using kitchen scissors or a sharp knife, remove the heads and wing tips from the squab, then spatchcock the birds by cutting them down the spine and, with the cut-side down on the bench, squashing them as flat as you can with the palm of your hand. Cut the legs away a little from the breast frame so the bird is as flat as possible (this will ensure that the legs and breasts cook evenly). Ease your fingers between the skin and flesh of the breast and legs of each squab, then take just over a quarter of the prepared butter and push it under the skin of each bird, smoothing it gently over the flesh. Spread the remaining butter over the skin of the squabs, and sprinkle with sea salt.

In a large heavy-based frying pan, heat a little extra virgin olive oil over high heat and quickly seal the birds, skin-side up. Carefully turn them skin-side down, and seal them for 2–3 minutes, until the skin has caramelised. Transfer the birds, skin-side up, to a shallow roasting pan, and roast for 6–8 minutes. Remove the dish from the oven and turn the birds skin-side down again, pour over the warm chicken stock, and set aside to rest, covered, for 10 minutes.

Meanwhile, toss the figs in the same frying pan over medium heat with a little butter and the rosemary, and season.

Cut the birds in half and serve with the pan-fried figs alongside, drizzling over any juices from the roasting pan.

VIGNERON'S SQUAB

6 × 450 g squab, livers removed and reserved

sea salt flakes and freshly ground
   black pepper

juice of ½ lemon

1 tablespoon butter

2 onions, unpeeled, cut in half and
   roughly chopped

2 small carrots, roughly chopped

1 stick celery, roughly chopped

2 sprigs flat-leaf parsley

2 sprigs thyme

100 ml verjuice *or* white wine

2 cups (500 ml) reduced Golden Chicken
   Stock (see page 178)

1 bunch fresh, large, seedless green grapes
   (*or* muscatels dried on the stem
   if grapes are out of season)

CROUTONS (OPTIONAL)

80 g butter, softened

6 slices baguette

2 tablespoons sparkling white wine

sea salt flakes and freshly ground
   black pepper

Preheat the oven to 230°C or the maximum temperature for your oven. Season the cavity of the birds with salt and pepper and squeeze a little lemon juice inside. In a frying pan, seal the birds in nut-brown butter with a dash of oil over medium heat to a gentle golden brown, turning on all sides. Sit them in a roasting pan with the juices from the frying pan and roast for 8–12 minutes (depending on the heat of the oven). Check them after 8 minutes. Remove the squab from the oven and turn them upside-down to rest for a good 15 minutes before carving. After carving the meat off the carcasses, set the squab meat aside, cut-side down, on a baking tray with just enough of the cooking juices to keep it moist.

Meanwhile, skim the fat off the juices in the roasting pan and brown the onions, carrots, celery, parsley and thyme, drizzled with extra virgin olive oil, in the pan over high heat. While they are browning, roughly chop the carcasses and set aside. Once the vegetables are caramelised, add the carcasses back to the pan, then deglaze it with verjuice or white wine. Add the stock and cook vigorously over high heat for about 20 minutes or until the sauce is sufficiently reduced. Strain the sauce and keep it warm until ready to serve.

If you're making the croutons, melt half the butter in a heavy-based frying pan over medium heat, then fry the bread until golden brown on both sides. Drain on kitchen paper. Sauté the reserved livers in a little of the butter, then add the sparkling wine and deglaze. Mash the livers and the reduced pan juices with the rest of the soft butter and season. Spread on the croutons.

To serve, warm the carved meat in the oven for about 3 minutes, divide the squab meat among 6 plates, then spoon over a little of the sauce, place a crouton to the side and add the grapes at the last minute. Drink the rest of the sparkling wine!

PORK

 UNTIL A WONDERFUL HOLIDAY WITH EIGHT FRIENDS IN Umbria in 1995 I had little interest in eating pork, finding it dry and tasteless unless smoked to make bacon. Two simple meals on that holiday turned my lack of interest into a need to relive those sublime taste experiences when I returned home.

As friends, we were united by a love of food and, as the produce was so fabulous, there was a fair bit of competition to get to the stoves. We took turns in deciding what to eat, and shopping for food became a daily expedition. Our lives seemed to revolve entirely around who was cooking what. On market day Stephanie Alexander came home with pork to cook as brochettes. I was lukewarm about the prospect, but fortunately it was not my day to decide what we would eat. Grilled over an open fire with no extra attention, the meat was positively ambrosial.

Stephanie then led us to a simple trattoria, following notes her mother had made on a journey there many years before. Pig's kidneys were on the menu. The grilling took place in a large open fireplace, the heat of which must have been amazing for the cook – the aromas certainly were! The kidneys were as wonderful as the brochettes.

This trip was quite extraordinary, and not only because it reawakened my interest in pork. We were staying in a farmhouse on the side of a misty mountain with views so spectacular that each day was like waking up in a dream. The few buildings in view were nothing short of centuries old and the olive trees almost seemed abandoned, so steep were the slopes. Every weekend morning we were woken by the sounds of hunters calling, dogs barking and shots ringing through the air – wild boar were being hunted. The less aggressive locals appeared with baskets on the backs of motorised bikes (that struggled up the steep hill) in pursuit of fungi. (We also looked for mushrooms, but less successfully – obviously, local knowledge counts for a lot.) Wild chestnut trees, with branches weighed down by their hoary fruit, flanked each side of the steep track along which we walked each day to the monastery at the top of the mountain.

Roast pork belly with verjuice and Seville marmalade glaze (see page 126)

The huge fig tree at the side of the house seemed two storeys high because of the way the house was built into the slope. This meant we could pick the fruit by leaning over the terrace outside our bedroom, or by the kitchen door on the bottom floor where we break-fasted. The tree provided enough ripe figs for us each day, no matter how many ways we used them – for breakfast with yoghurt, lunch with prosciutto, or for dinner with cheese or in a dessert.

This trip gave us such a taste for Italy that we all returned to Australia declaring our need to visit again and again, and this led to the 'Stephanie and Maggie in Italy' cooking workshops, held in Siena in September 1997. This amazing experience – life-altering both for ourselves and some of our students – led to the publication of our *Tuscan Cookbook*.

When I returned, I asked myself why my experiences of pork in Italy were so very different from those at home. I now know it was a combination of many factors, and not just because I romanticised the memory. The pork we ate in Italy had been raised by small farmers who fed the pigs a varied diet (if only because the family's scraps became the pigs' food) and gave them room to move about, while also providing shelter. Perhaps most importantly, these pigs were of a breed that had not had the fat bred out of them.

In Australia, until recently, we have been intent on breeding the fat out of pigs. The emphasis has been on leanness before all else, driven by the market's fear of fat. Obviously the larger the animal grows in the shortest space of time, the better the profit for the farmer, whether it has 'boar taint' or not. (Boar taint is a flavour or odour that can spoil the meat – it's not present in female pigs but can manifest at any age in a male pig, and the risk of it developing increases significantly for pigs over 75 kg. Whilst a huge amount of work is being done in the industry to reduce boar taint, the risk is still higher for leaner, heavier pigs.) Fat is flavour, and the lack of fat is the major reason – though there are many – why I never eat mass-produced pork, as I find the meat deficient in flavour, juiciness and texture.

To turn the situation around, the industry needs to breed pigs with intramuscular fat – which gives meat tenderness and flavour – rather than a slab of fat encasing the meat. The great thing is that there are now some small-scale farmers producing beautifully flavoured pork that lives up to the memory of my Italian experience.

The pig has always been central to the Barossa tradition, given the German heritage of the Valley. When I first settled here in 1973, almost every farm was mixed and included a vineyard. It was normal practice to have a couple of hundred chooks, fifty turkeys and geese for the Christmas market, and a pig or two, complete with mud holes for wallowing.

Over the years I've seen that mixed farming tradition become rare, but some small traditional farmers have survived. Colin and Joy Leinert of Sheoak Log, who breed rare Berkshire pigs, are an important example, not only influencing Australian pig breeding but the progeny of Berkshires all over the world. Even though I live close by, it was only in 2006 that I first visited their stud 'Lynjoleen', and it was a real privilege to have an insight into the lives of this industrious couple.

Both of them have much to say about their history and their industry, and they are committed to providing a good life and a good death for the animals they raise. The issue of flavour, and the importance of the marbling of fat throughout the meat, is paramount to their business. How wonderful it is that the pendulum is swinging back, as more farmers, chefs and producers understand these issues. Even more remarkable is the fact that the Leinerts have never wavered in their convictions – they rode out the twenty years when they were ostracised for keeping Berkshire pigs when the trend was to raise hybrid pigs with the fat bred out of them. That's true passion! However, this is not easy farming, as they believe in controlling the whole cycle, which means that Colin and Joy grow and mix their own feed: the wheat, the barley and the peas (although they do buy in the lucerne).

Colin told me proudly that the Emperor of Japan will eat only Berkshire pork and that his stud's progeny has been an important part of the Berkshire pork world from Japan to the United Kingdom and United States. A single stud like the Leinerts' can't possibly supply a large market, and with retail outlets being so successful in selling their pork, as well as a burgeoning market from the smallgoods they produce (the best I have tasted), there are necessary plans for expansion in place. After my visit, I drove away so excited by their energy and enthusiasm that I completely lost my way home – in my own stamping ground!

We are lucky to have a small group of producers Australia-wide who are already aware of the need for better-tasting pork. Of special note is Bangalow Sweet Pork (www.sweetpork.com.au) of Ballina, New South Wales, the winner of a *Vogue Entertaining and Travel* magazine Produce Award in 2005. They have had an enormous impact on creating a discerning market for quality pork. Then there is Otway Pork (www.otwaypork.com.au), a larger concern breeding free-range pork in Victoria. There are also a handful of other producers of free-range pork from rare breeds in each state, driven by a passion for flavour.

All animals and poultry reflect the feed they are given, but none more so than a pig. If you can buy from farmers who allow their pigs to range in a field of fallen figs, apples or even onions, you'll taste the difference. The added advantage of buying from a small producer is that the animal is likely to have been slaughtered in a small abattoir and will not have been as stressed as an animal processed in a larger set-up. We dedicated meat-eaters have a responsibility to ensure that the animals we eat have been raised happily and slaughtered humanely. To make sure we take the best care of our land and animals we should understand the processes, and influence the marketplace accordingly. Too often we'd rather not know the gory details, but that's passing the buck.

If you want to seek out better pork and do not have access to a small producer, go to a Chinese or Vietnamese butcher. The Chinese and Vietnamese are very fussy about their

pork and are intolerant of boar taint – in fact, they insist on sows and are prepared to pay a premium for them, since the meat is sweeter than that of boars. Both cultures also value the role fat plays in providing flavour and texture, so carcasses with a good covering of fat are sought out.

There are pockets throughout Australia where the tradition of the home pig kill remains, and the long weekend in June sees rural Australia's pig population decimated. Italian and German families (many more of the former than the latter these days) take advantage of the cool weather and the three-day break to have their pigs slaughtered and to make sausages and pancetta.

On one such weekend some years ago, knowing I had changed my thinking about pork after my Italian sojourn, the Fanto family welcomed my participation. The selection of the pig is of great importance. The Fantos prefer the sweeter meat of the sow but like the breeder to reassure them that the animal has just come off heat, since they believe the keeping quality of the meat can otherwise be affected (most of their pork is used in dried sausages, pancetta and capocollo – the latter two being lean meat rolled and then brined before being smoked). The butcher came out to their property and killed the pigs in situ.

I wasn't a witness to the killing, so my first sight on arriving was of three pigs hanging from the rafters of the shed. The hair had been removed before the pigs were strung up and the skin was rubbed all over with salt and lemon to whiten and clean it. The pigs were then gutted and the blood collected and put aside to set. (I have a photograph on my office wall of a typical Barossa pig killing of probably a century ago – the pig is hanging from a tree and the ladies of the household are standing on one side with enamelled bowls ready to catch the blood, while the men stand on the other side with their large aprons, knives and steel. Some might think it a strange thing to photograph, but the picture reveals so much of our past and it is one I treasure.)

The Fanto family got straight to work once the pigs were gutted, as the sooner the intestines are cleaned the easier they are to manage. While this was being done, a large pan of water was boiled ready to take the blood, which cooks for about an hour and a half before being sliced and fried. I haven't yet organised myself enough to make my own blood sausage with apples or chestnuts, but after a short holiday in the Basque country of Spain, the image of fat blood sausage served with caramelised onion and apple spurs me on.

The tradition is to use every part of the animal, and as so much is set aside to preserve, the delicacies that are left – all those tidbits that others may reject from lack of knowledge – are for eating immediately. They are the rewards, and as a guest there to observe, take notes and learn, I was offered my choice of these treats, which were hanging on the Hills Hoist to dry a little. The caul fat (the 'veil') hung like lace curtains; the 'lights', or lungs, were light in weight but otherwise bulky. The table was set for lunch with pastas, salads and last year's sausages – all within easy reach of the huge logs burning not only to keep us warm but to grill the liver I had picked out. The liver was wrapped in caul fat and cooked quickly on the barbecue hotplate so that it was still rare. Delicious!

Late on the first day, when the meat was set, the carcasses were taken down and cut, ready for the mincer much later that night. The salt, crushed chillies and fennel seed gathered from the paddocks and roadsides were put on top of the meat until it was cold enough to mince, ready for the sausage-making the next day. (The meat wasn't refrigerated at all, as the Fantos feel it gets too cold and oxidises if refrigerated, changing colour when it is taken out of the fridge.)

On the second day, the cleaned casings were filled with the spiced minced pork and the sausages were hung in the smoking shed to dry for four or five days until the weather was right for smoking to begin.

On the Monday, the Fantos minced the pork lard and pressed it into the sides of a gas-fired stainless steel 'copper', then added the trotters, skin and bones and cooked the whole lot very slowly, so that the fat didn't burn, for eight hours or so (it can require up to ten

hours cooking) – the cooking pot had to be stirred constantly. About five hours into the cooking, salt was sprinkled onto the surface of the fat and left to penetrate before the stirring was resumed. Some of the children and adults couldn't wait for dinner and devoured the shoulder bones (these have the sweetest meat of all) straight from the pot.

At the end of cooking, the fat was drained away. (The family used to bottle the lard and cellar it for use during the year, but these days they throw most of it out, worried about their fat intake and the threat of contamination after long storage.)

The bones and other goodies were served for dinner – no knives and forks for this – with lots of salads and pickled vegetables heavy with vinegar to help cut the super-rich morsels. As the final treat, the remaining cooked blood was added to the scrapings in the copper and cooked for half an hour before being served with a fried egg. This reminded me of my father's favourite breakfast of fried eggs and black pudding, and my German heritage peeped through as I revelled in the feast.

My time with the Fantos was inspiring: while quite a constitution was needed, I found the weekend a fascinating tradition to observe. Such traditions must be encouraged, especially since those who partake in them insist that their pigs provide flavoursome meat, and that can only have a good effect on the market for the rest of us.

I might have eschewed pork meat in the past (until I discovered what it could taste like), but I have always been very interested in piggy bits. My parents always made brawn with a pig's head at Christmas and, as an offal freak, I have always loved pig's liver and kidneys.

You can emulate the kidneys I enjoyed in Umbria using the oven instead of an open fire.

Because it is almost impossible to purchase kidneys encased in their fat, buy caul fat from the butcher and wrap this around them instead. Allow one super-fresh kidney per person, then season it and wrap it in the caul fat (this will melt away during the cooking), placing a fresh bay leaf in the parcel. Strip sprigs of rosemary of their leaves and push one leaf into the middle of each kidney. Stand the parcels on a wire rack in a roasting pan and roast them at 230°C for 15–20 minutes in all, turning the kidneys over halfway through the cooking. Let the kidneys rest for 5 minutes before slicing and serving them with a very piquant mustard. The kidney is very rich – it would make a good first course served on a bed of gratinéed potato.

My first experience of stuffed pig's ears was at Berowra Waters Inn many years ago. It was such an amazing dish, and it gave me the courage to put pig's ears on our restaurant menu. I served them much as Janni Kyritsis had done, partnered by a rémoulade sauce, except that I used pheasant meat with mushrooms rather than chicken for the stuffing. Even though I was lucky to sell five serves a weekend, each time they were ordered they were loved, which gave me a great thrill.

As a child I was always attracted to the crackling and apple sauce that came with roast pork, long before the hysteria about breeding fat out of pigs, but even so, I left the meat, which my mother had overcooked for fear of infecting us all with tapeworm and other nasties. Trichinosis (*Trichinella spiralis*) was the main concern – but I'm advised by the Australian Pork Council that this does not exist in Australian pigs. The Council tells me my mother's fears were based on hearsay and that we should be cooking our pork only until it is no longer pink but still moist.

The way to ensure crisp crackling and moist meat is to first choose a roasting pan that is only a little larger than the pork itself, so that the juices don't burn in the cooking. Score the rind with a sharp knife, then moisten it with a little extra virgin olive oil and rub it thoroughly with salt. Stand the piece of pork on a wire rack in the roasting pan and roast at 210°C for 20 minutes (for a 1.2 kg piece of pork), then pour verjuice, wine or water into the baking dish – this creates steam and will help the meat remain moist. Reduce the oven temperature to 180°C and roast for another 50 minutes, then remove the pork and allow it to rest for 20 minutes. Pork needs to be just cooked: if you are unsure, insert a skewer in the thickest part of the meat to see if the juices run clear.

For a delicious change, rub fennel seeds into the meat with salt, or insert slivers of garlic into it. This is the base of the *porchetta* you see for sale in Italian marketplaces or fairs, where great slabs of pork are sandwiched between slices of crusty bread; you're even asked whether you want your pork from a leaner part, with fat, or a bit of both.

Try pan-frying pork fillet or chops and then deglazing the pan with verjuice. Serve the meat with slowly roasted heads of garlic and squeeze out the sweet, nutty cloves. The aniseed flavour of caramelised fennel is a great counterpoint to the richness of pork too.

Potatoes are wonderful with pork: crispy pan-fried potato, garlic and rosemary; perfect mashed potato, but go easy on the cream; or boiled waxy potatoes sprinkled with salt to counteract the richness of the meat.

STEVE'S SAUSAGES IN GRAPE MUST   *Serves 4–6*

Friend and former Pheasant Farm Restaurant chef Steve Flamsteed used to talk of cooking
pork sausages in grape must for the first meal of each vintage when he worked in Bordeaux.
Grape must is what remains once grapes have been pressed for their juice. Doing this at
home, 1 kg of red wine grapes will give you the juice and must required – either put the
grapes through a food mill or push them through a sieve.

This is how I've translated Steve's tales of the dish. Remember that this is traditionally
a dish for vintage, and ideally you need wine grapes (preferably shiraz or mataro) rather
than table grapes.

1 kg sweet Italian pork and fennel seed sausages (about 12)	2 cups (500 ml) red grape juice
1 tablespoon extra virgin olive oil	2 cups (500 ml) grape must

Gently seal the sausages over a moderate heat in a deep, heavy-based frying pan that
has been brushed with the olive oil. Add ½ cup (125 ml) of the grape juice and cook for
10 minutes until reduced by half. Turn the sausages over, then add the grape must so
that the sausages are smothered, then tip in the balance of the juice. Simmer for another
10 minutes, or a little longer if the sausages are thick (longer cooking will also enhance
the flavour of the must). Serve the sausages on a bed of must with creamy mashed potatoes and finely sliced fennel drizzled with olive oil. (If you find the seeds in the must a
problem, then just squeeze the juice from it over the sausages on serving.)

BRAISED PORK BELLY, COTECHINO AND GREEN LENTILS   *Serves 4*

What an amazing trio of talents Steve Flamsteed has – trained chef, wine-maker and
cheese-maker – and, more than that, he is one of nature's gentle, beautiful people. Steve
has the ability to bring calm and thoughtfulness to any situation. It therefore wasn't hard
for him to talk me into being involved in a very special day for the Zonta Club of Toowoomba
in August 2004 that his sister-in-law, Vicki Flamsteed, was helping to organise. It wasn't
until after I arrived that I realised it was a far bigger occasion than I had envisaged.

Our responsibilities were to prepare lunch for the several hundred participants and do
a cooking demonstration. Steve and I planned the menu from afar and, as we were aware
that we would have to prepare all the ingredients in advance, this slow-cooked dish of
pork belly was ideal. I arrived the day before assuming there would be lots to do, but in
truth it was Steve who did all the work. Our cooking demonstration could have been a bit
scary, as we were centre stage with a huge screen and bright lights, as if in a TV studio.
But although Steve and I hadn't cooked together for eight years, we just slipped straight
back into our familiar pattern – that's what happens with teamwork when it comes from
intuition and not instruction. We were just a small part of a day that was a great success,

raising huge amounts of money for a selection of children's and youth charities in Queensland and South Australia.

Now Steve, who is so obviously passionately interested in flavour when you look at the combination of skills he has amassed, is pulling all those threads together into one tapestry in his role as wine-maker/manager for Giant Steps Winery in the Yarra Valley. The winery is diversifying to provide all the ingredients necessary for living a good life: firstly, there is the wine; secondly, they have a sourdough bakery baking bread for sale at the cellar door; they also have their own coffee roaster from Germany; and lastly, although they no longer make cheese, Steve buys young cheeses and ages them to sell once they mature.

sea salt flakes and freshly ground
    black pepper
2 fresh bay leaves
8 sprigs thyme
600 g pork belly
1 × 500 g piece cotechino
extra virgin olive oil, for cooking
12 golden shallots, chopped
6 cloves garlic, chopped
1 × 400 g can tomatoes, strained,
    reserving ½ cup juice
⅓ cup (80 ml) verjuice
1 litre reduced Golden Chicken Stock
    (see page 178)

½ cup (125 ml) chardonnay
5 baby carrots, cut into large pieces
2 small sticks celery, chopped
Salsa Agresto (see page 179), to serve

LENTILS
250 g Australian green lentils, rinsed and
    soaked in water for 30 minutes
2 cloves garlic, peeled
1 tablespoon chopped preserved lemon rind
½ cup freshly chopped flat-leaf parsley
100 ml extra virgin olive oil

Start preparing the pork the night before. Sprinkle a baking tray with salt and pepper, the bay leaves and 4 thyme sprigs. Lay the pork belly in one or two pieces on the tray and massage in the salt, pepper and herbs. Keep it covered in the refrigerator overnight.

The next day, wash the cotechino, then place in a saucepan of cold water and slowly bring to the boil over medium–high heat. Simmer for 15 minutes, then remove and set aside.

Lightly rinse the seasoning off the pork belly, reserving the herbs, then pat the meat dry. Heat a little olive oil in a large heavy-based cast-iron casserole over low–medium heat, then gently seal the meat. Remove from the pan and set aside. Add the shallots, garlic, reserved bay leaves and thyme to the pan and sauté for 5–10 minutes or until the shallots are golden and soft. Deglaze the pan with most of the verjuice, then return the meat to the pan along with the cotechino. Pour in the tomatoes and ½ cup of their juice, the stock and wine, then increase the heat to high and bring to simmering point. Reduce heat to as low as possible and simmer, covered, for 3 hours or until the meat starts to soften; use a simmer mat if possible.

After the pork has been cooking for nearly 3 hours, heat a little olive oil in a heavy-based frying pan over low–medium heat and sauté the carrots, celery and remaining thyme for

6–8 minutes or until golden. Deglaze the pan with a little verjuice. Transfer the vegetables and verjuice to the casserole, then season to taste with salt and pepper.

Meanwhile, place the drained lentils and garlic in a medium-sized saucepan and cover generously with water. Cook over medium heat for 20 minutes or until soft and most of the liquid has evaporated; the lentils should retain a little of the cooking liquid. Remove the garlic cloves.

Just before serving, gently stir the preserved lemon, parsley and olive oil into the lentils. Slice the cotechino and pork belly into large pieces. Place a ladleful of the lentils in the centre of 4 warm large, shallow bowls, then top with a piece of cotechino and a piece of pork and a few of the vegetables. Serve with a dollop of salsa agresto (I might well add another cup of basil and a little more olive oil to the salsa when I make it to accompany this dish), a side dish of boiled waxy potatoes and a salad of bitter green leaves.

ROAST PORK BELLY WITH VERJUICE AND SEVILLE MARMALADE GLAZE

Serves 12

1 large clove garlic, chopped	2 tablespoons verjuice
sea salt flakes	2 tablespoons extra virgin olive oil
1 tablespoon minced ginger	2 kg pork belly, skin removed
⅓ cup (115 g) Seville marmalade	1 tablespoon freshly ground black pepper

Using the flat of a large knife blade, crush the garlic and 1 teaspoon salt to form a paste. Combine the garlic paste, ginger, marmalade, verjuice and olive oil in a bowl to make the glaze.

Place the pork belly in a roasting pan and season with the pepper and salt. Pour the glaze over the pork and let stand for 10 minutes. Meanwhile, preheat the oven to 120°C.

Roast for 3 hours, or until tender and well-glazed and serve with rapini (a peppery green vegetable that tastes somewhere between turnip and broccoli) or any other robustly flavoured green vegetable.

RABBIT

 **RABBIT, BOTH WILD AND FARMED, IS A FAVOURITE** ingredient of mine. In the Pheasant Farm Restaurant days I often had wild rabbit on the menu – a tricky beast to prepare until you learn to cook each part separately with great care.

Since the arrival of the calicivirus in the mid-1990s, which significantly reduced the numbers of wild rabbits in Australia, a previously thriving export market of wild rabbit (vermin to some, but big business to others) has come to a standstill. This is such a shame, to my mind – I saw it as a delicious irony that we exported our vermin back to the countries from which they were originally introduced to Australia. However, the calicivirus will move through a district, but soon rabbits are breeding again, so it has not really solved the problem – and even if you too like the flavour of wild rabbit, it is now much harder to find as the businesses that used to sell it went broke when the virus was introduced.

The wild rabbit's decimation of the countryside is a pretty emotive issue. This year we have noticed a profusion of young rabbits sharpening their teeth on our orchard trees, and have lost some mature trees as a result. So, until my supply of wild rabbits was curtailed by this virus, I always thought I was doing my bit by cooking rabbit as often as I could. Certainly people who grew up in the country loved to eat the food of their childhood (does anyone cook quite like mother – even if her dishes were sometimes overcooked to blazes?) and rabbit was the food of the Depression. My husband's grandfather was a butcher, and during the Depression he became a rabbit trapper at Mannum in order to earn a few shillings to feed his family. My mother-in-law often talked of grilling rabbit livers over hot coals, and remembers her father grilling rabbit kittens – a great delicacy then – over an open fire after the coals had died down. Even though she ate rabbit every day for many years as a child, she still loved me to cook it for her. And I was always surprised by how popular it was at the Pheasant Farm Restaurant.

Fortunately, there is a growing industry in farmed rabbits, which differ quite markedly from their wild cousins. Reared in hutches, they do not roam the countryside, and they are much more forgiving of the cooking process as they are larger, fatter, and therefore juicier, than their wild counterparts.

I have to admit it took me a long time to switch from wild rabbit to farmed, as I always followed the mantra of 'eat a rabbit, save the land' – and, when well chosen and cooked with great care, wild rabbit remains special to me, as long as it is in good nick and hasn't been grazing on onion weed. But if I'm being honest, I'd have to say that the plump young flesh of the farmed rabbit, as well as being a lot more succulent, is a lot easier to cook, as any part can be grilled, pan-fried or baked.

I try to buy the largest farmed rabbit I can, which is around the 1.7 kg range; a rabbit this size will serve three adults, and given enough notice, your butcher should be able to order one in for you. The more common weight of the farmed rabbit seems to be around 1.5 kg. Specify if you want the kidneys and liver too. Rabbit livers are a treat in themselves when seared and deglazed, then eaten immediately. All those scared of fat can skip the next suggestion: when cooking the saddle separately, make sure you keep the kidneys enclosed in the fat of the underbelly – nothing could be more succulent.

To cook a rabbit perfectly, it is actually best to treat the front legs, back legs and saddle as different cuts, all requiring different cooking times and methods. (The exception to this is the rabbit kitten, which is best barbecued whole.) If the thought of dissecting a rabbit is too off-putting, you can buy specific portions from butchers and specialist suppliers. Otherwise, dissect the rabbit with a sharp knife by first cutting off its front legs and then the back legs. The remaining piece is the saddle, which has a silvery sinew covering it that will drastically interfere with the cooking if not removed.

There are three ways of removing the sinew. Firstly, you can run a sharp knife along the spine and around the ribs to free a fillet from each side of the spine – a thin, flexible fish-filleting knife is best for this job. The fillets will still have sinew on the outside and should be trimmed in the same manner as a fillet of beef. The fillets can then be sealed in foamy golden butter and literally just turned over before turning off the gas and letting the residual heat in the pan finish off the cooking. The second way to handle the sinew is to seal and bake the saddle as is, and then carve off the fillets and trim the sinew after cooking. The third and, to my mind, most successful way is to remove the whole sinew with a filleting knife before you cook the saddle. This way you can prevent any shrinkage during cooking, and the meat will not be tough. The saddle can then be served on the bone, cut through the middle, accompanied with a sauce.

I used to discard rabbit bones as I was always told they can turn a stock bitter, but as long as they are only cooked for a short time (a little like fish stock), they make a really good stock.

I cook the saddle of rabbit by browning it on both sides, taking care that the butter stays golden by adding a dash of oil, and then placing it in a small baking dish in the oven for 5 minutes at around 220°C; a wild rabbit will take 5 minutes and a farmed one 8–10 minutes,

Pot-roasted rabbit with garlic, rosemary, preserved lemon and bay leaves (see page 130)

depending on its size. Then remove it from the oven and let it rest, covered, for 10 minutes before carving the meat off the bone. If you want to make pasta or risotto using rabbit, you could cook it in this fashion and then carve off the meat, but only add the meat at the last moment, otherwise it will overcook.

One of the simplest ways to serve the saddle is to make a sauce of reduced verjuice, chicken stock and cream with some basil leaves thrown in for flavour.

The front legs have the sweetest meat of all. I often pot-roast them in a heavy-based saucepan on top of the stove with some stock, garlic, rosemary, preserved lemon and bay leaves. I cook them very slowly and turn them several times during cooking until the meat readily comes away from the bone. This meat is also perfect in sandwiches and for rillettes as it is very moist and sweet.

The back legs I either braise gently at a low temperature or cook in a pressure cooker or crockpot with carrots, celery, onions or leeks and some chicken stock. When the meat

is cooked so that it comes away easily from the bone, I use it in a casserole or make a small pie of rabbit pieces and prunes by reducing the cooking liquid and then adding pitted prunes and rendered bacon to taste.

I recently barbecued a farmed rabbit for the first time ever, and was surprised but really delighted by how good it was. I separated the front and back legs, leaving the saddle, in one piece, with the kidneys encased in fat. (I took the sinew off the saddle so it wouldn't become tough, but then had to be incredibly careful to make sure it didn't overcook on the barbecue.) Before cooking it, I sat the meat in a dish of extra virgin olive oil, rosemary and thyme and a good dash of verjuice for an hour.

I cooked the saddle and legs together over two burners of our six-burner barbecue, taking care to turn the legs to cook them evenly, and making sure the saddle wasn't on the hottest part of the plate so it didn't

burn. The total cooking time was just under 20 minutes. I then put all the pieces in a resting marinade of a little more extra virgin olive oil, some verjuice (just enough to moisten them well) and more fresh herbs for 15 minutes. The meat was really succulent, and I wished I'd made a prune mustard or aïoli to serve with it. I also thought it might have been a good idea to wrap the saddle in some pancetta or bacon as extra insurance that it wouldn't dry out.

Rabbit is marvellous when marinated in extra virgin olive oil, lemon juice and marjoram before cooking. It also has a good affinity with mushrooms. Farmed rabbit, even though it has a delicate taste, can be teamed with all kinds of bold flavours. Think of olives (either black or green), pancetta, anchovies, capers, globe artichokes, roasted garlic, prunes, figs, rosemary, thyme, bay or basil – all are winners. Remember not to overcook it and, as with all meats and poultry, leave it to rest. A ladleful of warm chicken stock, verjuice or a marinade, added as soon as the heat of the oven or flame is turned off, helps to keep rabbit meat moist.

RABBIT RILLETTES   *Makes 2 kg*

I like to serve rabbit rillettes with cornichons (see Glossary) together with crusty bread and lots of salt and freshly ground black pepper. Prunes soaked in tea or brandy, whichever is your tipple, and then puréed to a thick paste with a little wholegrain mustard also go down well, especially in concert with the crispness of the cornichons.

1 kg pork belly (with the rind and
    bones removed)
500 g pork fat
sea salt flakes
2 kg rabbit legs, front and back
    (if you have a choice, use all front legs
    as they are the sweetest – leave the
    saddle for other dishes as it overcooks
    easily and is wasted in rillettes)

1 clove garlic, crushed
4 sprigs thyme
2 sprigs rosemary, leaves stripped
    and finely chopped
freshly ground black pepper
⅓ cup (80 ml) stock *or* water
1 cup duck fat, melted (optional)

Rub the pork and fat well with salt and stand at room temperature overnight in winter (or in the refrigerator in summer or if you live in the hotter parts of Australia). Cut the pork into thick strips along the grooves where the bones were, and then again into small strips shorter than a match and about twice as thick. Cut the pork fat into small pieces.

Preheat the oven to 120°C. Leave the rabbit on the bone and put it into a heavy-based ovenproof dish with a lid, together with the pork strips and pork fat. Bury the crushed garlic, thyme and rosemary in the centre, season with pepper and add the stock or water. Cover the pan and cook in the oven for about 4 hours if you are using wild rabbit, and perhaps half the time if you are using farmed. The rabbit meat should be soft and falling off the bone. Taste to see if more salt and pepper are needed – rillettes can be insipid if not seasoned properly.

Turn the contents out of the pan into a wire sieve set over a large bowl so that the fat seeps through. When well drained, remove the rabbit bones. Using two forks, pull the rabbit and pork meat into fine shreds. Put the meat into a large jar, then pour the fat from the bowl into the jar, or use melted duck fat if you prefer. Rillettes will last for ages in the refrigerator if they are sealed properly.

RABBIT TERRINE

I like to serve this terrine with pickled figs, cornichons (see Glossary), wholegrain mustard and good crusty bread.

6 rabbit legs	¼ cup (60 ml) verjuice
250 g pork fat, diced	100 g white bread
1 tablespoon sea salt	milk, for soaking
1 tablespoon Quatre-Épices (see page 179)	2 egg yolks
1 tablespoon freshly ground black pepper	4 fresh bay leaves
2 tablespoons fresh thyme leaves	250 g thinly sliced smoked pork belly
¼ cup finely chopped lemon rind	*or* rindless bacon
butter, for cooking	80 g pitted prunes
250 g chicken livers	

Bone the rabbit legs and cut the meat into dice – you should have about 525 g. Combine the leg meat with the pork fat. Combine the salt, quatre-épices, pepper, thyme leaves and the lemon rind then grind in a spice grinder or using a mortar and pestle. Toss this spice mixture into the meat mixture and refrigerate for 1 hour.

Heat a little butter in a frying pan, then quickly sear the livers to just seal on both sides. Deglaze the pan with verjuice. Remove the livers while still quite rare and allow to cool.

Soak the bread in a little milk, then squeeze it out and combine it with the meat mixture. Pass the mixture through a meat mincer, choosing the largest plate so that the meat is coarsely minced. Place the mince and egg yolks in a large bowl and mix together, working the mixture to help release the proteins and bind it together. Return it to the refrigerator.

Line a terrine mould with baking paper and place the bay leaves on the bottom; this provides a nice presentation once the terrine is turned out. Line the terrine with the pork belly or bacon slices, leaving enough hanging over the edge of the mould to fold over the top of the terrine later.

Preheat the oven to 110°C. Add half the rabbit mixture to the mould and then layer in the prunes and livers. Add the remaining mixture then fold the pork belly or bacon slices over the top.

Wrap the terrine in foil and place in a water bath (a roasting pan half-filled with hot water). Place this in the oven and cook for approximately 3 hours, checking after 2 hours to see if the terrine is coming away from the sides. When the terrine is cooked, a meat thermometer inserted into the centre should read 65°C. If you don't have a thermometer, insert a skewer into the middle of the terrine and check that the juices that escape are clear rather than pink. Turn the oven off and let the terrine stand in the oven for another hour.

Remove the terrine from the oven and place on a tray or plate. Weight the top of the terrine down with cans and leave overnight in the refrigerator (this is essential to develop the flavours). The terrine will keep in the refrigerator for up to 1 week.

To serve, invert the terrine onto a plate, remove the mould, then slice and serve.

RABBIT WITH ROASTED GARLIC AND ANCHOVIES *Serves 6*

3 heads garlic

2 × 1.7 kg farmed rabbits
(including livers and kidneys)

extra virgin olive oil, for cooking

freshly ground black pepper

3 sprigs thyme, leaves stripped

2 sprigs rosemary, leaves stripped

6 fresh bay leaves

sea salt flakes

½ cup (125 ml) Golden Chicken Stock
(see page 178)

⅓ cup (80 ml) verjuice

1 × 45 g tin anchovies, freshly opened
and drained

½ cup roughly chopped flat-leaf parsley,
to serve

CROUTONS

30 g butter

extra virgin olive oil, for cooking

reserved rabbit livers *or* 120 g chicken livers

3 teaspoons red-wine vinegar

1 tablespoon tiny capers

sea salt flakes and freshly ground
black pepper

6 thick slices baguette

1 clove garlic, halved

2 tablespoons freshly chopped
flat-leaf parsley

Separate the garlic cloves, then blanch them in a saucepan of boiling water for 3 minutes to begin cooking and allow for easier peeling. Let cool a little, then peel and set aside.

Remove the legs from the rabbits and set aside. Reserve the livers, leaving the kidneys intact. Slip the top sinew off the saddles of rabbit (see page 128). Rub all the pieces of rabbit, including the livers and kidneys, with a generous amount of olive oil, then season with a little pepper and the thyme, rosemary and bay leaves. Toss together, then transfer to a tray and leave for 1 hour at room temperature.

Preheat the oven to 220°C. Select a roasting pan with shallow sides that will hold the meat in a single layer without crowding (or cook in two pans). Salt each piece of rabbit just before cooking. First add the hind legs, then the whole saddles, and then the garlic. Roast for 10 minutes, then turn the pieces over and add the front legs, seasoning them first with salt. Make sure the garlic isn't burning – remove it if it is – and cook the rabbit for another 8 minutes. Turn the front legs over and cook for another 6–8 minutes before testing for doneness.

Heat the chicken stock in a small saucepan and keep warm. Remove the rabbit from the oven and add the verjuice, up to 60 ml olive oil, and 80 ml of the warm chicken stock to the pan. Add the anchovies and lots of freshly chopped flat-leaf parsley and leave to rest for at least 10 minutes.

Meanwhile, to make the croutons, heat the butter and a little olive oil in a frying pan over high heat and quickly seal the livers on both sides. Deglaze the pan with the vinegar, then add capers and season with salt and pepper. Leave to cool a little, then chop the livers into pieces. Reheat when ready to serve, reducing any liquid. Meanwhile, brush the bread slices with a little olive oil and bake until golden, then rub with the cut clove of garlic while still warm. Add the chopped parsley to the liver mixture and pile onto the toasted bread slices.

Just before serving, using a cleaver or heavy knife, chop each saddle into three and place on a platter with the rabbit legs, drizzled with the juices from the roasting pan. Serve immediately with the warm croutons.

RABBIT RISOTTO
Serves 6

4 farmed rabbit saddles	80 g butter
¼ cup (60 ml) extra virgin olive oil	1.75 litres Golden Chicken Stock
3 cloves garlic, finely chopped	(see page 178)
3 sprigs lemon thyme, leaves stripped	425 g Arborio rice (see Glossary)
freshly ground black pepper	¼ cup (40 g) pine nuts
3 oranges	extra virgin olive oil, for cooking
3 fresh bay leaves	sea salt flakes
3 medium onions, finely chopped	¼ cup (30 g) green olives, pitted

Remove the sinew from the top of the saddles (see page 128) and carve the meat off the bones. Cut the rabbit into 4 cm × 5 mm strips. Toss in a bowl with the olive oil, garlic, plenty of thyme and pepper. Shave the rind from one of the oranges, making a few long curls, and finely chop the rind of the remaining two oranges, then squeeze the juice from all three. Add all the orange rind and bay leaves to the bowl and stir to combine with the other ingredients. Cover and leave in the refrigerator for at least 1 hour.

Half an hour before you plan to serve the risotto, soften the onion in a saucepan in 60 g of the butter. Bring the stock to simmering point in a separate saucepan. Stir the rice into the softened onion, making sure the rice is coated with the butter mixture. Add the orange juice and cook over high heat, stirring regularly, until the rice absorbs most of the juice. Reduce the heat to low and add a generous ladleful of the hot stock, stirring until it is absorbed. Continue cooking gently, stirring occasionally and adding another ladleful of stock each time the previous one has been absorbed. After 15–20 minutes of cooking, the rice should be ready – creamy and tender with just a hint of bite at the centre of each grain.

While the risotto is cooking, lightly toast the pine nuts in a dry frying pan then set them aside. Heat the remaining butter in the frying pan and add a dash of olive oil. Remove the rabbit from its marinade, season with salt and sauté over medium heat for about 1 minute, shaking and stirring as necessary to cook the meat and lightly brown it. Only cook a small amount at a time so as not to poach the meat.

When the rice is almost cooked, tip the rabbit into the risotto. Use a spatula to ensure you scrape in every drop of the flavoursome rabbit juices. Add the pine nuts and olives. Mix well, check the seasoning and serve immediately with a crisp green salad.

ROAST SADDLE OF RABBIT   *Serves 4*

2 × 1.7 kg farmed rabbits
   (including livers and kidneys)
⅓ cup (80 ml) extra virgin olive oil
2 bay leaves
1 sprig rosemary, leaves stripped
6 sprigs thyme, leaves stripped
sea salt flakes and freshly ground
   black pepper
50 g butter
½ cup (125 ml) reduced Golden Chicken
   Stock (see page 178)
100 ml verjuice

ANCHOVY BUTTER
1 × 45 g tin anchovy fillets
250 g unsalted butter, softened
juice of 1 lemon
freshly ground black pepper

To make the anchovy butter, mix the anchovy fillets with the butter and lemon juice and add pepper to taste. Form the mixture into a log the diameter of a 20 cent piece, then wrap it in baking paper and refrigerate.

Remove the legs from the rabbits and set aside for use in another dish. Reserve the livers, leaving the kidneys intact. Slip the top sinew off the saddles of rabbit (see page 128). Trim the saddles to form two compact rectangles, then marinate the meat in olive oil, bay leaves, rosemary, thyme and pepper for at least 1 hour or overnight.

Preheat the oven to 220°C. Salt and gently seal the saddles in 2 tablespoons of butter until they are a pale golden-brown colour. Place the saddles meat-side up in a large roasting pan and roast for 6 minutes, then turn over and roast for another 6 minutes. Check for doneness and return to the oven for another 4–6 minutes if required. Meanwhile, heat the stock in a small saucepan. Remove the pan from the oven, then pour over the verjuice and the warm stock, cover the dish, and leave it to rest in a warm spot for 20 minutes. This will create a beautiful jus to serve with the saddle.

In a separate pan, sauté the rabbit livers on both sides in the balance of the butter (2 minutes on one side, 1 minute on the other). Rest the cooked livers for 5 minutes.

To serve, top the saddles and liver with a slice of anchovy butter and briefly return them to the oven until the butter just starts to melt.

RIVERFISH

 **THE GREAT MURRAY RIVER IS NOT ONLY SOUTH AUSTRALIA'S** major water supply, it also nurtures grapes, citrus fruits, almonds, pistachios, olives and other crops important to the state. It is almost our lifeline, our umbilical cord – but, as ancient as the river system is, it is as fragile as a newborn baby. Only 45 minutes from the Barossa at its closest point, the Murray is another world, and is quite addictive if you've a passion for old wooden boats, riverfish and quiet times.

Riverfish are of immense value to recreational and commercial fishermen in South Australia, and are a well-managed resource. Each licensed fisherman is responsible for an area or 'reach' of the river, and for recording the daily catch; these records provide a long-term overview of the ebb and flow of both native and introduced fish.

But there is much that could be done to develop the river's full potential, and nothing more so than encouraging people to eat carp. European carp were introduced into lagoons in 1961, but when the Murray floods carp find their way into the river system, where they feed on the eggs of native fish and muddy the water, which in turn threatens aquatic vegetation. I call carp 'the rabbit of the river'.

Like the rabbit, carp is seen as a pest and so there is little encouragement for commercial fishermen to catch it since the returns are so low. But, when caught small (1–1.5 kg) from the deep running water of the river, and cooked with knowledge, carp can be highly desirable – in fact it is prized in China, Japan and Eastern Europe, places with strong food cultures in which every ingredient is maximised. It is a point of honour with me to find ways of cooking carp to satisfy a wide spectrum of tastes, from the adventurous to the conservative. We must stop seeing carp as vermin and market it as the viable and inexpensive food source it is, and then we will have a chance of eradicating it from our river systems. I would go so far as to say that, prepared by a good cook, using simple ingredients and eaten fresh, I'd prefer carp to redfin any day. I am determined to convert as many people as I can to carp – as the saying goes, 'eat a fish, save a river'.

Sweet-and-sour flavours are popular with carp in Asian and European countries, and the Mediterranean combination of olives, anchovies and capers also works well.

If you are camping by a river, try cooking carp on the campfire. Gut a 1 kg carp and stuff it with lemon and onion, season thoroughly with salt and freshly ground black pepper, then wrap it in about eight pages of wet newspaper and barbecue for 15 minutes a side or until the paper dries out. When you open the parcel, the skin will peel away, exposing the steamed flesh. Don't be worried about bones – use your fingers.

While the carp is the most reviled of our fish, the king of the river is the Murray cod. Fossils of fish identical to our modern Murray cod have been found in New South Wales, dating back 26 million years. It is thought possible that the species is as old as the Murray–Darling itself – some 50 to 60 million years. Prior to European settlement, Murray cod was not only a food source for Aboriginal people, but also central to their mythology, including their creation stories. It was the largest, most abundant and most beautiful of all our native fish.

Even though Murray cod is now listed as a 'vulnerable species', it can still be fished, but is subject to bag and size limits and closed seasons which vary from state to state. For South Australia the closed season is from 1 September–31 December.

Cod live to a grand old age and can wait out a bad drought in dried-up riverbeds until a flood brings food and scatters predators. However, there were very few floods in the 1980s and seven breeding years were lost. The pressure of excessive recreational fishing over centuries has been exacerbated by many other factors: the regulation of the river flow; the lack of spring flooding in so many years, which is essential to their breeding; the removal of the natural snags of red gum in the river, which are critical to their habitat; and degradation caused by stock grazing on the river bank.

I had heard of the delights of Murray cod for years, but my first taste surpassed my expectations. In March 2003, I had the privilege of sharing an amazing meal with two friends at the Grand Hotel in Mildura, during a weekend conference at which we discussed a national plan for growing olives in Australia. The chef was Stefano de Pieri and, from beginning to end, the meal was one of the 'greats' of my life.

Stefano takes seasonal local produce and cooks according to whim, offering his customers no choice. It's the perfect way to run a country restaurant – here was the food we had dreamed of finding in Italy in 1995 but which had often eluded us in restaurants.

We walked down to the hotel cellar, where Stefano had his 'cave'. The pristine white-clothed table was laid with nothing more than a bottle of Laudemio extra virgin olive oil that had a napkin around its neck, as one would do for a precious bottle of wine. It set the tone for the evening. Stefano cooked one course after another (small courses, I hasten to add), beginning with a slice of polenta and the finest salami and Parmigiano Reggiano, served with the olive oil. Then came a sublime pigeon broth with the breast, livers and croutons floating side by side; freshly grated Parmigiano Reggiano was to hand, as was the oil once more. A mushroom risotto, a quail ravioli and *bollito misto* with mustard fruits followed – and then came the Murray cod.

The fish was displayed on a bed of ice on the table in front of the kitchen, and fillets were cut from the side that wasn't on show. It was a true statement, and the flavour of the fish . . . ! It was sweet and dense, and mingled magnificently with the earthiness of the artichokes Stefano had included in the dish: a combination that was meant to be.

Murray cod is being farmed, although it's not easily available. Even though wild Murray cod have a superior flavour, I hope that the farmed version will succeed, so we can continue to have access to this fish.

The first time I handled a Murray cod myself was under the tutelage of Stefano, for the inaugural Barossa Slow Food Luncheon in 1996. The lunch marked the release of Michael Burr's Wild Olive Oils, so I served pickled wild olives, wild Murray cod and wild hare. Stefano and his wife, Donna, contributed the fish itself. This amazing fish, as long as a man's arm, was enough to feed fifty! I discovered it had a layer of fat, like chicken. So as not to waste anything, I braised the 'wings' in this fat and verjuice – much as I would for a confit. Although there was plenty of fish for all, it was the helpers in the St Hallett's winery kitchen who scored those prized morsels.

It was also Stefano who taught me about freshwater catfish. Another treat of the Murray River, catfish is in such short supply that the South Australian Government is considering legislation that will protect the wild population, while leaving those fish in dams for fishermen. However, at the time of writing, catfish can still be legally fished. Our catfish belongs to a different family from the fish of the same name that is farmed extensively in the United States. Bryan Pierce, one of Australia's most respected fisheries scientists, has eaten many 'catties' and says ours are superior in flavour and oil content. Certainly, under the sure hand of Stefano, catfish is a great delicacy. The flesh is sweet and slightly less dense than that of a rock lobster (catfish is sometimes called 'the crayfish of the poor'). The fish must

be skinned before it is cooked, since the skin is very fatty and has a bad smell – this is one fish from which Stefano doesn't make stock. But he loves to use catfish in a risotto, in which case he uses chicken stock. His favourite way of cooking catfish, however, is to fry floured fillets gently in nut-brown butter and then to deglaze the pan with verjuice. He serves these fillets with wild fennel – how often it is that the simplest way is the best.

What I call callop or yellow belly is now being marketed nationally as golden perch. Whatever the name, this fish is alive and well in the Murray River. I'm very partial to it and even love the jellied fat line that runs along its spine. I bake golden perch whole, gutted but not scaled, and stuff it with preserved lemons and wild fennel. I rub some of the salty, oily pulp from the preserved lemons into the skin, too, so that the flavour penetrates from both sides. I wrap the fish in foil and cook it at 210°C for 15 minutes

and then turn the parcel over and cook it for another 15 minutes. Once removed from the oven, I let the fish rest for a while, then peel away the skin. If you have scaled the fish, open the foil for the last 5 minutes of cooking, and drizzle the skin with extra virgin olive oil to brown it.

Friends of ours from the Barossa have a tradition they enjoy every time they camp by the river: a sandwich of freshly caught, filleted and cooked golden perch. It absolutely must be served with white bread, butter, lemon, salt and freshly ground black pepper. Golden perch can also be cooked whole on a campfire.

Less successful, I find, are silver perch, which are in decline in the river system but are being farmed extensively, particularly in New South Wales. I find them a coarser fish than golden perch, with less oil and flavour. Similarly, while many fishermen claim the introduced redfin to be their favourite to barbecue, I find it a very bland fish. It has good texture, but for me it needs strong spices to make it interesting.

My first taste of bony bream, a freshwater herring, was a revelation. Henry Jones, a keen supporter of riverfish who fishes carp commercially at the mouth of the Murray near Clayton, gave me some bony bream to try. Unfortunately the excellent flesh is full of the tiniest bones imaginable, making eating them nigh on impossible, but they were so delicate, and the flesh whiter even than that of whiting, that I feel I simply must find a way around the bones. Henry Jones and Bryan Pierce were working on a solution to this problem, but I suspect it isn't high enough on a long list of priorities.

You'll often hear it said that riverfish are 'muddy' in flavour. In fact, this is caused not by mud but by algae living in the fat under the skin. This so-called 'muddiness' is not as obvious in winter, when all riverfish are at their best. If you really want to avoid this muddy flavour, you could always have your fish swim in clean water in the bath for a couple of days! An easier option is to remove the skin when cleaning the fish and then soak the fillets in verjuice, or a mixture of 1 part vinegar to 4 parts water, for 30 minutes. The advantage of using verjuice is that it won't mask the flavour of the fish as vinegar can.

It is worthwhile briefly mentioning the two types of crustaceans that inhabit the Murray River, as their respective numbers reflect the state of this waterway. Yabbies have good years and bad years, but are still very much part of the ecosystem – they are also now being farmed in most states. The same cannot be said of the Murray River crayfish, which is rarely seen now. Crays prefer clear, cool, running water, while yabbies thrive in poor-quality backwaters. Crays also need more oxygen than yabbies. As Bryan Pierce puts it, until the river habitat is improved, we can't expect Murray River crayfish to do well. But don't just blame the carp. The number of people who use the river, the eroding wash from speedboats, the overgrazing of river flats, the lack of tree regeneration, and the indiscriminate use of super-phosphates in the past have all contributed to the decline of the Murray, from its upper reaches in Victoria and New South Wales to where it meets the sea in South Australia. Things are improving in South Australia (farmers have to meet stringent criteria for new irrigation proposals and many are moving stock off riverbanks after floods to encourage regeneration, for example), but the three states that use the river must work in unison. We *must* look after our river!

PAN-FRIED CARP WITH ANCHOVY BUTTER   *Serves 2*

1 small carp, filleted
plain flour, for dusting
sea salt flakes and freshly ground
   black pepper

butter, for cooking
generous dash of verjuice *or* lemon juice
Anchovy Butter (see page 135), to serve

Dust the carp fillets with flour seasoned generously with salt and pepper.

Heat a knob of butter in a frying pan until nut-brown, then pan-fry the fish for about 3 minutes over medium–high heat. Turn the fish over and cook for 2 minutes on the second side, then deglaze the pan with the verjuice or lemon juice.

Serve the fish with a slice of anchovy butter on top and a salad of peppery green leaves alongside.

THAI FISH BALLS

Makes 20

This is one of my favourite carp dishes. While it includes chilli, remember that I am not a fan, so it's not overly hot.

1 × 250 g carp fillet

1 × 2.5 cm piece ginger, peeled and grated

3–4 spring onions, finely chopped

½ cup firmly packed coriander leaves, roughly chopped

¼ cup basil leaves, roughly chopped

1 clove garlic, finely chopped

½ teaspoon chilli paste

2 teaspoons fish sauce

1 teaspoon soy sauce

2 teaspoons mirin

1 tablespoon coconut milk

vegetable *or* peanut oil, for shallow-frying

Make sure the fish is free of bones, then purée it in a food processor. Add the remaining ingredients, except the oil, to the fish and blend to a smooth paste. Scoop the mixture into little balls and shallow-fry in a frying pan in the hot oil until crisp. Serve with thinly sliced lemon as an appetiser with drinks.

CAMPFIRE MURRAY COD IN A SALT CRUST

Serves 10

It is important to coordinate the preparation of this dish so that you do not make the dough too far ahead. I like to accompany this with damper and some Joseph Foothills Extra Virgin Olive Oil, Russell Jeavons' dukkah, sea salt and native pepper, all of which can be bought from gourmet food stores. If Murray cod is unavailable, you could use snapper instead.

1 large fennel bulb, trimmed and shaved

1 lime, sliced

sea salt flakes

extra virgin olive oil, for cooking

1 × 1.4 kg farmed Murray cod

freshly ground black pepper

¼ cup (60 ml) verjuice

DOUGH

1 kg plain flour, plus extra for dusting

1 kg cooking salt

800 ml cold water

Toss the fennel and lime with sea salt and a little olive oil and set aside. Rub the fish with some olive oil, pepper and verjuice, and set aside to stand while dough is being made.

To make the dough, combine the flour, salt and cold water in a large bowl until a dough forms, then leave to rest for 10 minutes.

Sprinkle the fish with salt. Roll out dough on a piece of baking paper until it is about 6 mm thick. Stuff the fish cavity with the fennel and lime mixture until quite full so it holds its shape. Wrap the fish in the dough, folding the dough like a parcel and tucking the ends in – make sure the dough is not too thick or the crust will crack. Use off-cuts to decorate, brushing them with water to help them stick. Dust the parcel liberally with flour and rest it for 10 minutes in the refrigerator.

Meanwhile, preheat the oven to 180°C. Bake the fish parcel for 35 minutes only. Remove from the oven and rest for at least 35 minutes, preferably 1 hour. Carve the fish at the table, cutting into the dough and peeling it right back, taking the fish skin with it. The flesh will be very moist – use a fork and spoon to serve each portion.

STEFANO'S MURRAY COD

Serves 6

1 onion, chopped

1 carrot, chopped

2 cloves garlic, chopped

extra virgin olive oil, for cooking

6 globe artichokes

1 lemon, halved

sea salt flakes

¼ cup freshly chopped flat-leaf parsley

2 tablespoons white wine *or* verjuice

2 cups (500 ml) Golden Chicken Stock (see page 178)

100 g butter

6 × 100 g Murray cod fillets

extra virgin olive oil, to serve

Gently sauté the onion, carrot and garlic in a little olive oil in a stainless steel or enamelled saucepan over low–medium heat until softened.

Meanwhile, trim the artichokes by cutting away the top third of the bulb, then squeeze the juice of the lemon over. Remove the outer leaves from the base and rub the cut surfaces with lemon. Halve the artichokes if they are large, then add them to the pan with the vegetables, along with salt and the parsley. Increase the heat to high and add the wine or verjuice and chicken stock, then cover the pan with a tight-fitting lid, reduce the heat to low and cook for about 30 minutes.

Preheat the oven to 220°C. Melt the butter in a roasting pan on the stove over low heat. Remove from the heat and slip in the fillets, then season with salt and add the vegetables and some of their cooking juices. Roast for about 7 minutes (depending on the thickness of the fillets), then remove from the oven and swirl the butter and juices to amalgamate. Put the fish on a warm serving plate and spoon over the juices and vegetables, then add a drizzle of your best extra virgin olive oil and serve immediately.

ROOT VEGETABLES

ROOT VEGETABLES HAVE LONG BEEN FAVOURITES OF MINE, PERHAPS because of their special affinity with game. Their warm flavours and distinct earthiness complement so many dishes, and they are at their very best in winter, when there is a smaller variety of fresh vegetables available.

JERUSALEM ARTICHOKES

The Jerusalem and globe artichoke come from the same plant family, although they are very different species. The globe is part of the thistle genus and grows proudly above the ground, whereas the Jerusalem is a tuber and member of the sunflower genus. Yet this knobbly specimen does share a delicious earthy and nutty sweetness with the heart of the globe artichoke.

Jerusalem artichokes are prolific growers that require little attention and will spread like wildfire. Pristine white when they are first dug up, the tubers darken with age, but as long as they feel firm and crisp, they will be fine.

Most cookbooks won't overwhelm you with ideas for using Jerusalem artichokes. So when in doubt, turn to Stephanie Alexander's *The Cook's Companion*. I was aware that Jerusalem artichokes are particularly suitable for diabetics but it wasn't until I read this book that I learned why. Stephanie writes that these tubers 'contain no starch, so their carbohydrates are well tolerated by diabetics and hypoglycaemics. However, these same carbohydrates are of a type that cannot be broken down by any enzymes we possess. The undigested carbohydrates pass into the gut intact, where they produce great quantities of gas!' It seems these health benefits aren't without their side effects, and it pays never to accept a second helping, particularly in soup, as you'll really notice it.

Jerusalem artichokes have a unique flavour, particularly when they are baked until almost melting. To achieve this, roast halved artichokes (if left whole, they may explode in the oven)

Jerusalem artichoke and pink grapefruit salad with walnuts (see page 146)

at a high temperature (say 200°C) until the skin is golden on both sides and they are fully cooked. For a change, try roasting the artichokes in butter with fresh thyme, lemon rind or thinly sliced meyer lemon, sea salt and freshly ground black pepper.

Boiled artichokes, scrubbed but unpeeled, can be mashed and creamed with knobs of unsalted butter and a good dash of cream – the mash won't have the consistency of potato, so the cream and butter need to be added judiciously so that it doesn't become too runny. Boil or steam unpeeled Jerusalem artichokes and cut them in half as soon as they are cool enough to handle. Drizzle the artichokes with extra virgin olive oil and toss through a tiny bit of finely diced garlic, some flat-leaf parsley or chervil, lemon rind, sea salt and freshly ground black pepper, and serve warm with grilled meat or fish.

Simmer Jerusalem artichokes whole and then slice them thinly with a mandolin into a salad of spinach and pine nuts. As sweet as they are cooked, raw Jerusalem artichokes add a delightful crunch to salads (although some may find them difficult to digest). To peel or not to peel is very much a personal question, but if you do peel them, drop the peeled artichokes into acidulated water to prevent discolouration.

One of my great culinary discoveries was the affinity that Jerusalem artichokes have with seafood. I had two meals within weeks of each other that combined these ingredients. The first was at bel mondo restaurant in Sydney, when Steve Manfredi was chef, where silky tagliatelle overflowed with mussels and slightly crunchy Jerusalem artichokes – a great balance. A dish at the Landhaus restaurant at Bethany in the Barossa Valley (sadly no longer in existence) presented a tart of puréed Jerusalem artichokes topped with poached oysters. The pastry melted in the mouth and a sharp yet rich beurre blanc completed this magical marriage. The earth and sea combination just works so well – try Jerusalem artichokes with marron or scallops.

Jerusalem artichoke soup, perhaps the most familiar use for this vegetable, is simply a purée of the steamed, boiled or even baked vegetable that has been thinned with a little chicken or vegetable stock. To make the soup truly velvety, add a good slug of cream.

JERUSALEM ARTICHOKE AND
PINK GRAPEFRUIT SALAD WITH WALNUTS   *Serves 2*

This recipe could easily be made into a light meal with the addition of prosciutto or grilled pancetta.

2 tablespoons butter	40 g gorgonzola dolce
extra virgin olive oil, for cooking	(see Glossary), crumbled
3 Jerusalem artichokes, peeled and sliced	1 small bunch rocket
widthways (about 160 g)	1½ tablespoons walnut oil
1 small ruby grapefruit, peeled and sliced	1½ tablespoons verjuice
widthways, juice reserved	sea salt flakes and freshly ground
40 g walnuts, toasted	black pepper

Heat the butter with a dash of olive oil in a frying pan until nut-brown, then add Jerusalem artichokes and quickly toss until lightly coloured. Deglaze the pan with the reserved grapefruit juice, then transfer artichokes to a large bowl and leave to cool for a few minutes. Add the remaining ingredients and toss to combine, then serve.

PARSNIPS

Of all root vegetables, parsnips in particular speak to me of late autumn and winter, of warming food and crackling fires. Their rich, nutty, sweet butteriness is perfect with that ultimate cold-weather meal, the stew (or do we not have stews any more, just casseroles and pot-roasts?). I developed a love for parsnips after moving to South Australia over 33 years ago, as our neighbour grew them and always offered us their excess produce. I soon found parsnips to be wonderfully compatible with game, and so during the cooler months, parsnip was the vegetable of the day in our restaurant, coming to the table in many different guises.

Parsnips require a coldish winter to reach their peak. As with many other vegetables, frost plays a part in converting stored starch to sugar, giving that desirable rich, sweet flavour. Early-season parsnips cannot be passed up, however the flavours develop even further from July onwards, but watch out for woody end-of-season produce. When choosing parsnips, don't go for size but look for crisp flesh and pale skin, both of which indicate freshness. A parsnip that has travelled from afar and been displayed for a long time will darken and become limp, the most tell-tale sign of tiredness of all.

I rarely peel parsnips, but then I have access to the freshest specimens possible. I do peel them if making a purée, or the legendary Parsnip Puff (see page 149).

If mashing freshly dug parsnips, I simply give them a scrub and cut them into chunks then steam or boil them until just cooked, before mashing roughly with good extra virgin olive oil, freshly ground black pepper, sea salt and flat-leaf parsley. Leaving the skin on adds to the flavour and texture of the mash, however it's a good idea to peel the parsnips though if they are anything but young and fresh.

To make a purée to rival the creamiest of mashed potato, I peel and chop parsnips into rounds and then seal them in nut-brown butter in a frying pan. I then cook the parsnip until tender in a saucepan with just enough milk to cover, then drain it. I add a spoonful of butter and mash the parsnip, adding cream as I go, until the desired consistency is reached, then season it with salt and freshly ground black pepper.

A great way to use up large parsnips is to make parsnip chips. Peel and cut the tops off the parsnips and slice very thinly lengthways with a sharp knife and a steady hand (or use a mandolin if you have one). Soak the slices in cold water for 10 minutes, then drain and dry very well with a clean tea towel. Heat extra virgin olive oil to about 190°C and fry in small batches until crisp. Drain, salt and serve.

My favourite parsnip combination of all is roasted parsnips with hare – either the saddle, rare-roasted, or the legs, slowly cooked with red wine, bacon or mushrooms and fresh

Roast parsnips

herbs. Roasted parsnips are also great with beef or kangaroo cooked on the barbecue, or with slow-roasted mutton or grilled lamb chops. Whether I peel parsnips for roasting depends on their freshness. I cut them in half lengthways, par-boil them in a little salted water and drain them well. I melt a good amount of butter in a heavy-based roasting pan in a 220°C oven, then just before the butter turns nut-brown I add a little oil to stop it from burning. I put the par-cooked parsnips cut-side down in the melted butter, well spaced so they become crisp rather than soggy and butter-soaked, and then bake them for about 20–30 minutes until caramelised. Roast parsnips are addictive – I've even been known to eat them as a meal in themselves.

PARSNIP PUFF
Serves 4

In the early 1980s, before I knew her, Stephanie Alexander first visited my restaurant. I remember being delighted by her comment in the visitors' book, 'Parsnips were wonderful.' I suspect that it might have been a less-than-perfect day, particularly in those very early years of the restaurant, and finding something positive to say was her way of encouraging me.

That day I had served parsnip puff, a Beverley Sutherland Smith recipe, from her book *A Taste for All Seasons*. This is my adaptation of her recipe. I like the texture obtained from using the food processor but the trick is to start with good parsnips – they should be crisp, not wilted, and as smooth and creamy white as possible. I avoid really large parsnips and the woody ones found near the end of the season.

6 medium parsnips, 10–12 cm long
 and 3 cm wide, unpeeled
75 g butter, chopped
¼ cup (60 ml) cream
pinch freshly grated nutmeg
1 egg
sea salt flakes and freshly ground
 black pepper

TOPPING
1 tablespoon breadcrumbs made from
 stale bread
30 g melted butter

Preheat the oven to 180°C. Cook the parsnips in a saucepan of boiling salted water until tender. Drain well and purée in a food processor or put through a mouli while still warm. Add the butter, cream, nutmeg and egg to the parsnips and season with salt and pepper. Spoon into a buttered ovenproof dish.

Sprinkle the breadcrumbs over the top, then pour over the melted butter and bake in the oven for 20 minutes. This dish can be prepared in the morning and reheated at dinner time.

PARSNIP QUENELLES WITH WALNUTS   *Serves 6*

This dish combines two of winter's greatest offerings – parsnips and walnuts. It can be served with beef, lamb or kangaroo – warming fare on a chilly day. It will also stand on its own as an entrée, and makes a good luncheon dish with a leafy salad.

¼ cup freshly shelled walnuts

1 kg young parsnips

milk, for cooking

75 g unsalted butter

2 egg yolks

freshly grated nutmeg

sea salt flakes and freshly ground
    black pepper

plain flour, to combine

olive oil, for frying

Preheat the oven to 200°C. Roast the walnuts on a baking tray for 10 minutes or until coloured but not burnt. Rub the hot nuts in a clean tea towel to remove the bitter skin; if you are using local new season's nuts, you can skip this step.

If the parsnips are really small, just scrub them; if they are medium-sized, peel them. Cut the parsnips into even chunks, then put them into a smallish saucepan and cover with milk. Boil until tender, about 5–10 minutes. Drain well, then add butter and let it melt. Mix in the egg yolks, nutmeg, salt, pepper and roasted walnuts and add just enough flour to pull the mixture together.

Make quenelles using two dessertspoons: take a spoonful of the mixture, then use the other spoon to mould it into a smooth oval shape (this looks attractive, but is optional – any shape will do). Refrigerate the quenelles on a baking tray lined with baking paper for at least 20 minutes, or until ready to cook.

Pour olive oil into a heavy-based saucepan to a depth of 5 cm and heat until very hot. Fry the quenelles, a few at a time, until golden brown on both sides. Drain on kitchen paper and serve hot.

SALSIFY AND SCORZONERA

A vegetable that you have might only have seen in a book rather than a greengrocer's is salsify. To my knowledge, no one in South Australia is growing it in commercial quantities, though I sometimes hear of it on restaurant menus, which means it is being grown for specific markets. This is a vegetable we should all be demanding – it has a wonderful oyster-like flavour and is known by some as the oyster plant.

Scorzonera belongs to the same family as salsify but is a brownish-black colour, whereas salsify is whitish in appearance, like a fresh parsnip. Both have hairy roots that resemble those of ginseng.

Salsify grow in a similar way to carrots but take much longer to mature. To be honest, it's been years since I've grown salsify myself, having got out of the habit when a grower in Greenock supplied it to me in the Pheasant Farm Restaurant days.

Cut the tops off the salsify as you would a carrot and scrub the soil away under running water. Salsify can be peeled and tossed in acidulated water to keep them white, but I just leave them whole, with the skins on, and either steam or cook them in salted water. When tender, slip the skins off the salsify whilst they are still warm. I like to serve them on their own with a little butter and freshly ground black pepper. French and Italian dishes often team salsify with chicken, and it makes a terrific soup.

The flowers of the salsify are also edible. The buds taste a little like asparagus. They can be pickled: put alternate layers of the flowers in a jar with layers of sugar and pack down firmly. Cover with cider vinegar that has been boiled and cooled. Leave to mature for a week, then use in salads.

SALSIFY WITH COFFIN BAY OYSTERS AND OYSTER MUSHROOMS WITH A SPARKLING WINE SAUCE *Serves 6*

A simple yet very special dish is this one featuring a combination of oyster flavours.

juice of 2 lemons

12 salsify

sea salt flakes

18 medium–large oyster mushrooms

butter, for cooking

freshly ground black pepper

18 large Coffin Bay oysters (preferably
 unopened, with their juices)

SPARKLING WINE SAUCE

1 × 375 ml bottle Yalumba Brut de Brut *or*
 other dry sparkling white wine

1 cup (250 ml) rich double cream

80 g unsalted butter

Add the lemon juice to a large saucepan of water, then add the salsify and cook with a pinch of salt until tender. Drain and leave until cool enough to handle, then slip the skins off the salsify while still warm. Cut in half lengthways.

In a large frying pan over medium heat, toss the oyster mushrooms in butter until golden brown, then toss in the salsify to both warm and gently brown. Season to taste with a little pepper. Transfer mushrooms, salsify and any pan juices to a bowl, then set aside and keep warm.

Make the sparkling wine sauce by reducing the wine over high heat in a frying pan. At the last minute, open the oysters and drain the juices into the pan, along with any juices from the mushrooms bowl. Add the cream and reduce to the desired consistency.

Slip the oysters into the warm sauce and toss for just a few seconds. Remove the oysters and set aside with the mushrooms and salsify, then quickly whisk the cold cubed butter into the sauce.

To serve, spoon a little sauce into the centre of 6 plates, then stack the salsify on top. Arrange the oyster mushrooms on top, with the oysters cascading over.

SWEET POTATO, SWEDE AND TURNIP

Sweet potato is perfect simply par-boiled then baked, though it needs to be handled carefully so it is not oversweet – I like to add a little lemon juice for balance.

Swede is a vegetable that is often ignored but is delicious when dug fresh from the ground and simply boiled and mashed with a little butter and sprinkled with some freshly grated nutmeg and freshly ground black pepper. It makes a wonderful addition to any meal, from a piece of boiled silverside to a grilled lamb chop. In the restaurant I used to serve it with vegetable soup or lamb stew, and I found people either loved or hated its sweet earthiness.

Turnips are easy to grow. They are a little like radishes, in that they seem to mature very quickly – or perhaps it is just that I like them fairly small, as their sweetness is then at its peak, especially when they are pulled fresh from the ground. The bonus with turnips is that turnip greens have a lovely, sharp flavour which contrasts well with the sweetness of the vegetable. Turnips have a particular affinity with duck and, of all vegetables, they work best at the 'baby' stage. They look attractive whole, either caramelised or just boiled and tossed with butter and freshly ground black pepper.

CARAMELISED TURNIPS OR PARSNIPS *Serves 4*

75 g butter

juice of 1 lemon

500 g turnips *or* parsnips, peeled
   and cut into strips

1 tablespoon sugar

1 tablespoon red-wine vinegar

sea salt flakes and freshly ground
   black pepper

Melt the butter in a frying pan or other shallow pan with a lid, add lemon juice and vegetables, then cover and simmer gently over low heat until just cooked (turnips will take about 5 minutes, parsnips a little longer).

In a saucepan, heat the sugar until it melts, then add the vinegar and simmer gently over low heat until the sugar caramelises. Add the vegetables and cooking juices to the caramel, season to taste, toss and serve.

GARDEN GREENS SOUP WITH PURÉE OF TURNIP *Serves 4*

This soup was hastily created one Sunday in winter during the restaurant days, when I had run out of ingredients and, in desperation, turned to the greens growing in a very small vegetable patch. I made a soup of the fresh greens and spooned the puréed turnips into the centre instead of cream. I remember it as wonderful. Freshness is of paramount importance in this recipe, so don't try it if your turnips and greens aren't crisp.

450 g turnips, peeled

120 g unsalted butter

2 tablespoons cream

sea salt flakes and freshly ground
   black pepper

1 bunch spring onions, chopped

2–3 cups turnip greens, washed and
   finely chopped

3 sprigs flat-leaf parsley, leaves picked

10 leaves sorrel

3 cups (750 ml) Golden Chicken Stock
   (see page 178) *or* vegetable stock

Cook the turnips in a saucepan of boiling salted water until tender, then purée in a food processor. Add 40 g of the butter, the cream and salt and pepper to taste. Keep warm.

Melt the remaining butter in a saucepan, add the spring onions and cook over low heat until translucent, then toss in the turnip greens and herbs and stir to combine. Add chicken stock and cook for a few minutes until tender. You could purée the greens and swirl through the turnip purée but I choose to serve it ladled into bowls with the greens just wilted, and spoon the purée into the centre.

SMOKED FOODS

SMOKED FOODS ARE THE BASIS OF THE BAROSSA CULINARY tradition. The Silesians who settled the Valley and other parts of South Australia in the mid-1800s brought with them their sausage-making and smoking skills. Smokehouses were built as a matter of course, and many Barossa cottages and farms still boast them.

Our first Barossa home, across the river from the Pheasant Farm Restaurant, had one such smokehouse. In my enthusiasm for country life, soon after moving in I declared that we must raise, kill and smoke our own pigs. Step one was easy; steps two and three took some doing. We called upon Lachlan Marcus McKinnon, my husband Colin's uncle, and an old bushy who was an extraordinary man and the last of the packhorse bagmen. Uncle Lachie lived with us for six months, and the small challenge of killing and smoking a pig was easily within his grasp. Colin had organised the logistics – the bathtub in the paddock and other essentials – but on the morning of the 'occasion' he was nowhere to be seen. His uncle had to handle it all alone, and I suspect he never forgave Colin for disappearing when the deed was to be done.

Lachie's bad temper vanished, though, when he and I came to smoking the pig – we were so excited that the talk was of nothing else. We bought a brine pump especially for the occasion (the only time it was ever used), our neighbour, a saw-miller, supplied the sawdust, and we started the fire with eucalyptus twigs. Lachie kept the fire smouldering day and night, which interfered with his drinking, but he was a man with a mission. The pig smoked for days – the old smokehouse was so black from generations of use it was obvious it had produced successes in the past. The resulting bacon was the best I have ever eaten (Col thinks I got sawdust in my eyes); we fried it in great slabs every morning for breakfast and felt so indulgent and clever. There was no doubt it was very smoky bacon, but then I was looking for a smack-between-the-eyes experience – and I got it!

The smoking tradition is still alive and well in the Barossa. In each town the butcher smokes in his or her own distinctive style, and there is much discussion and debate about

who makes the best mettwurst, ham, pork hocks, sheep's or calf's tongue, lachschinken (a smoked fillet of pork sliced super-fine like prosciutto) and so on. Everyone has their favourites, often travelling to one butcher for a particular speciality, and on to a neighbouring town for another product. Until my daughter Saskia began making bacon and smallgoods from the Leinerts' Berkshire pigs, I relied on Schulz's Butchers of Angaston – Schulz's then made the best sugar-cured bacon but, as every butcher in the Valley smokes their bacon traditionally, it is really a matter of individual taste. In the Barossa hams are brined and then smoked a little before being cooked in a copper and given a final smoking. This technique imparts a wonderful flavour quite different from that of some commercial hams, which are often smoke-injected. The sugar-cured hams of the Barossa are sought after from far afield, as are the other products of traditional smokers committed to the smoking tradition Australia-wide. As in all food manufacture, you get what you pay for – the mass-produced market cannot afford the costs of traditional production.

Most products for smoking are brined first, whether they are to be cold- or hot-smoked. Cold-smoking is a long, slow process that preserves rather than cooks. Bacon, mettwurst, and lachschinken are cold-smoked for two to three days, depending on weather conditions. The temperatures at which the meat is smoked are carefully regulated. It is imperative, for example, that mettwurst is smoked at below 28°C for the first 24 hours; the next day it rises to 30–35°C. The art, of course, is maintaining the temperature when the smokehouse is unattended at night. Natural fermentation gives cold-smoked meat its acidic flavour, and a starter culture (which reduces pH levels to a level unattractive to bacteria) used in the commercial manufacture of mettwurst does the same.

As the term suggests, most hot-smoked food is smoked relatively quickly and at a higher temperature. This process effectively cooks the ingredient. While meat, poultry and game can all be hot-smoked successfully, the best results are to be had when a fat animal or bird is used, as the process can be very drying.

We used to brine and hot-smoke our breeders at the end of each pheasant season when they were at their fattest. They made a delicious salad with bitter greens, sautéed mushrooms and sweet-and-sour mustard apricots. As these birds were both old and fat, it was only the ample breasts that were tender enough for use in a salad; the smoked legs became such a great addition to our classic poultry stock that we always froze them for later use.

Although many of the Barossa smokehouses are still standing, lives have become so busy that many of us make special requests of our butchers, who, given enough notice, are happy to oblige. Smoked pork belly, tongues, pork fat, and legs or saddle of lamb can be ordered, and I have had Schulz's smoke a whole suckling pig for a banquet to great effect. I scored the skin and painted on a marinade of wholegrain mustard and brown sugar first and then borrowed my neighbour's blow torch to glaze it.

I was always indebted to Schulz's Butchers for allowing me to smoke my kangaroo saddle there for so many years. This smoked kangaroo was an integral part of our restaurant and epitomised my philosophy of using traditional Valley techniques and local (and in this case indigenous) produce. My Smoked Kangaroo and Duck Egg Pasta (see page 58) became the most famous of the Pheasant Farm Restaurant dishes, but was only one of the ways in which I used the roo.

What Colin misses most about the restaurant is the Sunday afternoons. After lunch service, our extended restaurant family would all eat leftovers and put the world right over good wine, basking in the glow of a successful day or blotting out a bad one. Whenever the cupboard was really bare, because we'd been incredibly cost-efficient and everything had sold, or we'd lingered on long past the afternoon and needed supper, we'd always be left with two ingredients: bread and a reserve supply of smoked kangaroo. Sometimes crusty bread, smoked roo, aïoli, squeezed cloves of slowly roasted garlic and slivers of pickled quince would come together with salad greens. On other occasions we'd feast on a salad of smoked kangaroo, sliced pear, rocket and Parmigiano Reggiano. Roasted capsicum, rocket and extra virgin olive oil were always favourites with the roo and bread too.

Chef and close friend Cheong Liew and I once spent a wonderful few days cooking and experimenting with my produce in my Barossa kitchen. He served smoked kangaroo on a bed of witlof and rocket with salmon roe and local fresh oysters alongside and a dressing of extra virgin olive oil, finely chopped garlic and balsamic vinegar. The sweet, sour and salty combination was great.

Chilled foods are fragile in nature, and it's important that the public is aware of this. I encourage everyone to carry an esky in the boot of their car, in order to ensure that any meat or smallgood on its way home from the butcher or being taken on a picnic is adequately chilled. After the tragic Garibaldi affair in 1995, when contaminated mettwurst resulted in the death of a child and the hospitalisation of several others, the South Australian Government moved quickly to upgrade all meat-processing as part of a quality-assurance program. The rest of the states followed suit, so that now every meat, pâté and smallgoods producer in Australia is regulated by heavily audited programs to ensure food safety. But some of the changes to food production have resulted in a change of flavour and texture in the interests of safety. As mentioned earlier, it is now mandatory to use a starter culture under controlled conditions when making mettwurst and salami commercially – natural fermentation no longer takes place. Mettwurst used to be made by allowing the seasoned minced meat to sit for a few days in a coolroom before it was put into skins to ferment naturally in the smokehouse. The wooden barrels in which the mixture was traditionally kept were replaced many years ago by plastic, at the request of health authorities – no one realised then that the wood had properties that helped with fermentation.

I understand the need for these changes in the mass-production of mettwurst and salami but I would dearly love to see the regulations revised to allow the operation of small producers bound by the highest standards of hygiene and the ability to maintain control via traditional methods (just like those cheese-makers who wish to make unpasteurised cheeses). These producers would stand apart as artisans. These changes represent a loss of our heritage and I think we should be able to strike a balance between maintaining safety and retaining flavour; traditional methods seem to offer us both. Food prepared by traditional methods meets the highest safety standards if these methods are followed properly.

GLAZED LEG OF HAM   *Serves 12*

There is a world of difference between traditionally made and smoke-injected hams and it's worth seeking out specialist suppliers of the traditional product. I have been spoilt by having easy access to sugar-cured Barossa hams. Schulz's have always been my favourite, but all the Barossa butchers traditionally smoke theirs, as do smokehouses elsewhere. Although there are some in each state, the standout was probably the late Jonathon Gianfredo, of Jonathon's of Collingwood in Melbourne.

Traditionally cloves are often dotted over the glazed surface of a ham, but I find them too strong and use dried figs instead. The figs almost burn in the cooking, which gives their sweetness a slightly bitter edge.

1 × 7 kg leg ham
175 g brown sugar
½ cup (125 ml) Dijon mustard

1½ cups (375 ml) verjuice *or* white wine
400 g dried figs, halved

Preheat the oven to 220°C. Strip the skin off the ham but leave on the fat (you need 5 mm–1 cm). Score the fat quite deeply into a diamond pattern but be careful not to cut through to the meat.

Mix the sugar and mustard into a paste and pat it evenly over the top and sides of the ham. Pour half of the verjuice or wine into the base of a baking dish and bake the ham for 15 minutes. Reduce the temperature to 200°C.

Carefully fix the fig halves into the corners of the diamonds with toothpicks. Pour the remaining verjuice over the ham. Add a little water to the baking dish to prevent the juices from burning, if necessary. Bake the ham for another 10 minutes, then let cool before serving.

SMOKED LAMB'S TONGUE WITH RÉMOULADE SAUCE *Serves 4*

The basis for this recipe for rémoulade sauce comes from Elizabeth David's *French Provincial Cooking*, although I've added to it over time. It was my friend Peter Wall who first made it with me – he added the cornichons – to serve with a brined and baked hand of pork for one of our picnic extravaganzas. After that, rémoulade became a favourite, especially with smoked food or offal. This is one instance where I might use a combination of grapeseed or vegetable oil and extra virgin olive oil, as the latter could be overpowering unless it was a ripe and mellow one.

You will need to order the smoked tongues in advance from your butcher. You could use a pressure cooker to speed up the cooking of the tongues – or a crockpot to make it very much slower. I find my crockpot handy for putting food on to cook in the morning to be ready that night.

12 smoked lamb's tongues, soaked overnight in cold water	RÉMOULADE SAUCE
1 onion, roughly chopped	2 hard-boiled egg yolks
1 carrot, roughly chopped	red-wine vinegar, to taste
1 bay leaf	1 egg yolk
3 black peppercorns	1 teaspoon Dijon mustard
butter, for cooking	sea salt flakes and freshly ground black pepper
	150 ml extra virgin olive oil
	2 cornichons (see Glossary), finely chopped
	1 tablespoon tiny capers
	1 tablespoon freshly chopped tarragon
	1 tablespoon freshly chopped chives
	squeeze of lemon juice (optional)

Place the drained tongues, onion, carrot, bay leaf and peppercorns into a stockpot. Cover with water and cook at a simmer for 1–2 hours or until the tongues yield to pressure when squeezed. Allow the tongues to cool in the cooking liquid.

To make the sauce, pound the hard-boiled egg yolks with a drop of vinegar using a mortar and pestle (or carefully and slowly in a food processor) to make a paste, then stir in the raw egg yolk and mustard and season with salt and pepper. Pour the olive oil in slowly in a thin stream, incorporating it into the sauce as you go (this is the same technique used for making mayonnaise). Once all the oil has been incorporated and the sauce is thick, fold the cornichons, capers and herbs into the sauce. If necessary, adjust the flavour with a little more vinegar (or a squeeze of lemon juice) – it should be piquant.

To serve, skin the tongues and then cut them in half lengthways. Heat a little butter in a frying pan over high heat until nut-brown, then seal the tongues on both sides for a minute or so. Serve the hot tongues with the rémoulade sauce and some peppery greens.

POLENTA WITH SMOKED KANGAROO
AND PARMIGIANO REGGIANO

Serves 4

This came from one of our Sunday nights with the restaurant family. I sometimes add goat's cheese to this dish as well.

150 g Parmigiano Reggiano

3 cups (750 ml) Golden Chicken Stock
   (see page 178)

185 g polenta

1½ teaspoons salt

butter, for cooking

⅓ cup (80 ml) extra virgin olive oil

200 g very thinly sliced smoked
   kangaroo *or* super-thinly sliced
   raw beef or venison fillet

2 handfuls rocket leaves

good-quality balsamic vinegar
   (optional), to serve

Preheat the oven to 150°C. Grate 100 g of the Parmigiano Reggiano and set it aside. Heat the stock in a deep, heavy-based saucepan until simmering, then pour in the polenta and salt, stirring constantly. Stir the polenta over very low heat for about 20 minutes or until it begins to come away from the sides of the pan, then add the grated Parmigiano Reggiano and stir through. Tip the polenta into an ovenproof bowl, then dot with a little butter and put it in the oven, covered, to keep warm.

When you are ready to serve, warm the olive oil gently in a frying pan over low–medium heat and toss the kangaroo in it quickly. The pan should not be too hot or the kangaroo will discolour and spoil. Turn the warm polenta out onto a serving platter and mound the roo and rocket around it, then shave the remaining Parmigiano Reggiano over the lot with a potato peeler. Add a drizzle of balsamic vinegar, if desired.

VENISON

WHEREAS VENISON WAS ONCE ONLY WITHIN THE AMBIT OF restaurateurs, who either bought a whole animal and butchered it themselves or imported specific cuts from New Zealand, it is now available from most specialty butchers and is usually sold off the bone and vacuum-packed. It is, admittedly, still expensive by the kilogram, but a piece of trimmed meat with no waste can be bought well within reason – and you only need about 150 g per person. Don't think, however, that you should only consider the prime cuts: shoulders or shins, surrounded by tendons, are full of flavour when slow-cooked and are a lot less expensive.

A promotional book called *Gold on Four Feet*, published in the late 1970s, encouraged dangerously high expectations for venison farming in this country, but the industry, although still small, is now settling in for the long haul. Fallow deer are the most common breed in South Australia, Victoria and New South Wales, while red deer are raised in Queensland and smaller numbers of rusa and chital deer are farmed in parts of northern Australia.

The red deer is my favourite, although the diet of the animal determines the meat's flavour – and those from the wild have a more distinctive flavour than those farmed. The fallow deer is less than half the size of the red deer; its meat is milder and finer in texture when young, and tends to be preferred by most Australian consumers. The rusa is closer to the red in flavour and texture and may even be a little stronger. The chital is proving not to be commercially viable, as it is a nervous animal; its meat is mild, pale and a little like veal.

In the Pheasant Farm Restaurant days, my venison supplier used to talk with regret of the 'old days', when he had a licence to shoot in the wild – although the powerful flavour imparted by the saltbush on which the deer had fed was too much for him and his customers of the time. I used to have access to such animals, shot in the field without stress and hung for weeks. I thought the flavour was superb, but I must admit I was in the minority.

Game and poultry producer Ian Millburn, of Glenloth Game in northwest Victoria, is now supplying wild field-shot venison. In truth it's the only venison I'm really excited about – I love the flavour of game and am not looking for the gaminess of an animal to be diluted, as some are. To me, the animals being shot in the field is the most humane way of killing them, and no stress for the animal means quality of meat.

The practice of harvesting farmed deer in their first year can result in the meat having a much less developed flavour than that of an older animal. To me it is like yearling beef – lacking in character – although this is a very personal opinion, as the venison I've tasted that has been shot in the wild has set a very high benchmark.

The industry has been pushing the notion that the flavour of today's venison is not as confronting as that of old or wild venison. This is not an issue for me: I love the gamy flavour of venison and like the carcass to be well hung to enhance that flavour and to tenderise the meat. When I had the restaurant I was able to make such demands of my suppliers, usually individual farmers, but I now let specific cuts age in their vacuum-packaging. (In fact, vacuum-packaging replaces the ageing and hanging process that so few butchers are able to undertake themselves because of lack of space.) If you choose to do this too, remember to

turn the package over every couple of days. The recommended shelf-life of vacuum-packed venison is three weeks; after four weeks the flavour of the meat is much gamier and more 'livery', encouraging some to keep the meat for up to six weeks. Just remember to keep it refrigerated throughout. When you come to use the meat, remove it from its packaging about an hour in advance to rid it of any plastic smell. Once out of its packaging, the meat needs to be used within a couple of days.

There is no shortage of ideas for cooking venison in European books but you'll have to keep in mind that farmed venison needs less cooking than meat from a wild animal. Overcooking venison (as with most game) ruins it, unless, of course, you are slow-cooking or braising the so-called lesser cuts. If you can't accept your meat rare, or medium–rare at the most, you'd be better off forgetting the prime cuts of venison from the saddle and the trimmed cuts from the leg muscles, as the meat will be tough, dry and mealy in texture. Because all venison is almost devoid of fat, if cooked beyond this it's important to protect it by marinating it in extra virgin olive oil before cooking, after it has been trimmed of all sinew. I like to add some bruised juniper berries, bay leaves and freshly ground black pepper to the olive oil.

When roasting or pan-frying venison, you need to cook the meat quickly at a high temperature and allow a long resting time. For pan-frying, the small eye fillet is the most tender cut, while hind cuts, trimmed from the leg or the saddle, are also suitable. Cut the meat across the grain to produce 1.5–2 cm-thick steaks, and cook them over high heat for about a minute a side in nut-brown butter with some fresh rosemary or sage leaves, then rest them for 5 minutes. A sharp jelly or Cumberland sauce added to the pan when the meat has been removed to rest is an easy way of making a sauce.

The saddle, on which the loin and fillet are joined, can be ordered on the bone (it comes as a rack with eight or ten chops) and is considered the best cut of all for roasting. Cooking on the bone retains moisture; the meat is tender and, I find, sweeter. A saddle of about 1 kg should be sealed before it is roasted at 230°C for 10–15 minutes, and then rested for about 15 minutes before it is carved.

Thicker pieces for roasting require more cooking and basting after the initial searing. For cuts off the bone, allow about 30 minutes per kilogram at 220°C. The resting time is a crucial part of the cooking process – rest the meat for the same length of time as it took to cook.

Pickled cumquats or pickled native currants have a piquancy that's attractive with venison. They can be added to the marinade before the venison is cooked, or rubbed into the meat with a little extra virgin olive oil and freshly ground black pepper before sealing and roasting it. Or throw some pickled cumquats or currants into the sauce in the final stages of cooking and add a little of the pickling liquid (but be judicious, as the liquid will be very vinegary).

Jane Casey's chestnuts and Brussels sprouts (see page 17) would be a perfect side dish for roasted or pan-fried venison, as would any form of root vegetable, such as roasted or puréed parsnips or swedes, or baked beetroot. Wide sheets of Duck Egg Pasta (see page 58) or spätzle (short German noodles that are made by forcing dough through the holes of a colander into a simmering sauce) provide a great contrast in textures.

Diced shoulder, blade, chuck or shin meat is great to use in braises – just seal small batches over high heat first. Braising venison slowly for a couple of hours at 180°C with lots of wine, juniper berries, bay leaves or rosemary, and orange rind or tamarind, produces wonderful results. Don't be afraid of adding strong flavours like field mushrooms and sugar-cured bacon or pancetta either, as venison can take them well.

Venison shoulder makes a great pie. I like to use mushrooms, as dark and old (but not slimy) as I can get them, lots of small onions or golden shallots, pancetta, rosemary, garlic and veal stock and perhaps some tomato paste. I then gently braise chunks of venison in these flavourings for about 2 hours. When the filling has cooked, I make a simple lid with Sour-cream Pastry (see page 62) and bake the pie for 20 minutes at 200°C.

In late 1996 I roasted five double saddles of venison on the bone at the Tokyo Park Hyatt for a dinner held to launch our pâté in Japan. The trimmed meat rested overnight smothered with olive oil and seasoned with lots of rosemary, bruised juniper berries and cracked black pepper. The next day we prepared a sauce along the lines of that served with stuffed loin (see page 168) – except that we started with 10 kg of venison bones and veal stock made by executive chef Rainer Becker, and we used 1991 Mountadam pinot noir to deglaze the baking dish! (In total we used two magnums of this wonderful wine, which also accompanied the dish.) More juniper, rosemary and pepper were added to the sauce as the meat was resting. The beautifully rare venison was then served with this fabulous

sauce, duck egg pasta (which took one patient cook the whole day to prepare) and Brussels sprouts and chestnuts caramelised with a touch of sugar, veal stock and wine. It was a huge hit.

Venison also saved the day in the restaurant on one memorable occasion. It was the longest Sunday lunch service I can remember: we had a power failure, and a full house. It was the middle of summer and no electricity meant no cooling, no ovens and no water, since we relied on pumps to supply bore or rainwater to the restaurant. Thankfully I noticed the lights flicker hesitantly, so we were able to fill stockpots with rainwater for making coffee and cooking vegetables, pasta and so on before we actually lost the power. (Later we formed a human chain to the dam to quickly fill huge plastic containers with water that was then heated over gas for washing the dishes.) The silence in the kitchen was amazing: no exhaust fan whizzing in our ears like an aeroplane about to take off and no whirr of the oven, just the hissing of the gas flames.

My menu was very oven-focused and most of the dishes were cooked to order and carved off the bone, particularly the pheasant. But suddenly, no ovens! I had just put a large haunch of venison into the oven at its usual high temperature minutes before the power failure and actually forgot about it in the drama (the clock had stopped too and, without the usual noise, the whole tempo of the kitchen had slowed). There was enough residual heat to cook the venison to perfection, yet it must have been in the oven for more than an hour and a half. The menu was hastily changed to include slow-cooked venison and, with my honour intact, I was relieved to learn that you can successfully cook a prime cut in a slow oven.

The use of venison meat is well documented, but as the Deer Association points out, there is also a market, particularly in Asia, for the tails, pizzles (penises), tongues, eyes, brains, blood and sinews of deer and, of course, the velvet from the antlers. While we're talking of things normally only whispered across the table, Jane Grigson gives a wonderful recipe for brawn in her book *Charcuterie and French Pork Cookery*. It's called *fromage de tête*, and I made it once using deer's penis and other parts of the animal, along with a pig's head. Suffice to say this was not a popular creation, and nearly caused a divorce in the family.

A quote that tickles my fancy comes from one of the few game books I respect, *Gourmet Game*, by Philippa Scott. (In many other game books I've come across the cooking times seem way off the mark, making me wonder if the authors actually cook.) Philippa explains that 'the edible entrails of a deer are known as umbles. These used to be made into a pie, usually a "below stairs" provision, which gave occasion to the expression "eating humble pie". The entrails were cooked with ginger, nutmeg, dates, raisins and currants, then baked in a pastry case in the oven.' Wonderful!

CARPACCIO OF VENISON WITH
PARMIGIANO REGGIANO AND ROCKET   *Serves 6*

Raw venison lends itself well to carpaccio. I've had it with fresh truffles shaved over it, and the earthiness of the truffles against the sweetness of the raw meat was sensational. Although truffles are very much a luxury, perhaps they will become more accessible and affordable in Australia as farmers in Tasmania and Victoria become more successful. In the meantime, truffles from Italy and France are imported by a handful of people, if you are willing to be extravagant.

1 clove garlic	1 × 300 g fillet of venison
1 small sprig rosemary, leaves stripped	2 handfuls rocket leaves
½ cup (125 ml) extra virgin olive oil	180 g Parmigiano Reggiano
freshly ground black pepper	sea salt flakes

Make a paste of the garlic, rosemary leaves and 1 tablespoon of the olive oil using a mortar and pestle, then add the pepper. Smear the paste over the venison, then wrap the meat in plastic film and put it in the freezer for 20 minutes.

Carve the chilled meat (it should not be frozen) into paper-thin slices. Arrange a layer of meat over the base of each serving plate and allow it to return to room temperature. Drizzle over the remaining olive oil, then add the rocket leaves and shavings of Parmigiano Reggiano. Season and serve immediately.

LOIN OF VENISON STUFFED WITH
MUSHROOMS AND HERBS

Serves 8–10

2 × 1 kg loins of venison (off the bone)

extra virgin olive oil, for cooking

2 tablespoons juniper berries, bruised

2 bay leaves

freshly ground black pepper

1 kg field mushrooms, finely chopped

2 bunches spring onions, finely chopped

2 sprigs thyme, chopped

10 stalks flat-leaf parsley, finely chopped

butter, for cooking

sea salt flakes

2 small carrots, roughly chopped

2 onions, roughly chopped

1 stick celery, roughly chopped

¼ cup (60 ml) brandy

1 litre reduced veal stock

Remove the venison from its packaging at least an hour in advance of cooking, then trim it of any sinews and even up its shape. Keep the trimmings for making a sauce later on. Put the meat in a bowl and smother it with olive oil, then add the juniper berries, bay leaves and lots of pepper.

Combine the chopped mushrooms, spring onions, thyme and parsley. Season generously, then cook small batches of this mixture at a time in a frying pan over medium heat, in a little butter until softened. Reduce any juices and add them to the mushroom mixture, which should be like a thick paste.

Preheat the oven to 230°C. In a roasting pan, toss the carrots, onions and celery with a little olive oil and the reserved meat trimmings and caramelise in the oven for 20 minutes. Meanwhile, cut a pocket the length of each piece of meat down the middle of the loin and stuff with the mushroom mixture, then tie up the meat with string if necessary. Season the meat and seal it on all sides on the stove in a heavy-based roasting pan, then transfer it to the oven and roast for 10 minutes. Turn the meat over and cook it for another 5–10 minutes. Remove from the oven and transfer the meat to a warm plate to rest for 20 minutes, loosely covered with foil.

While the meat is resting, tip the caramelised vegetables into the pan used to roast the meat and scrape every bit of goodness off the bottom with a spatula. Place the roasting pan over high heat and deglaze it with the brandy. Add the veal stock and reduce the resulting sauce to the desired consistency, then strain it into a hot jug for serving, discarding the vegetables. Don't forget to add the juices from the resting meat to the sauce at the last moment. Check the sauce for seasoning, then carve the meat and serve with the sauce.

WITLOF

I HAVE ALWAYS BEEN PARTICULARLY PARTIAL TO BITTER flavours. As Angelo Pellegrini writes in *The Food Lover's Garden*, 'my own fondness for chicory approaches addiction'. I love Pellegrini's writing and echo his sentiments here. What I know as witlof, a form of chicory, is called Belgian endive elsewhere. In case you are in any doubt, the vegetable I am referring to is shaped a little like an elongated tulip, with more tightly packed leaves. Witlof has been forced – that is, it is shielded from light in the latter stages of its growth by earth which is banked up around the roots and trimmed heads. Grown like this, its leaves remain tightly furled and white with just a flush of yellow or apple-green. The more green that is evident, the more bitter the witlof will be. Although by rights a winter vegetable, it is now available year-round.

Witlof is bitter and cleansing at the same time. In fact, it is so refreshing eaten raw that it can be used as a palate cleanser instead of a sorbet, since it acts as a balance to anything sweet. When cooked, it becomes bittersweet as it caramelises.

Witlof needs to be handled delicately or it turns brown on the edges. It is transported in a large tray, indented to give each individually wrapped 'bulb' maximum protection from bruising and light, which makes the leaves turn green and consequently more bitter. It has a fairly short shelf-life, becoming soft with age, but if you find yourself with witlof that is no longer crisp, bake them whole rather than waste them. However, fresh, crisp witlof is the most desirable of all and is absolutely essential for certain salads.

Fresh witlof is quite beautiful to look at. By pulling the leaves off one at a time you can make an extravagant-looking salad from just one bulb. Try combining witlof and rocket leaves: the mixture is as attractive as it is tasty. Witlof also goes really well with sliced fennel, blood orange and toasted walnuts. Dress the salad with a vinaigrette of walnut oil, garlic, Dijon mustard, red-wine vinegar and a little cream.

Witlof leaves, taken carefully from the bulb, make a natural cup for hors d'oeuvres. Swirl prosciutto-thin slices of smoked kangaroo brushed with some extra virgin olive oil onto witlof leaves and top with salmon roe. The combination of the bitterness of the witlof, the sweetness of the kangaroo and the saltiness of the roe is fantastic. Use the leaves, too, to encase rich pork, duck or Rabbit Rillettes (see page 131) and add a dab of quince chutney on top.

Fresh witlof leaves can become the base for a warm salad of pan-fried scallops (deglaze the pan with verjuice and use it as a dressing). Or try warm sweetbreads on a base of witlof, topped with salty, freshly shucked oysters.

Picking up a treasured cookbook is like visiting an old friend: memories come flooding back and ideas from past seasons are refreshed. It was the rereading of *Stephanie's Seasons*, in which Stephanie Alexander writes about, among many other things, a month spent at Patricia Wells' beloved Vaison-la-Romaine in Provence, which evoked the memory of a wonderful guinea fowl dish that Patricia had cooked for us the year before, in a tiny wood oven built into the stone wall of her courtyard. I re-created this dish at home and teamed it with braised witlof. Turning to Patricia's book *Simply French*, which presents the food of Joël Robuchon, I found a quote many will find relevant. Patricia prefaces the recipe for witlof with: 'I admit that until I began preparing it this way, I was not much of a fan of cooked witlof . . . even though I love this popular winter vegetable raw in salads.'

Patricia suggests cooking witlof in well-acidulated water with some sugar and salt for 20 minutes, then sprinkling it with a tablespoon of sugar and seasoning with salt and pepper, before setting it aside until cool enough to handle. She next squeezes the witlof firmly to extract any bitter liquid from the cooking water, then sautés it in butter until it caramelises. The witlof certainly caramelises quickly this way. My method for braising witlof (which is included in the recipe for Witlof Tart on page 173) differs only in that it is a one-step operation – but I should warn you that I use considerably more butter.

You needn't dose the witlof with butter and sugar as I've described. Instead, try baking witlof cut in half lengthways (the cut side brushed with extra virgin olive oil) with fresh thyme, garlic cloves and a little more olive oil at 220°C until well caramelised (about 25 minutes), turning the witlof halfway through. I expand this idea into a pasta dish on page 172.

Braised witlof makes a powerful side dish to roast duck, pheasant or other game. Many years ago, pheasant with a liver glaze and braised witlof appeared on the menu of a tiny restaurant run by Cedric Eu in the Adelaide Hills. Given my love of game and offal, there was never any doubt I would order it. The real surprise of the day was my first taste of bittersweet witlof. It married so well with the richness of the liver sauce and the flavour and texture of the pheasant.

Try adding a couple of tablespoons of freshly grated Parmigiano Reggiano and a handful of walnuts (roasted and rubbed free of their bitter skins) to six braised witlof. Or add strips of prosciutto, or you could crisp pancetta in the oven and bundle it on top.

The bitterness of witlof and the richness of smoked tongue are a great combination too, but be sure to go lightly on the sugar when braising the witlof as sugar is usually included in the brine for the tongue.

GRILLED ORANGE, ASPARAGUS AND WITLOF SALAD WITH VINO COTTO DRESSING

Serves 2

1 large orange, cut into wedges

⅓ cup (80 ml) extra virgin olive oil

1 bunch asparagus, trimmed

1 tablespoon butter, melted

2 tablespoons vino cotto (see Glossary)

sea salt flakes and freshly ground
   black pepper

2 witlof, bases trimmed and leaves separated

Toss the orange wedges in a little of the olive oil. Heat a chargrill plate over high heat and grill the wedges on both sides until caramelised. Fill a sauté pan or deep frying pan with salted water, bring to the boil, then add the asparagus and poach until bright green and just tender. Drain and toss with melted butter.

Make a vinaigrette with the vino cotto and remaining olive oil, then season with salt and pepper. Toss the witlof, orange wedges and asparagus in a bowl with the vinaigrette and serve immediately.

PASTA WITH BAKED WITLOF AND RADICCHIO

Serves 4–6

6 cloves garlic

extra virgin olive oil, for cooking

3 plump witlof

2 heads radicchio

sea salt flakes and freshly ground
   black pepper

2 sprigs thyme

12 thin slices mild pancetta

2 teaspoons balsamic vinegar *or*
   vino cotto (see Glossary)

500 g penne

¼ cup flat-leaf parsley leaves

1 × 45 g tin anchovies, drained

squeeze of lemon juice

125 g freshly shaved Parmigiano Reggiano

Preheat the oven to 220°C. Caramelise the garlic slowly in a small saucepan over low heat with 1 tablespoon olive oil for about 20 minutes. Meanwhile, cut the witlof and the radic-chio into quarters lengthways, then toss them in a bowl with 1 tablespoon olive oil, salt, pepper and the thyme. Crisp the pancetta slices on a baking tray in the oven, not too close together, for 10 minutes, then drain on kitchen paper.

Bake the witlof and radicchio, spread out on a shallow baking tray with the caramelised garlic and brushed with a little more olive oil if necessary, for 10 minutes. The cut surfaces of the vegetables will have begun to caramelise. Turn the vegetables, then cook for another 10–15 minutes or until cooked through. Sprinkle with the balsamic or vino cotto and return to the oven for 5 minutes.

To cook the pasta, bring plenty of salted water to the boil in a tall saucepan. Slide the pasta gently into the pan, then partially cover with a lid to bring it to a rapid boil. Take the lid off and cook the pasta following the instructions on the packet (the cooking times can differ), stirring to keep it well separated – a tablespoon of olive oil in the water can help this too. If using fresh pasta, it only needs to cook for about 3 minutes. Drain the pasta, reserving a little of the cooking water in case you want to moisten the completed dish. Do not run the pasta under water or you'll lose the precious starch that helps the sauce or oil adhere.

Toss the pasta with the hot vegetables, pancetta, parsley, anchovies, lemon juice and a sprinkling of extra virgin olive oil. Serve immediately with the shaved Parmigiano Reggiano.

WITLOF TART
Serves 6

This recipe includes my favourite way of braising witlof in butter.

1 × quantity Sour-cream Pastry (see page 62)	125 g butter
6 witlof	80 g Heidi Farm Gruyère, grated
1 teaspoon sugar	2 eggs
sea salt flakes and freshly ground black pepper	1 cup (250 ml) cream
	freshly grated nutmeg, to taste

Make and chill the pastry as instructed, then use to line a 20 cm loose-bottomed flan tin. Chill the pastry case for 20 minutes.

Preheat the oven to 200°C. Line the pastry case with foil and cover with pastry weights, then blind bake for 15 minutes. Remove the foil and weights and return the pastry case to the oven for another 5 minutes.

Pack the witlof tightly into a small enamelled or stainless steel roasting pan, then sprinkle on the sugar and season with salt and pepper. Melt the butter in a small saucepan and pour it over the witlof to cover them. Tightly cover the dish with foil and bake for 20 minutes, then turn the witlof over and bake for another 10 minutes. Remove the witlof from the butter and reset the oven to 180°C.

Mix the Gruyère, eggs and cream, then season with salt, pepper and nutmeg. Fan the witlof out over the warm pastry case and carefully pour in the egg mixture. Bake for about 20 minutes or until set, then serve at room temperature.

BASICS

FISH STOCK

Snapper heads make the best fish stock, and if you have fish stock in the freezer you can make a simple soup or a rustic fish stew without a second thought. It also gives you a base for a sauce, or with the addition of the tiniest amount of gelatine (see Glossary) can become a quivering jelly – you could even serve it with poached seafood encased in it.

The addition of ginger to the stock gives an extra dimension to risottos. Just add 1 bruised knob of ginger to the stockpot before simmering. If I'm making a stock for a fish stew I use some fennel if it is in season (if it's not, I add a star anise). If the stock is to be used for a strongly flavoured dish you could use Pernod, and if you don't want to use wine at all you can add verjuice, which has a natural affinity with seafood. Just don't forget to label and date your stock before freezing it, and use it within 3 months.

1 kg snapper heads	2 tablespoons butter
1 large onion, finely chopped	½ cup (125 ml) dry white wine
1 leek, finely chopped	1.5–2 litres cold water
1 carrot, finely chopped	10 stalks flat-leaf parsley
½ stick celery, finely chopped	1 sprig thyme
¼ small fennel bulb (optional), finely chopped	½ fresh bay leaf

To clean the snapper heads, cut around the pointed underside of the head and the gills, then pull away the whole bottom part of the head and discard. Scrape out any trace of blood or innards, then rinse the head carefully and repeat with the remaining heads. Put all the vegetables into an enamelled or stainless steel stockpot with the butter and sweat them over low heat for 2 minutes; the vegetables should not brown. Add the fish heads to the stockpot and sweat them for 1 minute more, then increase the heat to high, pour in the wine and boil vigorously for a few minutes. Pour in the cold water, then add the herbs and simmer gently over low heat for 20 minutes, without allowing the stock to boil at any stage – it will become cloudy if allowed to boil.

Strain through a fine sieve or muslin to give a good clear stock. Allow the strained stock to cool and then freeze or refrigerate it if you are not using it within the day. A good fish stock will set into a jelly after refrigeration.

GOLDEN CHICKEN STOCK

Makes about 2 litres

I just can't cook without a good stock, and a chook stock is the one I use most of all. While there are a few good stocks on the market, usually made by small producers (ourselves included), for me nothing touches the homemade. There is something incredibly reward-

ing about having a pot of stock simmering on the stove, especially knowing that, either reduced or frozen, it might keep you going for a month. It takes so little work and adds so much to your cooking that I urge you to do it.

The better the quality of the original chook the better your stock will be. The skin and bones (with a generous amount of meat still attached) of a mature, well-brought-up bird has not only better flavour but more gelatinous quality. It's truly important not to overcook a stock; your benchmark should be that the meat on the bones is still sweet. An overcooked stock has all the goodness cooked out of it, and the bones have a chalky flavour.

I tend to make my stock in a large batch and then freeze it in 1-litre containers. Using fresh 'bright' vegetables rather than limp leftovers, and roasting the bones and veg before simmering them, gives the stock a wonderful golden colour and a deeper flavour. You only need use enough water to cover the bones and veg by about 7 cm in your stockpot (this way in most cases your stock won't need reducing). Never allow your stock to boil, just bring it to a good simmer, and don't skim it as you'll take the fat – and the flavour – off with it (you can remove the fat easily after the cooked stock has been refrigerated.) Don't let the stock sit in the pan once it is cooked: strain it straight away, then let it cool before refrigerating.

1 large boiling chicken (about 2.2 kg), cut
    into pieces (if you are using bones only,
    you will need 3 kg)
2 large onions, unpeeled and halved
1 large carrot, roughly chopped
extra virgin olive oil, for cooking
100 ml white wine (optional)
1 large leek, trimmed, cleaned and
    roughly chopped

1 stick celery, roughly chopped
1 bay leaf
6 sprigs thyme
6 stalks flat-leaf parsley
1 head garlic, halved widthways
2 very ripe tomatoes, roughly chopped

Preheat the oven to 200°C. Place the chicken pieces, onion and carrot in a roasting pan and drizzle with a little olive oil. Roast for 20 minutes or until chicken and vegetables are golden brown.

Transfer the chicken and vegetables to a large stockpot, then deglaze the roasting pan with wine over high heat, if using. Add the wine with the remaining vegetables and herbs to the pot, and cover with about 2.5 litres water. Simmer, uncovered, for 3–4 hours.

Strain the stock straight away through a sieve into a bowl, then cool by immersing the bowl in a sink of cold water. Refrigerate the stock to let any fat settle on the surface, then remove the fat.

The stock will keep for up to 4 days in the refrigerator or for 3 months in the freezer. To reduce the stock, boil in a saucepan over high heat until it is reduced by three-quarters. When the reduced stock is chilled in the refrigerator, it should set as a jelly; if not, reduce again. Jellied stock will keep in the refrigerator for 2–3 days, and in the freezer for 3 months.

QUATRE-ÉPICES *Makes 1 tablespoon*

This spice mixture is used for pâtés, rillettes and terrines. Although meant to be made of four spices, it can be modified to suit personal taste. Spices are much better freshly roasted and used straightaway than stored for a long period.

10 cloves	¾ teaspoon ground ginger
1 tablespoon white peppercorns	¾ teaspoon freshly grated nutmeg
1 cinnamon stick	

Grind all ingredients to a fine powder in a spice mill.

SALSA AGRESTO *Makes 700 ml*

1 cup (160 g) almonds	1 ½ teaspoons sea salt flakes
1 cup (100 g) walnuts	freshly ground pepper
2 cloves garlic	¾ cup (180 ml) extra virgin olive oil
2 ¾ cups flat-leaf parsley leaves	¾ cup (180 ml) verjuice
½ cup firmly packed basil leaves	

Preheat the oven to 200°C. Roast the almonds and walnuts on separate baking trays for about 5 minutes, shaking to prevent burning. Rub walnuts in a tea towel to remove bitter skins, then leave to cool. Blend the nuts, garlic, herbs, salt and 6 grinds of black pepper in a food processor with a little of the olive oil. With the motor running, slowly add the remaining oil and verjuice last. The consistency should be like pesto. (If required, thin with more verjuice.)

SORREL MAYONNAISE

Makes 375 ml

2 egg yolks

1 cup trimmed sorrel

pinch salt

juice of ½ lemon

½ cup (125 ml) mellow extra virgin olive oil

½ cup (125 ml) grapeseed oil

freshly ground black pepper

There is no need to chop the sorrel if you are using a blender, though you may need to if using a mortar and pestle. Blend the egg yolks with the sorrel and salt, then add a squeeze of lemon juice. When amalgamated, pour in the combined oils very slowly with the motor running until the mixture becomes very thick. Add a little more lemon juice, if required, and grind in some pepper, then continue pouring in the oil (it can go in a little faster at this stage). When the mayonnaise has emulsified, check whether any extra lemon juice or seasoning is required.

MAGGIE'S AÏOLI

Makes 1 cup

I have calmed down about the amount of garlic I use these days and would now only use 2 cloves to every 250 ml extra virgin olive oil, but those who really want to have that hit of raw garlic can use up to 6 cloves. At times I roast the garlic before adding it to the mayonnaise, in which case it could be called roasted garlic aïoli. For this, I would use 6 or more cloves of garlic, as its flavour when roasted is sweet and nutty.

2 cloves garlic, or to taste

½ teaspoon salt

2 free-range egg yolks

1 cup (250 ml) extra virgin olive oil

lemon juice, to taste

Mash the garlic using a mortar and pestle, mixing in the salt until it forms a thick paste. Add the egg yolks, then proceed with adding the oil, remembering to proceed very slowly until at least one-third of the oil has been used. Continue adding the oil slowly until an emulsion forms. Add lemon juice to taste.

ROUILLE

A pungent and particularly more-ish way of using garlic is to make this paste to serve with a fish soup, stew, braised oxtail, lamb shanks or with a crudité of fresh vegetables. For those who like spicy heat, it can be adjusted by including a chilli with the red capsicum. Rouille is French for 'rust' – and this should be the colour of your sauce.

1 large, very red capsicum	4 cloves garlic
200 ml extra virgin olive oil,	50 ml red-wine vinegar
plus extra for roasting	a few saffron threads (optional)
2 slices bread, crusts removed	3 free-range egg yolks
milk, for soaking	sea salt flakes and freshly ground
½ teaspoon cayenne pepper	black pepper

Preheat the oven to 200°C. Cut the top off the capsicum and remove the seeds. Rub with some olive oil and roast in the oven until it collapses and seems to be burnt – usually about 20 minutes. Take the capsicum from the oven and let it rest for a few minutes before putting it in a plastic bag to sweat. When it is cool enough to handle, peel, removing all traces of blackened skin.

Soak the bread in a little milk for 10 minutes, then squeeze it thoroughly.

Place the capsicum, cayenne pepper, garlic, bread, vinegar, saffron threads, if using, and egg yolks in the bowl of a food processor and purée well. Season, then with the motor running, slowly pour in the olive oil in a stream as you would for mayonnaise, processing until emulsified.

GLOSSARY

Wherever possible, I've explained any less familiar ingredients and techniques in the relevant recipes, but I've also included brief notes here on some ingredients and procedures that are used throughout the book.

Arborio rice

What distinguishes this pearly-white, short-grained rice is the amount of starch it releases during cooking, and it is this starch that makes a risotto creamy. Arborio rice should be cooked until it is *al dente*, which takes about 20 minutes, depending on the quality of the rice.

Blind baking

Baking a pastry case 'blind', or without its filling, helps to stop the filling from making the pastry soggy. Lining the pastry case with foil and holding it down with pastry weights prevents the pastry case from rising and losing its shape as it cooks. Special pastry weights are available at kitchenware shops, but dried beans work just as well.

Caul fat (*crépine*)

This is the lining of a pig's stomach, and can be used to wrap cuts of meat or delicate food such as kidneys before baking or pan-frying, to help retain moisture and add flavour.

You'll need to order caul fat in advance from your butcher.

Cheese

see Gorgonzola; Labna; Parmigiano Reggiano

Chocolate

The flavour of chocolate is determined by the amounts of chocolate liquor and cocoa solids it contains.

Bitter chocolate has the highest percentage of cocoa liquor and no added sugar, so it has a strong chocolate flavour, which adds depth to savoury dishes.

A good bittersweet chocolate may contain 70 per cent cocoa solids, and the best even more. Because it has sugar added, it is mostly used for sweet dishes – or eating.

Couverture chocolate is the name given to high-quality chocolate that melts well and dries to a glossy finish, making it perfect for covering cakes and for making fine desserts. I aways use this in any recipe calling for chocolate, since its high cocoa butter content gives it a fine flavour and texture, as opposed to compound chocolate.

Cornichons

Cornichons are tiny, crisp gherkins pickled in the French manner: picked when they are 3–8 cm long, and pickled in vinegar or brine. They are crunchy and salty, and are perfect to serve with rillettes, pâtés or terrines, to accompany a charcuterie plate, or as part of a ploughman's lunch.

Cream

In Australia, most cows are kept to produce milk rather than cream, so the fat content of their milk needs to be supplemented at various times of the year to bring it up to the 35 per cent fat content that is needed for pure cream. With nothing else added, this cream is good for enriching sauces.

Any cream labelled 'thickened cream' also has a thickener such as gelatine added. Because of the extra stability that the thickener provides, this is the best cream for whipping – just remember that reduced-fat thickened cream (with around 18 per cent fat) won't usually be whipped successfully.

Double cream is very rich, with a fat content of 45–60 per cent. Some of the thicker ones are perfect for spooning alongside a dessert. Try to find farmhouse versions that have been separated from unhomogenised milk.

Flour
Strong flour, also known as bread flour or baker's flour, is my staple flour. What differentiates strong flour is its high gluten content, which allows dough to stretch rather than break during kneading and rolling, making it particularly suitable for making pasta and bread. The gluten in strong flour also helps to ensure an extensive and even rise in bread.

Flours are further classified according to the percentage of wheat grain present. Wholemeal flour contains the whole grain, and so has a wonderful nutty taste, while brown flour contains about 85 per cent of the grain and white flour between 75 and 80 per cent. The flour industry has moved to unbleached flour; bleached flour must be specially requested. I prefer unbleached flour as it contains slightly more nutrients; it also has a more robust texture, which works well in breads and pizza bases.

Self-raising flour is plain flour with baking powder and salt added during the milling process, in the proportions of about 1¼ teaspoons of baking powder and a pinch of salt for every cup of flour.

It is used for making pancakes, cakes and muffins.

Gelatine
Gelatine leaves have a better flavour and texture than powdered gelatine. However, confusion can arise from the fact that the gelling strength of gelatine leaves is measured by their 'bloom' rather than their weight. All my recipes have been developed using Alba brand Gold-strength leaves, which weigh 2 g each and have a bloom of 190–220 g.

As gelatine will set more firmly over time, you may be able to use less gelatine if you can make the jelly the day before it is needed. A couple of other things to note: gelatine takes twice as long to dissolve in cream or milk as it does in water; and sugar can inhibit setting, so the higher the sugar content, the softer the set will be.

Gorgonzola
This Italian blue cheese comes in sweet (*dolce*) and spicy (*piccante*) versions. Gorgonzola dolce is soft and ripe, with a creamy, spreadable texture. Gorgonzola piccante is earthier in flavour, firmer, and has a more powerful aroma, having been washed repeatedly in brine during its year or more of cave-ageing.

Labna
Also referred to as yoghurt cheese, labna in its purest form is simply thick drained yoghurt. You can make it yourself by stirring 5 g salt into 500 ml plain yoghurt (the kind with no pectin, gums or other stabilisers) then placing it in a sieve lined with muslin or a clean Chux and leaving it to drain for at least 4 hours or overnight – the longer you leave it, the thicker it will get. Commercial labna is tart and tangy: some versions are thick enough to hold up a spoon, while others are more like soft sour cream.

Oils
As you will probably have gathered by now, I use extra virgin olive oil liberally in my cooking, and consider it vital to my food – and, indeed, my life. The only other oils I occasionally use are nut oils to flavour a salad dressing, and grapeseed oil in dishes where a more neutral-flavoured oil is desirable, such as in desserts, or to combine with extra virgin olive oil when making mayonnaise, to avoid a bitter after-taste.

Parmigiano Reggiano
Authentic aged parmesan cheese made in Italy according to specific traditional practices, Parmigiano Reggiano is my first choice for use in risottos, polenta, soups, and sauces such as pesto. I also love it as part of a cheese board or freshly shaved in salads. Grana Padano has a similar flavour to Parmigiano Reggiano, but has not been aged for as long, so can be a useful, less expensive alternative.

Pastry weights *see* Blind baking

Rice *see* Arborio rice

Sterilising jars and bottles
To sterilise jars that are to be used for storing or preserving food, wash the jars and lids in hot, soapy water, then rinse them in hot water and place them in a 120°C oven for approximately 15 minutes to dry out. This method also works for bottles.

Sugar syrup
Sugar syrup is a simple solution of 1 part sugar dissolved in 1–2 parts water (depending on its intended use) over low heat. It is great to have on hand if you are keen on whipping up your own cocktails at home!

Vino cotto
Literally meaning 'cooked wine' in Italian, this traditional Italian preparation is made by simmering unfermented grape juice until it is reduced to a syrup. The one I produce is finished with traditional red-wine vinegar to make it truly *agrodolce* (sweet–sour). With a much softer flavour than vinegar, vino cotto can be used to make sauces for meat or salad dressings or even drizzled over strawberries. In fact, it can be used anywhere you would normally use balsamic vinegar.

LIST OF SOURCES

The author and publisher would like to thank the following people and companies for allowing us to reproduce their material in this book. In some cases we were not able to contact the copyright owners; we would appreciate hearing from any copyright holders not acknowledged here, so that we can properly acknowledge their contribution when this book is reprinted.

Extracts
Alexander, Stephanie, *The Cook's Companion*, Lantern, Melbourne, 2004; Andrews, Colman, *Catalan Cuisine*, Headline, London, 1989; Pellegrini, Angelo M., *The Food Lover's Garden*, Lyons & Burford, New York, 1970; Scott, Philippa, *Gourmet Game*, Simon & Schuster, New York, 1989; Wells, Patricia and Robuchon, Joël, *Simply French*, William Morrow, New York, 1991.

Recipes
Stefano's Murray cod: Stefano de Pieri.

BIBLIOGRAPHY

Alexander, Stephanie, *The Cook's Companion* (2nd edition), Lantern, Melbourne, 2004.

—— *Cooking and Travelling in South-West France*, Viking, Melbourne, 2002.

—— *Stephanie's Journal*, Viking, Melbourne, 1999.

—— *Stephanie's Seasons*, Allen & Unwin, Sydney, 1993.

—— *Stephanie's Australia*, Allen & Unwin, Sydney, 1991.

—— *Stephanie's Feasts and Stories*, Allen & Unwin, Sydney, 1988.

—— *Stephanie's Menus for Food Lovers*, Methuen Haynes, Sydney, 1985.

Alexander, Stephanie and Beer, Maggie, *Stephanie Alexander & Maggie Beer's Tuscan Cookbook*, Viking, Melbourne, 1998.

Anderson, Ronald, *Gold on Four Feet*, Ronald Anderson, Melbourne, 1978.

Andrews, Colman, *Catalan Cuisine*, Headline, London, 1989.

The Barossa Cookery Book, Soldiers' Memorial Institute, Tanunda, 1917.

Beck, Simone, *Simca's Cuisine*, Vintage Books, New York, 1976.

Beck, Simone, Bertholle, Louisette and Child, Julia, *Mastering the Art of French Cooking, Volume One*, Penguin, Harmondsworth, 1979.

Beer, Maggie, *Maggie's Table*, Lantern, Melbourne, 2005.

—— *Cooking with Verjuice*, Penguin, Melbourne, 2003.

—— *Maggie's Orchard*, Viking, Melbourne, 1997.

—— *Maggie's Farm*, Allen & Unwin, Sydney, 1993.

Beeton, Mrs, *Mrs Beeton's Book of Household Management*, Cassell, London, 2000.

—— *Family Cookery*, Ward Lock, London, 1963.

Bertolli, Paul with Waters, Alice, *Chez Panisse Cooking*, Random House, New York, 1988.

Bissell, Frances, *A Cook's Calendar: Seasonal Menus by Frances Bissell*, Chatto & Windus, London, 1985.

Boddy, Michael and Boddy, Janet, *Kitchen Talk Magazine* (vol. I, no's 1–13), The Bugle Press, via Binalong, NSW, 1989–92.

Boni, Ada, *Italian Regional Cooking*, Bonanza Books, New York, 1969.

von Bremzen, Anya and Welchman, John, *Please to the Table: The Russian Cookbook*, Workman, New York, 1990.

Bureau of Resource Sciences, *Marketing Names for Fish and Seafood in Australia*, Department of Primary Industries & Energy and the Fisheries Research & Development Corporation, Canberra, 1995.

Carluccio, Antonio, *A Passion for Mushrooms*, Pavilion Books, London, 1989.

—— *An Invitation to Italian Cooking*, Pavilion Books, London, 1986.

Castelvetro, Giacomo, *The Fruit, Herbs and Vegetables of Italy*, Viking, New York, 1990.

Colmagro, Suzanne, Collins, Graham and Sedgley, Margaret, 'Processing Technology of the Table Olive', University of Adelaide, in Jules Janick (ed.) *Horticultural Reviews* Vol. 25, John Wiley & Sons, 2000.

Cox, Nicola, *Game Cookery*, Victor Gollancz, London, 1989.

David, Elizabeth, *Italian Food*, Penguin, Harmondsworth, 1989.

—— *An Omelette and a Glass of Wine*, Penguin, Harmondsworth, 1986.

—— *English Bread and Yeast Cookery*, Penguin, Harmondsworth, 1979.

—— *French Provincial Cooking*, Penguin, Harmondsworth, 1970.

—— *Summer Cooking*, Penguin, Harmondsworth, 1965.

De Groot, Roy Andries, *The Auberge of the Flowering Hearth*, The Ecco Press, New Jersey, 1973.

Dolamore, Anne, *The Essential Olive Oil Companion*, Macmillan, Melbourne, 1988.

Ferguson, Jenny, *Cooking for You and Me*, Methuen Haynes, Sydney, 1987.

Field, Carol, *Celebrating Italy*, William Morrow, New York, 1990.

Fitzgibbon, Theodora, *Game Cooking*, Andre Deutsch, London, 1963.

Glowinski, Louis, *The Complete Book of Fruit Growing in Australia*, Lothian, Melbourne, 1991.

Gray, Patience, *Honey From a Weed*, Prospect Books, London, 1986.

Gray, Rose and Rogers, Ruth, *The River Cafe Cook Book*, Ebury Press, London, 1996.

Grigson, Jane and Fullick, Roy (eds), *The Enjoyment of Food: The Best of Jane Grigson*, Michael Joseph, London, 1992.

Grigson, Jane, *Jane Grigson's Fruit Book*, Michael Joseph, London, 1982.

—— *Jane Grigson's Vegetable Book*, Penguin, Harmondsworth, 1980.

—— *Good Things*, Penguin, Harmondsworth, 1973.

—— *Jane Grigson's Fish Book*, Penguin, Harmondsworth, 1973.

—— *Charcuterie and French Pork Cookery*, Penguin, Harmondsworth, 1970.

Halligan, Marion, *Eat My Words*, Angus & Robertson, Sydney, 1990.

Hazan, Marcella, *The Classic Italian Cookbook*, Macmillan, London (rev. ed.), 1987.

Hopkinson, Simon with Bareham, Lindsey, *Roast Chicken and Other Stories*, Ebury Press, London, 1994.

Huxley, Aldous, *The Olive Tree*, Ayer, USA, reprint of 1937 ed.

Isaacs, Jennifer, *Bush Food*, Weldon, Sydney, 1987.

Kamman, Madeleine, *In Madeleine's Kitchen*, Macmillan, New York, 1992.

—— *The Making of a Cook*, Atheneum, New York, 1978.

Lake, Max, *Scents and Sensuality*, Penguin, Melbourne, 1991.

Manfield, Christine, *Christine Manfield Originals*, Lantern, Melbourne, 2006.

McGee, Harold, *The Curious Cook*, Northpoint Press, San Francisco, 1990.

—— *On Food and Cooking*, Collier Books, New York, 1988.

Ministero Agricoltura e Foreste. D.O.C. *Cheeses of Italy* (trans. Angela Zanotti), Milan, 1992.

Molyneux, Joyce, with Grigson, Sophie, *The Carved Angel Cookery Book*, Collins, 1990.

Newell, Patrice, *The Olive Grove*, Penguin, Melbourne, 2000.

del Nero, Constance and del Nero, Rosario, *Risotto*, Harper and Row, New York, 1989.

Olney, Richard, *Simple French Food*, Atheneum, New York, 1980.

Peck, Paula, *The Art of Fine Baking*, Simon & Schuster, New York, 1961.

Pellegrini, Angelo M., *The Food Lover's Garden*, Lyons & Burford, New York, 1970.

Pepin, Jacques, *La Technique*, Hamlyn Publishing Group, New York, 1978.

Perry, Neil, *The Food I Love*, Murdoch Books, Sydney, 2005.

Pignolet, Damien, *French*, Lantern, Melbourne, 2005.

Reichelt, Karen, with Burr, Michael, *Extra Virgin: An Australian Companion to Olives and Olive Oil*, Wakefield Press, Adelaide, 1997.

Ripe, Cherry, *Goodbye Culinary Cringe*, Allen & Unwin, Sydney, 1993.

Santich, Barbara, 'The Return of Verjuice', *Winestate*, June 1984.

Schauer, Amy, *The Schauer Australian Cookery Book* (14th ed.), W.R. Smith & Paterson, Brisbane, 1979.

Scicolone, Michele, *The Antipasto Table*, Morrow, New York, 1991.

Scott, Philippa, *Gourmet Game*, Simon & Schuster, New York, 1989.

Silverton, Nancy, *Nancy Silverton's Pastries from the La Brea Bakery*, Random House, New York, 2000.

Simeti, Mary Taylor, *Pomp and Sustenance*, Alfred A. Knopf, New York, 1989.

Stobart, Tom (ed.), *The Cook's Encyclopaedia*, Papermac, London, 1982.

Studd, Will, *Chalk and Cheese*, Purple Egg, Melbourne, 2004.

Sutherland Smith, Beverley, *A Taste for All Seasons*, Lansdowne, Sydney, 1975.

Sweeney, Susan, *The Olive Press*, The Australian Olive Association, Autumn 2006.

Symons, Michael, *One Continuous Picnic*, Duck Press, Adelaide, 1982.

Taruschio, Ann and Taruschio, Franco, *Leaves from the Walnut Tree*, Pavilion, London, 1993.

Time-Life Fruit Book, Time-Life, Amsterdam, 1983.

Wark, Alf, *Wine Cookery*, Rigby, Adelaide, 1969.

Waters, Alice, Curtan, Patricia and Labro, Martine, *Chez Panisse Pasta, Pizza and Calzone*, Random House, New York, 1984.

Waters, Alice, *Chez Panisse Café Cookbook*, Random House, New York, 1999.

—— *Chez Panisse Menu Cookbook*, Chatto & Windus, London, 1984.

Weir, Joanne, *You Say Tomato*, Broadway Books, New York, 1998.

Wells, Patricia, *At Home in Provence*, Scribner, New York, 1996.

Wells, Patricia and Robuchon, Joël, *Simply French*, William Morrow, New York, 1991.

Whiteaker, Stafford, *The Compleat Strawberry*, Century Publishing, London, 1985.

Wolfert, Paula, *The Cooking of the Eastern Mediterranean*, Harper Collins Publishers, New York, 1994.

—— *The Cooking of South-West France*, The Dial Press, New York, 1983.

—— *Mediterranean Cooking*, The Ecco Press, New York, 1977.

Zalokar, Sophie, *Picnic*, Fremantle Arts Centre Press, Perth, 2002.

ACKNOWLEDGEMENTS

Maggie's Harvest represented the culmination of a life's work, so it's not easy to conjure up all the people who have been instrumental in so many ways over the years.

My husband, Colin, is my rock – a true partner in every sense of the word. My daughters, Saskia and Elli, have grown into strong, independent women and we share regular boisterous meals with their partners and our much-loved grandchildren, Zöe, Max, Lilly, Rory and Ben – and one more on the way.

The indomitable Julie Gibbs, originally suggested an update of *Maggie's Farm* and *Maggie's Orchard*, an idea which developed over time into *Maggie's Harvest*. I always had faith in Julie's extraordinary ability to know just what will make a book special.

Photographer Mark Chew effortlessly captured the essence of the produce in the book – it feels so Barossan! Daniel New, the book's designer, weaved his magic with the design. Marie Anne Pledger not only helped out on the shoots, but provided paraphernalia from her own kitchen and that of her friends for us to use.

There are so many in the team at Penguin I'd like to thank. My editors Kathleen Gandy and Virginia Birch and Nicole Brown for keeping us all on track, Anouska Jones for proofreading, and Jocelyn Hungerford and all at Penguin for eleventh-hour assistance.

Over the years I have had an incredible array of staff who have contributed so much to both my business and my life. First and foremost was the lovely Hilda Laurencis, who sadly died as I wrote the very last pages of *Maggie's Harvest*.

From the Pheasant Farm Restaurant days, Sophie Zalokar, Steve Flamsteed, Nat Paull and Alex Herbert remain part of our extended family, and more recently Victoria Blumenstein and Gill Radford have both done much to ease my daily life.

The friendly, hard-working team at the Farmshop are the public face of our business and help to keep the tradition of the farm alive. I have so much to thank them for. Our customers, from the early days of the Pheasant Farm Restaurant, to those who buy our products all over the world today, have believed in us and what we've done.

I would also like to thank the following people who have lent their expertise in specific areas: Louis Glowinski; Geoff Linton of Yalumba; Dr Rod Mailer, Principal Research Scientist at the NSW Department of Primary Industries (who I'm delighted to say works exclusively with the olive oil industry now); and Richard Gunner of Coorong Angus Beef, for his passionate endeavours and wealth of knowledge on beef and lamb.

INDEX

A

acidulated water 7
Aileen's Olive Bread 266
aïoli 38
  Maggie's Aïoli 180
  Rouille 38
Alexander, Stephanie 9, 116,
  118, 144, 149, 170
almonds
  Orange and Almond Tart 108
  Salsa Agresto 179
anchovies
  ~ pissaladière 97
  Anchovy Butter 135
  Rabbit with Roasted Garlic
  and Anchovies 133
  Squid with Onion, Parsley
  and Anchovy Stuffing 100
Apex Bakery 42
apples
  Celeriac, Apple and Walnut Salad 9
artichokes see globe artichokes;
  Jerusalem artichokes
asparagus
  Grilled Orange, Asparagus and
  Witlof Salad with Vino Cotto
  Dressing 172
Australian Olive Association 33

B

Baby Onions Roasted in Vino
  Cotto 99
bacon 154
  see also pancetta
Bangalow Sweet Pork 119
Barbecued Sugar-cured
  Kangaroo 67
Becker, Rainer 165
Beer, Colin 18, 24, 26, 45,
  96, 119, 154, 158
Beer, Saskia 84, 87, 157
Bilson, Tony 83
Blanc, Georges 70
blind baking 61–2, 183
blood sausage 121
Blue Swimmer Crab Risotto
  with Verjuice 28
Blumenstein, Victoria 10, 55, 63, 84
bony bream 140

brains (lamb's)
  ~ preparing 89
  Brains in Caper Butter 90
braises
  ~ venison 165
  Braised Cavolo Nero 5
  Braised Celeriac 10
  Braised Pork Belly, Cotechino
  and Green Lentils 124
bread 41–53
  ~ butter in 48
  ~ crusty 48
  ~ flour 47
  ~ freezing 48
  ~ improvers 48
  ~ poolish 49
  ~ problems and
  solutions 47–8
  ~ salt in 48
  ~ water 47–8
  ~ wood-fired ovens 41, 42
  ~ yeast 48
  Bread and Butter Pudding 53
  Croutons 114, 133
  Grape and Walnut Bread 50
  Mustard Bread 27
  Piquant Bread Salad 40
  Sophie's Farmhouse Loaf 49
  see also bruschetta; flatbread;
  sandwiches
brioche
  Olive Oil Brioche with
  Candied Seville Peel 107
bruschetta
  ~ with cavolo nero 4
  ~ making 45, 47
  ~ toppings 47
brussels sprouts with
  chestnuts 17, 165
Burr, Dr Michael 31, 139
butters
  Anchovy Butter 135
  Caper Butter 90
  Ginger and Lemon Butter 113
  Sea Urchin Butter 85
Byrne, Lee 105

C

cake
  Chestnut Cake 21

Campfire Murray Cod
  in a Salt Crust 142
candied orange peel 105
Cantrell, Deb 15
capers
  Caper Butter 90
  Spaghettini with Parmigiano
  Reggiano, Garlic, Capers
  and Flat-leaf Parsley 37, 40
capsicums
  ~ rouille 38
caramelised onions 94, 96
  Caramelised Onion Salad 66, 99
Caramelised Turnips or
  Parsnips 153
Carluccio, Antonio 92
carp 137–8, 141
  ~ campfire-cooked 138
  ~ sweet and sour 138
  Pan-fried Carp with Anchovy
  Butter 141
  Thai Fish Balls 142
Carpaccio of Venison with
  Parmigiano Reggiano
  and Rocket 167
Casey, Jane 15, 17, 165
catfish 139–40
  ~ 'crayfish of the poor' 140
  ~ in risotto 140
  ~ skinning 140
caul fat 121, 123, 183
cavolo nero 2–6
  ~ on bruschetta 4
  ~ campfire-cooked 138
  Braised Cavolo Nero 5
  Cavolo Nero with Golden
  Shallots and Quince 4
  Minestrone with Cavolo
  Nero 5
  Ribollita 4, 6
celeriac 7–11
  ~ with apple 8
  ~ chips 8
  ~ choosing 7
  ~ discolouration 7
  ~ with game 7
  ~ raw in salads 7, 8
  Braised Celeriac 10
  Celeriac, Apple and Walnut
  Salad 9
  Celeriac Rémoulade 7, 9

Purée of Celeriac to Accompany
  Game 10
Victoria's Celeriac and Chestnut
  Pie 10
cheese
~ gorgonzola 184
~ parmesan 184
Pears, Parmigiano Reggiano
  and Green Extra Virgin
  Olive Oil 39
Pizza with Goat's Cheese,
  Semi-dried Tomatoes and
  Basil 55
Polenta with Smoked Kangaroo
  and Parmigiano Reggiano 162
Spaghettini with Parmigiano
  Reggiano, Garlic, Capers and
  Flat-leaf Parsley 37, 40
Cheong Liew 12, 158
chestnuts 12–22
~ with brussels sprouts 17, 165
~ with chocolate 18
~ choosing 12, 14
~ dried 15
~ flour 16–17, 21
~ freezing 16
~ freshness 12, 15
~ grilling 16
~ industry 15
~ panfried with herbs 17
~ peeling 15–16
~ with pigeon 111
~ purée 17, 18
~ roasting 16
~ soup 17
~ in stir-fries 17
~ storing 12, 15
~ in stuffings 17
Chestnut Cake 21
Chestnut and Chocolate Pots 21
Chestnut Soup 17, 18
Ravioli with Chestnuts,
  Mushrooms and
  Mascarpone 19
Seared Duck Breasts with
  Chestnuts, Bacon and Vino
  Cotto-glazed Radicchio 20
Victoria's Celeriac and Chestnut
  Pie 10
Cheznuts restaurant 15, 17
chicken
Chicken Wings with Orange
  Peel 106
Golden Chicken Stock 178
Chickpea Flatbread 53
chickpea flour 53
chips
celeriac 8
parsnip 147
chocolate
~ bitter 183
~ with chestnuts 18
~ couverture 183
Chestnut and Chocolate Pots 21
Chocolate and Chestnut Log 22

Ganache 21
Choux Pastry-style Gluten-free
  Pastry 63
cold-smoking 157
confit
duck fat confit 97
Lime Confit 86
Coorong Angus Beef 87
cornichons 183
crabs 23–9
~ blue swimmers 23–4
~ buying 24, 26
~ cooking 24, 26
~ freezing 26
~ 'mustard' 27
~ with pasta 26
~ shelf-life 24, 26
~ soft shell 24
~ vacuum-packed 26
Blue Swimmer Crab Risotto
  with Verjuice 28
Port Parham Crab Sandwich 27
Potted Crab 26
Salad of Blue Swimmer Crab,
  Fennel and Pink Grapefruit 28
cream 183–4
Crisp Gluten-free Pastry 64
Croutons 114, 133
cumquats with venison 165
currants
Spinach with Lemon and
  Currants 443

David, Elizabeth 160
de Pieri, Stefano 88–9, 138, 140
de Rohan, Maurice 68
dressings
Grilled Orange, Asparagus and
  Witlof Salad with Vino Cotto
  Dressing 172
Vin Cotto Dressing 172
see also mayonnaise; vinaigrette
duck
duck fat confit 97
Roast Duck with Seville Orange
  and Prosciutto Stuffing 106
Seared Duck Breasts with
  Chestnuts, Bacon and Vino
  Cotto-glazed Radicchio 20
Duck Egg Pasta with Smoked
  Kangaroo, Sun-dried Tomatoes
  and Pine Nuts 58, 158
Dunn, Gavin 47
Eu, Cedric 170

extra virgin olive oil 31–7
~ choosing and using 36–7
~ extraction 33
~ grades 36–7
~ quality 33–4
~ rancidity 34, 36, 37

~ research into 31–2
~ shelf life 36
~ storing 37
Mayonnaise 38
Pears, Parmigiano Reggiano
  and Green Extra Virgin
  Olive Oil 39
Piquant Bread Salad 40
Salmon Poached in Olive
  Oil 39, 40

Fanto family 121–2
Farmshop 10
Fechner family 42, 44–5
fennel
Salad of Blue Swimmer Crab,
  Fennel and Pink Grapefruit 28
figs
Squab with Fresh Figs and
  Ginger and Lemon Butter 113
fish
Fish Stock 177
see also specific fish
Flamsteed, Steve 16, 18, 49, 124
Flamsteed, Vicki 124–5
Flannagan, Zany 54
Flatbread 52
Chickpea Flatbread 53
flour 41–2, 53, 184
~ chestnut 16–17, 21
flour products 41–64
bread 41–53
pasta 57–60
pastry 61–4
pizza 54–7
Four Leaf Milling 47, 54
Fresh Pasta 57
frittata
Leek Frittata 75

game
~ with celeriac 7
~ with parsnips 147
Purée of Celeriac to
  Accompany Game 10
see also venison
Ganache 21
Garden Greens Soup with Purée
  of Turnip 153
garlic
Rabbit with Roasted Garlic
  and Anchovies 133
Rouille 38
Spaghettini with Parmigiano
  Reggiano, Garlic, Capers
  and Flat-leaf Parsley 37, 40
see also aïoli
Geering, Adrian 55
gelatine 184
Gianfredo, Jonathon 159
Ginger and Lemon Butter 113

Glazed Leg of Ham 159
globe artichokes 144
gluten-free
    Choux Pastry-style Gluten-free
      Pastry 63
    Crisp Gluten-free Pastry 64
Golden Chicken Stock 178
golden perch
    ~ cooking in foil 140
    ~ sandwich of 140
grapes
    Grape and Walnut Bread 50
    Steve's Sausages in Grape
      Must 124
Grigson, Jane 167
Grilled Intercostals 93
Grilled Orange, Asparagus and
    Witlof Salad with Vino Cotto
    Dressing 172
Grilli, Joseph 68
guinea fowl, chestnuts with 17
Gunner, Richard 87

H

ham
    ~ sugar-cured 157
    Glazed Leg of Ham 159
hare with parsnips 147, 149
Herbert, Alex 49
herbs
    ~ in mayonnaise 38
    Loin of Venison Stuffed with
      Mushrooms and Herbs 168
    Pizza with Goat's Cheese,
      Semi-dried Tomatoes
      and Basil 55
hot-smoking 157

I

Inauen, Urs 12

J

Jeavons, Russell 54–5, 142
Jerusalem artichokes 144–7
    ~ boiling 146
    ~ health benefits 144
    ~ peeling 146
    ~ roasting 144, 146
    ~ in salads 146
    ~ and seafood 146
    ~ soup 146
    Jerusalem Artichoke and
      Pink Grapefruit Salad
      with Walnuts 146
Jones, Henry 140–1
Jones, Quentin 15

K

kangaroo 65–9
    ~ with Asian flavours 66
    ~ with beetroot 66

~ with caramelised onion 96
~ vchar-grilling 66
~ fillets 65
~ glaze for 66
~ rare 67
~ smoked 58, 65, 157, 158
~ spoilage 66
Barbecued Sugar-cured
    Kangaroo 67
Duck Egg Pasta with Smoked
    Kangaroo, Sun-dried Tomatoes
    and Pine Nuts 58, 158
Kangaroo Tail Pie 68
Polenta with Smoked Kangaroo
    and Parmigiano Reggiano 162
Salad of Smoked Kangaroo 67
Kennedy & Wilson Chocolates 18
Kyritsis, Janni 87, 123

L

labna, making 184
Laucke Flour Mills 42, 47
Laurencis, Hilda 108
leeks 70–5
    ~ overcooking 72
    ~ pencil leeks 70
    ~ with pheasant 72
    ~ roasting 72
    ~ as side dish 72
    ~ soup 72–3
    ~ washing 72
    ~ 'woodiness' 72
    Leek Frittata 75
    Leek and Oyster Pies 74
    Leek and Pancetta Tart 73
    Leeks Poached in Verjuice 73
Leinert, Colin and Joy 118–19, 157
lemons 76–83
    ~ cordial 84
    ~ juice 76, 78
    ~ growing 76, 78
    ~ Meyer 78
    ~ pectin in 76
    ~ rind 76, 78–9
    ~ varieties 76, 78
    Ginger and Lemon Butter 113
    Lemon Tart 83
    Meyer Lemon Risotto with
      Mascarpone and Scampi 81
    Spinach with Lemon and
      Currants 81
    see also preserved lemons
lentils
    Braised Pork Belly, Cotechino
      and Green Lentils 124
light olive oil 36
limes 84–6
    ~ cordial 84
    ~ juice 78, 84
    ~ Tahitian 84
    Lime Posset with Lime Confit 86
    Lime Vinaigrette 84
    Scallops with Lime Rind and
      Sea Urchin Butter 85

Loin of Venison Stuffed with
    Mushrooms and Herbs 168
Luján, Néstor 97

M

McKinnon, Lachlan Marcus 154
Maggie Beer Seville Marmalade 102
Maggie's Aïoli 180
Mailer, Dr Rod 31–2
maltaise mayonnaise 102
maltaise sauce 102
Manfredi, Steve 146
marmalade
    ~ cumquat 102
    ~ oranges for 102, 109
    ~ overcooking 109
    ~ in pressure cooker 109
    ~ setting point 109
    ~ unwaxed fruit 102
    Maggie Beer Seville
      Marmalade 102
    Marmalade-à-la-Lizzy 108
    Roast Pork Belly with Verjuice
      and Seville Marmalade
      Glaze 126
    Seville Orange Marmalade 109
mascarpone
    Ravioli with Chestnuts,
      Mushrooms and
      Mascarpone 19
Mayonnaise 27
    ~ adding herbs 38
    ~ with crab mustard 27, 28
    ~eggs in 38
    ~ handmade 38
    ~ maltaise 102
    ~ thinning 38
    ~ with verjuice 38
    Sorrel Mayonnaise 38, 180
    see also aïoli
Meyer Lemon Risotto with
    Mascarpone and Scampi 81
Millburn, Ian 110, 163
Milligan, Tom 12
Minestrone with Cavolo Nero 5
Moxham, Richard 15
Murray cod
    ~ closed seasons 138
    ~ farmed 139
    Campfire Murray Cod in a Salt
      Crust 142
    Stefano's Murray Cod 139, 143
Murray River crayfish 141
mushrooms
    Loin of Venison Stuffed with
      Mushrooms and Herbs 168
    Ravioli with Chestnuts,
      Mushrooms and
      Mascarpone 19
    Salsify with Coffin Bay Oysters
      and Oyster Mushrooms with
      a Sparkling Wine Sauce 151
Mustard Bread 27

N

Nirvana, Adelaide Hills 15
nuts *see* almonds; walnuts

O

offal 87–93
~ caul fat 121, 183
~from pig 88
~ sweetbreads 87, 88
~ from venison 167
Brains in Caper Butter 90
Grilled Intercostals 93
Smoked Lamb's Tongue with
  Rémoulade Sauce 160
see also tripe
oleic acid 33
Olive Oil Brioche with Candied
  Seville Peel 107
olives
~ farming in Australia 31–2
~ milling 32
~ pissaladière 71
~ varieties 32
~ when to pick 32, 33–4
Tripe with Tomatoes and
  Olives 92
olive oil
~ cold-pressed 33
~ light 36
~ pomace oil 36
~ virgin 34
see also extra-virgin olive oil
onions 94–100
~ baked with filling 97
~ peeling 96
~ pissaladière 97
~ red Spanish 94
~ sofregit 96–7
~ storing 96
Baby Onions Roasted in Vino
  Cotto 99
Squid with Onion, Parsley
  and Anchovy Stuffing 100
see also caramelised onions;
  shallots
oranges 101–9
~ blood 101–2
~ candied peel 105
~ green-tinged 105
~ juice 101, 105
~ navels 101
~ poor man's 102, 105
~ rind 105
~ Seville 102, 105
~ Valencia 101, 105
Chicken Wings with Orange
  Peel 106
Grilled Orange, Asparagus and
  Witlof Salad with Vino Cotto
  Dressing 172
Olive Oil Brioche with Candied
  Seville Peel 107
Orange and Almond Tart 108

Roast Duck with Seville Orange
  and Prosciutto Stuffing 106
see also marmalade
Otway pork 119
oysters
Leek and Oyster Pies 74
Salsify with Coffin Bay Oysters
  and Oyster Mushrooms with
  a Sparkling Wine Sauce 151

P

pancetta
Leek and Pancetta Tart 73
Tripe with Surprise Peas,
  Verjuice and Pancetta 90
Pan-fried Carp with Anchovy
  Butter 141
parsley
Spaghettini with Parmigiano
  Reggiano, Garlic, Capers
  and Flat-leaf Parsley 37, 40
Squid with Onion, Parsley and
  Anchovy Stuffing 100
parsnips 147–50
~ chips 147
~ choosing 147
~ with hare 147, 149
~ mashing 147
~ peeling 147
~ purée 147
~ roasting 149
~ woody 147
Caramelised Parsnips 153
Parsnip Puff 147, 149
Parsnip Quenelles with
  Walnuts 150
pasta 57–60
~ making your own 57–8
~ not rinsing 58
Duck Egg Pasta with Smoked
  Kangaroo, Sun-dried Tomatoes
  and Pine Nuts 58, 158
Fresh Pasta 57
Pasta with Baked Witlof
  and Radicchio 172
Ravioli with Chestnuts,
  Mushrooms and
  Mascarpone 19
Spaghettini with Parmigiano
  Reggiano, Garlic, Capers
  and Flat-leaf Parsley 40
pasta machine 57, 58, 60
pastry 61–4
~ blind baking 61–2, 183
~ making 61–2
Choux Pastry-style Gluten-free
  Pastry 63
Crisp Gluten free Pastry 64
Sour Cream Pastry 62
Paull, Natalie 49
Pears, Parmigiano Reggiano and
  Green Extra Virgin Olive Oil 39
peas
Tripe with Surprise Peas,
  Verjuice and Pancetta 90

Pellegrini, Angelo 169
pheasant
~ brining/hot-smoking 157
~ with leeks 72
Pheasant Farm Restaurant 22,
  127, 150, 158, 163
Pie, Betsy 61
Pierce, Bryan 140, 141
pies
~ pigeon 110
~ venison 165
Kangaroo Tail Pie 68
Leek and Oyster Pies 74
Victoria's Celeriac and Chestnut
  Pie 10
pigeon 110–15
~ chestnuts with 111
~ confit cooking 111
~ in crockpot 112
~ differences from squab 110
~ done-ness 112
~ pies 110
~ in pressure cooker 111, 112
~ serving pink 111
~ slow-cooking 111
~ stuffed 111
~ wild 110
Wild Pigeon 112
see also squab
pink grapefruit
Jerusalem Artichoke and
  Pink Grapefruit Salad
  with Walnuts 146
Salad of Blue Swimmer Crab,
  Fennel and Pink Grapefruit 28
Piquant Bread Salad 40
pissaladière 97
pizza 54–7
~ base 56
Pizza with Goat's Cheese,
  Semi-dried Tomatoes and
  Basil 55
Plane, Mike 2
Polenta with Smoked Kangaroo
  and Parmigiano Reggiano 162
pomace oil 36
Poolish 49
porchetta 123
pork 116–26
~ boar taint 118, 121
~ buying 119, 121
~ caul fat 121, 123
~ cooking 123
~ crackling 123
~ done-ness 123
~ home-killing 121–2
~ intramuscular fat 118, 119
~ kidneys 122–3
~ lard 122
~ pan-frying 123
~ potatoes with 123
~ producers 118–19, 121
~ sausage-making 122
~ stuffed ears 123
Braised Pork Belly, Cotechino
  and Green Lentils 124

Roast Pork Belly with Verjuice
  and Seville Marmalade
  Glaze 126
Steve's Sausages in Grape
  Must 124
Port Parham 23, 24, 26
Port Parham Crab Sandwich 27
potatoes with pork 123
Potted Crab 26
preserved lemons
  ~ unwaxed lemons 80
  ~ uses 79
  Preserved Lemons 80
  Preserved Lemon Vinaigrette 80
prosciutto
  Roast Duck with Seville Orange
    and Prosciutto Stuffing 106
pastry
  ~ 'bounding' 61, 62
  ~ cases 61–2
  ~ shrinkage 62
pudding
  Bread and Butter Pudding 53
purées
  ~ for desserts 17
  ~ parsnip 147
  ~ prune 131
  Purée of Celeriac to Accompany
    Game 10

Q
Quatre Épices 179
quinces
  ~ in caramelised onion 97
  Cavolo Nero with Golden
    Shallots and Quince 4

R
rabbit 127–35
  ~ back legs 130, 131
  ~ barbecued 130
  ~ bones 128
  ~ dissecting 128
  ~ farmed 128, 130–1
  ~ front legs 130, 131
  ~ kidneys 128
  ~ kittens 127, 128
  ~ livers 128
  ~ marinated 130
  ~ in pasta or risotto 130
  ~ with prunes 131
  ~ removing sinew 128, 130
  ~ saddle 128, 130
  ~ wild 127, 128
  Rabbit Rillettes 131
  Rabbit Risotto 134
  Rabbit with Roasted Garlic
    and Anchovies 133
  Rabbit Terrine 132
  Roast Saddle of Rabbit 135
radicchio
  Pasta with Baked Witlof
    and Radicchio 172

Vino Cotto-glazed Radicchio 20
Ravioli with Chestnuts,
  Mushrooms and Mascarpone 19
redfin 140
Reichelt, Karen 31
Rémoulade Sauce 160
  Celeriac Rémoulade 7, 9
Ribollita 4, 6
rice
  ~ arborio 183
  ~ chestnuts cooked with 17
  see also risotto
rillettes
  ~ keeping 131
  Rabbit Rillettes 131
risotto
  ~ catfish in 140
  Blue Swimmer Crab Risotto
    with Verjuice 28
  Meyer Lemon Risotto with
    Mascarpone and Scampi 81
  Rabbit Risotto 134
riverfish 137–43
  ~ carp 137–8, 141
  ~ 'muddy' flavour 141
  ~ Murray River crayfish 141
  ~ redfin 140
  ~ silver perch 140
  Pan-fried Carp with Anchovy
    Butter 141
  Thai Fish Balls 141
  see also catfish; golden perch;
    Murray cod
Roast Duck with Seville Orange
  and Prosciutto Stuffing 106
Roast Pork Belly with Verjuice and
  Seville Marmalade Glaze 126
Roast Saddle of Rabbit 135
Robuchon, Joël 111–12, 170
root vegetables
  ~ with Duck Egg Pasta 165
  ~ scorzonera 150
  ~ sweet potato 152
  ~ swede 152
  see also Jerusalem artichokes;
    parsnips; salsify; turnips
Rouille 38, 181

S
salad dressings see mayonnaise;
  vinaigrette
salad greens see radicchio; sorrel;
  witlof
Salad of Smoked Kangaroo 67
salads
  Caramelised Onion Salad 66, 99
  Celeriac, Apple and Walnut
    Salad 9
  Grilled Orange, Asparagus and
    Witlof Salad with Vino Cotto
    Dressing 172
  Jerusalem Artichoke and Pink
    Grapefruit Salad with
    Walnuts 146

Pear, Parmigiano Reggiano and
  Green Extra Virgin Olive
  Oil 39
Piquant Bread Salad 40
Salad of Blue Swimmer Crab,
  Fennel and Pink Grapefruit 28
Salad of Smoked Kangaroo 67
Salmon Poached in Olive
  Oil 39, 40
salsa
  ~ onions in 94
  Salsa Agresto 179
salsify 150–1
  ~ flowers 151
  Salsify with Coffin Bay Oysters
    and Oyster Mushrooms with
    a Sparkling Wine Sauce 151
sandwiches
  ~ golden perch 140
  Port Parham Crab Sandwich 27
Sassafras Nuts 15
sauces
  ~ bigarde 102, 105
  ~ maltaise 102
  Celeriac Rémoulade 99
  Rémoulade Sauce 160
  Rouille 38
  Sparkling Wine Sauce 151
Saunders, Alison 15
sausages
  ~ blood 121
  ~ home-made pork 121
  Steve's Sausages in Grape
    Must 124
Scallops with Lime Rind and
  Sea Urchin Butter 85
Schulz's Butchers 58, 65, 85, 157
scorzonera 150
Scott, Philippa 167
sea urchin roe
  Sea Urchin Butter 85
seafood see also crabs; oysters;
  scallops; scampi; sea urchins;
  squid
Seared Duck Breasts with
  Chestnuts, Bacon and Vino
  Cotto-glazed Radicchio 20
Seppelt Australian Menu of the
  Year 12
Seville oranges
  ~ sauce bigarde 102, 105
  Maggie Beer Seville
    Marmalade 102
  Olive Oil Brioche with Candied
    Seville Peel 107
  Seville Orange Marmalade 109
shallots
  ~ caramelised 94
  Cavolo Nero with Golden
    Shallots and Quince 4
silver perch 140
Silverton, Nancy 61–2
smoked foods 154–62
  ~ bacon 154
  ~ pheasant 157

~ safety regulations 158
~ sausages 158–9
Glazed Leg of Ham 159
Polenta with Smoked Kangaroo
    and Parmigiano Reggiano 158
Smoked Lamb's Tongue with
    Rémoulade Sauce 160
sofregit 96–7
Sophie's Farmhouse Loaf 49
Sorrel Mayonnaise 38, 180
soup
    ~ chestnut 17, 18
    ~ Jerusalem artichoke 146
    ~ leek 72–3
    Garden Greens Soup with
        Purée of Turnip 153
    Minestrone with Cavolo Nero 5
    Ribollita 4, 6
Sour Cream Pastry 62
Spaghettini with Parmigiano
    Reggiano, Garlic, Capers and
    Flat-leaf Parsley 37, 40
Sparkling Wine Sauce 151
spices
    Quatre Épices 179
Spinach with Lemon and
    Currants 81
squab 110, 111
    ~ cooked rare 111
    ~ spatchcocking 113
    Squab with Fresh Figs and
        Ginger and Lemon Butter 113
    Vigneron's Squab 114
squid
    ~ preparing 100
    Squid with Onion, Parsley and
        Anchovy Stuffing 100
Stefano's Murray Cod 139, 143
sterilising 185
Steve's Sausages in Grape Must 124
stock
    Fish Stock 177
    Golden Chicken Stock 178
Stonyfell Olive Oil Company 31
stuffing
    ~ chestnuts in 17
    Roast Duck with Seville Orange
        and Prosciutto Stuffing 106
    Squid with Onion, Parsley and
        Anchovy Stuffing 100
sugar syrup 185
Sutherland Smith, Beverley 149
swede 152
Sweeney, Susan 32
sweet potato 152
sweetbreads 87, 88

T

tarts (savoury)
    Leek and Pancetta Tart 73
    Witlof Tart 170
tarts (sweet)
    Lemon Tart 83
    Orange and Almond Tart 108

terrine
    Rabbit Terrine 132
    terroir 33
Tetsuya Wakuda 83
Thai Fish Balls 142
The Cook and The Chef 90, 92
The Cook's Companion 9
tomatoes
    Duck Egg Pasta with Smoked
        Kangaroo, Sun-dried Tomatoes
        and Pine Nuts 58, 158
    Pizza with Goat's Cheese,
        Semi-dried Tomatoes and
        Basil 55
    Tripe with Tomatoes and
        Olives 92
tongue 88
    Smoked Lamb's Tongue with
        Rémoulade Sauce 160
tripe 88
    ~ preparing 92, 93
    ~ risotto 88–9
    Tripe with Surprise Peas,
        Verjuice and Pancetta 90
    Tripe with Tomatoes and
        Olives 92
turnips 152–3
    Caramelised Turnips 153
    Garden Greens Soup with Purée
        of Turnip 153

V

venison 163–8
    ~ ageing 164
    ~ in braises 165
    ~ with cumquats 165
    ~ fallow deer 165
    ~ gaminess 164
    ~ marinating 164
    ~ offal 167
    ~ pan-frying 164–5
    ~ in pies 165
    ~ red deer 163
    ~ resting 165
    ~ roasting 164–5
    ~ saddle 165
    ~ with truffles 167
    ~ umbles 167
    ~ vacuum packed 164
    Carpaccio of Venison with
        Parmigiano Reggiano and
        Rocket 167
    Loin of Venison Stuffed with
        Mushrooms and Herbs 168
verjuice 28
    ~ in mayonnaise 38
    Leeks Poached in Verjuice 73
    Roast Pork Belly with Verjuice
        and Seville Marmalade
        Glaze 126
    Salsa Agresto 179
    Tripe with Surprise Peas,
        Verjuice and Pancetta 90

Victoria's Celeriac and Chestnut
    Pie 10
Vigneron's Squab 114
Vinaigrette 28, 100
    Lime Vinaigrette 84
    Preserved Lemon Vinaigrette 80
vino cotto 185
    Baby Onions Roasted in Vino
        Cotto 99
    Dressing 172
    Vino Cotto-glazed Radicchio 20

W

Wall, Peter 160
walnuts
    ~ pickled 111
    Celeriac, Apple and Walnut
        Salad 9
    Grape and Walnut Bread 50
    Jerusalem Artichoke and Pink
        Grapefruit Salad with
        Walnuts 146
    Parsnip Quenelles with
        Walnuts 150
    Salsa Agresto 179
Wells, Patricia 170
Wild Pigeon 112
Wilson, Peter 18
witlof 169–73
    ~ braising 170
    ~ caramelising 162, 170
    ~ fresh 169–70
    ~ with game 170
    Grilled Orange, Asparagus and
        Witlof Salad with Vino Cotto
        Dressing 172
    Pasta with Baked Witlof and
        Radicchio 172
    Witlof Tart 173

X

xanthan gum 63

Y

yabbies 141
yeast 48

Z

Zalokar, Sophie 49

LANTERN

UK | USA | Canada | Ireland | Australia
India | New Zealand | South Africa | China

Penguin Books is part of the Penguin Random House group of companies whose
addresses can be found at global.penguinrandomhouse.com.

Penguin
Random House
Australia

This paperback edition published by Penguin Group (Australia), 2015
This material was originally published as a section of *Maggie's Harvest* by Maggie Beer

1 3 5 7 9 10 8 6 4 2

Cover and text design by Daniel New © Penguin Group (Australia)
Design coordination by Hannah Schubert
Typeset in Cochin by Post Pre-Press Group, Brisbane, Queensland
Colour reproduction by Splitting Image, Clayton, Victoria
Printed in China by 1010 Printing International Limited

National Library of Australia
Cataloguing-in-Publication data:

Beer, Maggie.
Maggie Beer's Winter Harvest Recipes.
Bibliography.
Includes index.
ISBN 9781921384226 (pbk.).
1. Cookery, Australian. I. Chew, Mark. II. Title.
641.5

penguin.com.au/lantern